The Federal Reserve and its Founders

ABOUT THE AUTHOR

RICHARD A. NACLERIO has worked extensively in business operations and real estate investment in New York City and Denver, Colorado. He continues to manage his own real estate companies and stock portfolios. Although he enjoyed some financial success, personal fulfilment eluded him. So in 2010, at the age of 40, he decided to pursue his passion for history. Still lacking a college diploma, he received his BA and Masters from Iona College, graduating first in his class at the age of 43. He taught business communications and English at Monroe College in the Bronx, New York and worked for three years at Sacred Heart University in Fairfield, Connecticut as an adjunct history instructor and academic advisor. Awarded a fellowship to the history doctoral program of the Graduate Center at City University of New York, he is now, at 48, a third-year PhD candidate. He is also a graduate teaching fellow at Lehman College. He is married with four children and lives in Westchester County, NY. This is his first book.

The Federal Reserve and its Founders

Money, Politics and Power

RICHARD A. NACLERIO

agenda
publishing

First edition published in 2018 by Agenda Publishing

Agenda Publishing Limited
The Core
Science Central
Bath Lane
Newcastle upon Tyne
NE4 5TF

www.agendapub.com

ISBN 978-1-911116-03-5 (hardcover)
ISBN 978-1-78821-078-2 (paperback)

British Library Cataloguing-in-Publication Data
A catalogue record for this book is available from the British Library

Typeset by Patty Rennie
Printed and bound in the UK by CPI Group (UK) Ltd, Croydon, CR04YY

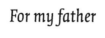

For my father

Contents

Acknowledgements

When your wife is your best friend and your Dad is your biggest fan, life is a wonderful thing.

Thank you to my family, all my friends, colleagues, professors who inspired me, and all the friends of Bill W. Because of all of you, I am the luckiest man I know.

"Let me issue and control a nation's money and I care not who writes the laws."

MAYER AMSCHEL ROTHSCHILD

"There comes a time when out of a false good there arises a true evil, since the encroachments of the rich are more destructive to the state than those of the people."

ARISTOTLE

"The hottest places in Hell are reserved for those who in time of moral crisis preserve their neutrality."

DANTE ALIGHIERI

Introduction

In these days of YouTube "New World Order" videos and illuminati chasers, a book on the Federal Reserve could be misconstrued as yet another conspiracy theory to add to the pile of blogs and web sites that choke our mainframes. This is not one of those books, and I am not one of those historians. You will find no satanic rituals, pentagrams, or lizard people from outer space here. You will find the Federal Reserve, money, politics, power, and the men who controlled them all.

I love the United States of America. I think a democratic form of capitalism is the best economic system for any nation. I like, in theory, what Wall Street provides the average American investor, as well as the corporate structure. I invest in the stock market, I own real estate, and I am even a private lender. The idea of an opportunity to better an individual's economic condition is one of the American ideologies that make this nation such a great place. However, this system can be and is abused on too many occasions, and that concept was the inspiration for my research.

I am against cupidity and the reckless nature in which those who are possessed by it slash and burn as a means to dictatorial or oligarchical ends. I am against the total lack of transparency and the destructive forces of corporate consolidation and monopolization that kills the spirit of free enterprise in this country. The scourge of deregulation since the Reagan years that has given Wall Street banking institutions a free pass to cannibalize their own market through derivative investment, synthetic portfolios, and notional commodity fixtures is an insult to average American investors and exemplifies the weakness and the culpability of the government, which was organized to protect them.

This book is about power. Those who possess it and those who channel it to the reservoirs of consolidated gain. This process has been going on since the pharaohs

1

of ancient Egypt. However, in this country, around the turn of the twentieth century, a politician, an economist, and a few Wall Street bankers overthrew the entire monetary system of the United States of America and produced an entity that for the benefit of the select few who built it, would wield more economic power than any other of its kind.

When the profits of private institutions begin to eclipse the GNPs of many countries, the argument that what is best for those companies is what is best for the nation that houses them, is a cogent one. The Wall Street bankers who created the Federal Reserve never made this argument. However, perhaps that was their motivation. Perhaps they only had the nation's best interests in mind when they revamped its monetary system. Admitting no benefit for themselves, the founders of the Federal Reserve made themselves out to be patriots, fighting for the economic freedom of a growing nation. They usurped control of America's currency and monetary policies, as they built a central banking system in which little to no government interference, regulation, or oversight was possible, with the banks they owned and represented, privately acting as the fiscal agents for every citizen of the United States. The founding of the Federal Reserve could be described as an economic *coup d'état*, with Wall Street as the insurgent, the US government as the assassinated leader, and the currency as the spoils.

There have been many books written about the Federal Reserve in recent years, and almost all of them cover its founding and its founders. William Greider's *Secrets of the Temple: How the Federal Reserve Runs the Country* was a *New York Times* best-seller in the 1980s, and an epic telling of the Fed's power and control over the nation's monetary system. Liaquat Ahamed's *Lords of Finance: The Bankers Who Broke the World* is a poignant source of information on the Federal Reserve and its founders, as are James Livingston's *Origins of the Federal Reserve System: Money, Class, and Corporate Capitalism*, Martin Mayer's *The Fed: The Inside Story of How the World's Most Powerful Financial Institution Drives the Markets*, and Allan H. Meltzer's *A History of the Federal Reserve*, which is a banking historian's bible. What makes this book different and, hopefully, a worthy addition to the scholarship that inspired it, is its aim to give insight into the men who created the Fed in order to better understand their creation.

The Federal Reserve System's one hundred year legacy has left no doubt of its vast monetary control, its far-reaching geopolitical power and its enigmatic secrecy. These defining features of the Fed remain a mirror of the men who created it. Wall Street barons and ambitious politicians vied for control over shaping the US Federal

Reserve to the specifications that suited the needs of both their country and themselves.

A vast number of Americans are focused on the Federal Reserve as of late. Along with the Fed's recent one-hundredth-year anniversary, economic and monetary globalization, the downward spiral of the economy and its subsequent stagnation has affected the entire nation. The collapse of the real estate market, backroom bailouts, interest rates, inflation and bank loans are on the forefront of US citizens' economic concerns. Given all this, I believe that mostly, people are clamouring for more transparency, clarity and honesty in politics, business and banking these days. Citizens are tired of being lied to and disillusioned by the small percentage of people and entities that seemingly run their lives. Yet, as the Federal Reserve has become slightly more exposed in its role in these affairs, the Fed remains as mythic and indecipherable as ever.

Although many people's livelihoods depend upon decisions the Fed makes, many people do not understand or have any knowledge of the inner workings of this institution. Many think the Fed is a government agency – it is not. Many think it was created by politicians for the benefit of the US economy – it was not. Many think it is stringently regulated by the government – it is not. Many think that the currency, which the Fed controls, is backed by something held in reserve, like gold – it is not. To fully understand the US Federal Reserve, one must familiarize oneself with its history. When we comprehend something's inception and its creators, we may then fully understand its nature, its capacities and its motivations.

This book will define the Federal Reserve and its power. It will then examine its founders separately and consider the ties that bound them through their banking or political careers. By examining their actions as individuals – a politician, an economist and four bankers – a deeper understanding is revealed of the politics, economics and the banking industry of the time, and the relationships that were formed within the web of fraternal and familial collectivism that was Wall Street. Armed with this information we may then make an honest appraisal of the men (and who or what they represented) who created and ran America's central banking system.

Asking "Who created the Federal Reserve?" is like asking "Who built the Empire State Building?". So many businessmen, companies, banks, politicians were involved with the finished product that it would be irresponsible to give credit to just one person. However, there was a small group of men who took the idea for a US central banking system and set the wheels of monetary change in motion for the country, and consequently, the world. They either were, or represented, the most dominant banking and business interests in the country, and six of them met, in secret, on a tiny piece of land off the coast of Georgia called Jekyll Island.

This book leaves the door open to many questions and the opportunity for further research on this subject and in the field of US banking and economic history from both a statistical standpoint and a biographical one. Continuing to track the Federal Reserve's impact on US and foreign economies throughout the twentieth century would be just as riveting and informative as tracing its lineage to the lives of men like J. P. Morgan, James J. Stillman, Jacob Schiff, or the Rockefeller and Rothschild dynasties. The US Federal Reserve was based on the many European central-banking systems of its time. Studying their births and comparing them to their neophyte, American cousin would be fascinating.

Senator Nelson W. Aldrich, Paul M. Warburg, Benjamin Strong, Jr, Frank A. Vanderlip, A. Piatt Andrew and Henry P. Davison were among the heavyweights of the American financial arena, and they did not acquire that reputation by being anything but merciless and single-minded in their nature and their actions. These men and the banking system they built had one singular goal: to gain as much money and power as possible. The longevity of the system; its cryptic, untouchable and unregulated hierarchy; and the immeasurable reach of its wealth and power are testaments to their success, and to many of the failures of the United States economy. This book is intended to hold a few feet to the fire, in an attempt to improve our economic system through an analysis of trust.

1

The Genesis

Historians often argue about what single civilizing occurrence had the most impact upon the history that succeeded it. The invention of the plow in ancient Egypt comes to mind. Or, it could be argued that the printing press was the largest historical game-changer. In terms of industry, the Sumerian ziggurat must be on the list, or for societal order, Hammurabi's Code, which first systematized the law in ancient Babylon. In the modern era, the invention of the home computer must be in the conversation, as well as the smart phone, perhaps.

However, there is one historical event, which to an economic historian can be argued as the most impactful on all of human kind. Everything else pales in comparison to the change brought about in the social, legal, cultural, military, labour, gender, and any other compartment of the historical landscape by one single innovation: the invention of money. Money is the greatest civilizing factor in history, and its existence remains the cornerstone of all power throughout history. Without money, nothing is possible, and for those who have most of it, anything is possible.

Before currency, the barter system was the means for purchasing goods and services. We would trade things like wheat and wood, goats and oxen, for other things like pottery and jewellery, oats and daughters. But the problem with many of the things we would trade like wheat, oats, oxen, and even daughters is the fact that they all die. Goods and services were greatly limited by the fact that they did not last long. The wealth of an individual could not be measured by his ownership of goods or his ability to produce. Even property was subject to the weather, the elements, and population adjustments.

Then, around 1100 BCE, in the era of the Palestinian civilization, a society of people in modern-day central and western Turkey, changed history forever. The ancient Lydians perfected the metallurgy of gold, silver, copper and bronze and became the first to mint coins from these metals and to create the first uniform accounting and record keeping system for the purposes of disseminating currency. Humankind was no longer subject to the shelf life of their tradable goods and services and with currency, came one thing never before possible: the storage of wealth.

As history progressed, currency quickly became the major means for the purchase of all goods and services, and currency led to the development of banking. All civilizations and societies exhibited a banking industry in one form or another. However, this field was consolidated and dominated by Jews in the early middle ages. Not because of some presently existing racist stereotype, but because of a very old racist attitude against the Jewish faith. Banking was seen as a lowly occupation in the centuries when land was everything and the Church of Rome held dominion over most of Europe. At that time it was considered sinful to charge interest for any loan. Since Jews did not fall under the same religious restrictions that Christians did, they were free to enter this plebian industry known as "moneylending", which they mastered among themselves. But, the church soon conceded to the boundless opportunities that banking had to offer and Europe became the centre of the financial universe for centuries to come, religious affiliation notwithstanding.

In America, banking played a major role in the new republic's inception. It would also be instrumental in changing the nation from what it was intended to be. The original structure of government, which was so closely tied to the founding fathers' constitution, was based on the individual freedoms of American citizens. The true intent of America's patriots was a commitment to a communal sense of neighbourly self-governance; their values of virtue and trust in each other reflected a disdain for self-promotion and the lust for profit, which today's America seems not only to be completely infected with, but steadily reveres and feeds upon under the guise of an "American dream". In economic terms, the Founding Fathers and American Patriots had a different understanding of what it meant to be a truly free American. It was not Herbert Spencer's social Darwinism and his "survival of the fittest" mantra that far too many Americans think is the oil with which their country's machinery works, but instead, a community of citizens, ruling themselves by committee. Nor was it François Quesnay's laissez-faire economic template from *Tableau Économique* or Adam Smith's "invisible hand". The Founding Fathers, including Thomas Jefferson, Benjamin Franklin, John Hancock and Benjamin Rush had a vision that was more akin to Thomas Paine's, *Common Sense*, wherein individual freedom was best achieved and protected by a communal effort towards building a republic.

Original American patriotism was steeped in the notion that we should feed each other, police each other, and consult with each other. The power of the local committee was the linchpin of the Patriot ideal and it allowed power to flow through the land "from the farmer and the cobbler to the merchant and the landlord". It was "a movement powerfully shaped by ordinary men, infused with ideals of mutual dependence and neighborly relations". It relied on "the political powers of ordinary free colonists", and it defended "popular presence as strongly as it defended representation".[1]

With all these good intentions and lofty goals for post-Revolutionary America, it was currency and debt that proved to be the undoing of the Patriot ideal. To pay for the Revolutionary War, currency finance was adopted. In June 1775 America issued its first $2 million in paper money. In July it added another million, and then another $3 million in 1776. This currency was earmarked for circulation among the Patriot population of the Thirteen Colonies and was to be integrated into their already established practices guided by ideals of interdependence and unity, within a policy of "commitment to consent in the marketplace". The Patriot Congress recommended new laws to be enacted to require creditors to accept these notes for all private and public debts.[2]

The Tory Party, entrenched in their conservative allegiance to Britain and its parliamentary procedure of imperial dominion over the colonies, would not accept the new Patriot currency and began to counterfeit it in order to lessen its value and impede the progress of the colonial war effort. Soon, refusal to accept the bills by predatory suppliers and merchants who were deemed as imperial sympathizers spread, as they also aggressively raised their prices. The new Patriot economy was marked for death, as "Men who sought a profit by weakening Patriot paper bills were guilty of the same greed and desire for power" as those who came before them, who resisted the Patriot ideal throughout the 1770s.[3]

The strength of the Tories in Congress led to Robert Morris's appointment as the financier of the Revolution. Morris, a Pennsylvania congressman, had been accused of seizing and withholding a massive shipment of dry goods in the port of Philadelphia in order to await the further value depletion of the Patriot currency, so as to sell the goods at higher prices to more desperate citizens. He was even brought up on charges, arrested, and went to court for the monopolization of goods. However, the evidence proved that since people bought up his product so quickly, there must have been a proper demand for the prices he set, therefore there was no illegality, only greed, laced in his actions.[4]

Morris quickly formed a "money connection" by pursuing the wealthier businessmen of the nation and began to carry out his vision of a powerful commercial empire, dominated by the elite sect of the new nation that would replace the Patriot economy. He removed government backing from the Patriot currency, enacted a program of heavy taxation, deregulated anti-monopoly laws, and set about creating a new money that would secure the confidence of the rich, in which money would be private instead of public (that currency would be issued by individuals and/or the banks they represented; not the US government). Large denominations of new currency were issued and "a majority of the certificates were concentrated in the hands of a limited number of commercial men in the states north of Maryland".[5]

These certificates were given value and Morris conspired with his monied allies to ensure that the new government would be indebted to him and his wealthy cohort. With this debt, came a strong central government, whose most important role was to pay the private creditors for the money they held. Thus, a strong lobby for the monied class was established and these men held control over the politicians running postwar America. The government was given the full authority to tax, which became its only option to pay back what Morris and the others had insisted to be both interest and principal, "all calculated on the face value of certificates often bought for a mere fraction of that amount".[6] The original Patriot vision for a currency that was to be distributed among the masses was gone, and the consolidation of currency into the hands of the wealthy few, their ability to loan it to a fledgling government (over which they had immense lobbying power), and their ensuing economic domination over America had begun.

By the 1790s the Founding Fathers went from battling creditors to battling each other over the existence of a central bank. Thomas Jefferson and Benjamin Franklin fought tirelessly to stop Alexander Hamilton from executing his plan for a central bank; Hamilton and his support of the First Bank of the United States was to set in motion an arduous process of controversy and embroiled debate surrounding central banking. A German banker by the name of James Rothschild was the bank's financial backer and helped to create it. He was the most powerful banker in France at the time, and he was a member of the most powerful banking family in the world.

On paper, the central bank was not a bad idea. It acted to provide currency, as a depository for federal funds, to control state bank note issuances, and was the fiscal agent for the country. It also loaned money to private, commercial and industrial interests and paid the government money, as a bonus, for the privilege of holding massive amounts of federal funds for the bank's use in making tremendous profits, interest and tax free.

What made central banks more palatable back then, was the fact that they were chartered. They would come into existence because there was a need for them at the time. The First Bank of the United States was necessary because of the debt the Republic had incurred after the Revolutionary War, and a financial plan was needed to pay back the creditors who held the loans and most of the currency. The federal government granted the bank's charter for a twenty-year term, from 1791–1811.

This charter system was how all corporations existed at the time. If a need arose for a project, like a bridge or a dam, businessmen and developers would create a corporation to commence and complete the project for a profit, and the government would allow them to incorporate for a specified term for the sole purpose of completing said project. The given project would benefit the common good of a city, state, town, or the entire country. Once the term of the charter was up, hopefully after the project was completed, the corporation would either disband or be asked to start another project under another charter with another specified term. In the case of the central bank, it was chartered to get the nation out of debt. The principle behind these fixed-term charters was to guard against a company (or bank) that was big enough to complete a job of such magnitude becoming too financially influential and powerful to be kept properly regulated. So the government issued these term-limited charters to benefit everyone involved without allowing for the size and scope of the corporation to spiral out of control.[7]

After the Civil War, massive rebuilding projects proved to be a prodigious opportunity for corporations to gain more power and profit. Thus, corporate lawyers used the Fourteenth Amendment to gain traction for the advancement of their interests. The Fourteenth Amendment was enacted in 1868 to protect the rights of ex-slaves from States impeding them from seeking life, liberty, or property. However, shrewd corporate lawyers began to bring cases to the US Supreme Court that argued the rights of corporations to be equal to the rights of a newly freed slave.

In 1888 the Supreme Court ruled in *Pembina Consolidated Silver Mining Co. v. Pennsylvania*: "Under the designation of 'person' there is no doubt that a private corporation is included in the Fourteenth Amendment".[8] According to Mary Zepernick, the head of the Program on Corporations, Law, and Democracy, 307 cases were brought before the US Supreme Court under the Fourteenth Amendment between 1890 and 1910; 288 of them were brought by corporate attorneys and only 19 by African American ex-slaves.[9]

The First Bank of the United States did its job. The country was almost out of debt and the bank's charter was up. However, the federal government enlisted central banking again, this time over the formation of the Second Bank of the United States. Why the need for another one? The First Bank was formed to help pay Revolutionary War debts, and its charter expired in 1811. The very next year the War of 1812 broke out. The United States military, unprovoked and in an expansionist effort, attacked the British and Indians in the North and Midwest. After this war, James Rothschild used Philadelphia banker and financier, Nicholas Biddle, to bid for the second bank's existence. With Rothschild's help, Biddle ended up forming the Second Bank of the United States, became its first president, and helped to create the powerful Independent Sub-Treasury System; another arm of private central banking.[10]

The Second Bank of the United States was chartered in 1816 to do the same job as the First – get the nation out of debt from war. The government used the bank to secure debt reduction so it did not have to put undue pressure on the existing money market of the country's currency. The bank, under Biddle, set interest rates higher and reduced loan volume to accommodate the country's payouts to defence contractors and other private bankers who had financed the war. The problem was that the new central bank, like the first one, did its job too well for its own good.[11]

In 1828, in his inaugural address, President Andrew Jackson pledged to eliminate the national debt under his administration. During his campaign, he accused the Second Bank of the United States of engaging in anti-Jacksonian politics. Jackson's plan was to pay off the country's existing debt by 1833, sell its shares in the central bank, and not renew its charter, which was up in 1836. He figured it would be counter-productive to sign another charter for a central bank, if the country was going to be out of debt. Historically, the role of a central bank is that simple. It exists to benefit the citizens and their government by means of aiding the economy so as to free the nation from debt. The problem for the bank is that if there is no debt, it is no longer necessary. The founders of the Federal Reserve System knew this.

Biddle proposed plan after plan to President Jackson. They benefited the public, the country's creditors, the government and the bank. They were sound ideas for the nation to end its debt by Jackson's deadline. However, Biddle wanted to be rewarded for doing a good job by having his charter renewed for a further fifteen or twenty years.[12] What Biddle had not understood was that the US government had given him and his banking colleagues the privilege of aiding their country in its time of need, and had paid them handsomely to do so. Also, Biddle and his Rothschild backer were certainly not the only bankers who could have done what they did. They were given an opportunity that any bank in the world would have grabbed. Jackson's stance was; job well-done, thank you for serving your country, you made tens of millions of dollars from this charter (and the US Treasury did most of the real work), now go back to the private sector and continue banking at the highest levels, thanks to the US government – you're welcome.

The United States would not have another central bank until 67 years later, under the provisions of the Federal Reserve Act of 1913. The Federal Reserve System became a new and much more powerful banking consolidation, which gave Wall Street control over the nation's monetary system. However, at the time of its inception this was nothing new. In fact, the banking industry was the last to get on board the vehicle of monopoly and corporate consolidation. Banking was the last bastion of the Wild West of the nineteenth century. Just as in the days of Jesse James and Billy the Kid, lawlessness seemed the norm on America's frontier. Bank-robbing and train-robbing scourged the country and small-town showdowns frightened the good people of post-Civil War United States. These outlaw practices brought lawmen from all over the country to get a tin star and fight the good fight for justice and the safety of the law-abiding American citizen. This, however, was not normal practice for the lawmen in charge of even more ruthless and destructive men.

The Reconstruction Era and "Gilded Age" of America exhibited a massive push towards the consolidation of corporate and banking power. The true Wild West of the American frontier was exhibited in the railroad, telegraph, oil well, and the less ostensible, stock offering. The men who rose to the top of these industries were just as dangerous, if not more, as the gunfighters of western lore. Names like Vanderbilt, Rockefeller, Morgan, Gould and Carnegie proved to be the most upwardly mobile.

Like the contested spaces of early America, the industrialization of the American West was an industrial occupation that contributed as much social dislocation as did the European occupation of Native American land during the historic age of exploration and discovery. As Ryan Dearinger has written, "Canals and railroads were not *ends* of progress but moving spaces of conflict and contestation."[13]

Legislative regulation of the corporate monopolies that formed over the course of a few decades after the Civil War was practically non-existent. This unfettered corporate landscape aided in the shifting imbalance of wealth and power to the select few of this time. Beginning with the railroads, the genesis of government support of corporate domination came when Leland Stanford drove the "Golden Spike" into the ground to commemorate the junction of the Union Pacific and Central Pacific railroads in Promontory Point, Utah Territory. This famous ceremony not only marked an American industrial triumph, but also a postwar beginning for the power of American corporate interests to rule over classes, races and the US government.

The more progress moved forward the more the uncivilized, non-white, lower class would be left behind. These dregs, as railroad managers, foremen and officers looked upon them, were the working classes who built the railroads for meagre wages under horrible conditions. A technology of whiteness was celebrated at Promontory Point, as, Dearinger again writes, "Slaves, convicts, Irish immigrants, Mormons, and the Chinese were best suited for the 'othering' that this experiment entailed".[14] Siloing workers into binary gender spheres promulgated infighting and divisive behaviour between the racial groups, and management homogenized them all as second-class citizens. As these employment and social practices led to strikes and riots, the news of a racially charged backlash was controlled not only by the officers of the railroads, but the federal government as well.

General Greenville Dodge, hired as a surveyor for the Union Pacific, and later mayor of Chicago, in his memoir, wrote disparaging lies about the immigrants who worked on the lines. Fearing immigrant takeover, *Harper's Weekly* published stories of drunkenness, fighting and attempted murder by the mixture of races that were marginalized and in some cases worked to death.[15] A substantial portion of the federal government's response to this cruelty, exclusion and libel was to turn the other way and allow the progress of big business to set the tone for the rest of the century, culminating in the Chinese Exclusion Act of 1882, "one of the most significant restrictions on immigration in United States history".[16]

In some ways greater than the federal government's social protection of US railroad business was its economic protection of it. Lack of regulation was ostensible, as railroad men became more and more powerful throughout the latter half of the nineteenth century. The National Board of Trade began pressuring the government to pass regulating legislation on the railroad industry. More than 30 bills were introduced in the House and the Senate from 1874 to 1885. All of them were killed. The railroad had revolutionized America, including its legislative branch.[17]

In response, New York merchants established the National Anti-Monopoly League, in 1881, to help launch the Hepburn investigation, which found that railroad magnate William Vanderbilt's New York Central had granted 6,000 special contracts in six months, and half of its local traffic was carried at special rates, including many to John D. Rockefeller's Standard Oil. However, it was a citizen's league, not the government that spurred this investigation. When regulation was considered, it was the corporate executive who initiated that as well. Vanderbilt sent his vice president, Chauncey Depew to speak at the New York Chamber of Commerce banquet on 8 May 1883. There, Depew explained the favourable conditions that government regulation could give to the railroad monopolies. Ray Ginger writes: "He proposed a National Tribunal to do two things . . . 'Impartial justice' to railroad shippers, and . . . protect the existing railroads 'against being pirated, by being unnecessarily harassed and paralleled'".[18]

Politicians were being used by monopolistic entrepreneurs, and in return politicians themselves found ways to capitalize on the progress of industry: Ginger again, "Businesses whose profits depended on the maintenance of a monopoly position were preyed upon by politicians as well as by other businessmen, and many was the nuisance bill introduced into city councils and state legislatures by men who had no intention of passing it but who wanted to be paid for not passing it."[19]

What were known as "Railway Congressmen" facilitated the great cause of railway expansion, and lined their pockets along the way. As the empire builders of the Union Pacific, men like Speaker of the House and future president, James Garfield, future vice-president, Schuyler Colfax and many other senators and congressmen gained wealth through the issuance of stock in Crédit Mobilier. This was, in effect, the Union Pacific Railway Corporation. Matthew Josephson writes: "Purchasing for nothing or little, through Oaks Ames, himself a representative of Massachusetts, who felt that the ownership in such a vast, patriotic venture should be distributed 'where it will do most good for us'".[20]

The men who were elected by ordinary citizens signed their allegiance over to the capitalists who scared the countryside, fixed prices, exploited workers and cannibalized their own industry. But why shouldn't they? Crédit Mobilier stock had cost the "Railway congressmen" nothing and the company's first dividend was "$2,500,000 in Union Pacific bonds, and the same in stock, or 100 per cent on the capital!".[21] These politicians were meant to serve their constituents and their country. Instead, they served themselves and the industry that made them rich.

Enter, the US banking industry. The banking industry was as culpable of cupidity as industrialists, and like the men of business, the bankers were aided by political legislation as well. It was the re-establishment of the gold standard that took the country off the greenback[22] redemption of the Civil War and onto a system that aided the wealthy class of hard-money bankers. As Rebecca Edwards has written: "Republicans failed to expand the money supply at a time when the economy was growing rapidly, a policy few economists today would endorse. The national banks, privately owned and run for profit, enjoyed special privileges but were under no obligation to issue notes."[23] Banks consistently exhibited a lack of urgency for ordinary classes of people who need liquidity: "Between 1882 and 1891 the number of bank notes declined by half."[24] The West and the South suffered most as much of the concentration of liquidity fell on Wall Street. "Not surprisingly, many protested a monetary system that enriched bankers and investors at the expense of those who grew wheat and cotton and crafted steel and textiles. Republican policies, they argued, impoverished these producers while rewarding men who shuffled papers or lived on accumulated wealth."[25]

Before this, the Specie Payment Resumption Act of 1875 was passed. This law was designed to keep the greenbacks in circulation, but make them fully redeemable in gold. Rural economies were crippled, and this law shrunk the money supply even before greenbacks were eradicated and the gold standard was in full force. Many saw this as a "malignant plot by eastern and foreign capitalists", as Democratic governor of Ohio, William Allen denounced the conspiracy of the "money power" that was draining "the life-blood of the American people".[26]

This law proved to overlook the downtrodden poor, and what was the middle class before the Panic of 1873. It was really designed to reassure Europe that US debt would ultimately be paid in gold. A syndicate made up of J. W. Seligman, J. P. Morgan and the Rothschild family took in foreign investors for a refinancing loan to the US government in 1876. As Strouse has stated: "Most of the bond sold at a premium, up to four points above the bankers' contract price . . . The syndicate earned over $3 million, plus $1 million in commission, plus the spread between their buying and selling price".[27]

By the 1890s, metal was the political and economic topic. A bimetal[28] approach to currency reform was adopted in the Sherman Silver Purchase Act of 1890. Farmers and miners, comprising the new populist movement of the working-class south, needed aid and the tight money policies that helped the monopolies and trusts of the "money power" were taking its toll on them and the rest of middle-class America. With silver being purchased along with gold, currency would become more accessible, inflation would ensue, and people could more readily pay their debts and sell their cultigens for a greater profit. The problem with adding silver to the reserve, as a currency-backing mechanism was that European investors began redeeming their securities for gold and "shipping it home". This affected the upper classes, bankers and corporate giants who relied on foreign money.

The newly elected President Grover Cleveland began a push to repeal the Silver Act, blaming it for the Panic of 1893. As Congress debated the fate of the Act, a young representative from Nebraska named William Jennings Bryan gave a three-hour oration, in which he described the uneven distribution of wealth in America in terms of the bimetal argument that lay before Congress:

> On the one side stand the corporate interests of the United States, the moneyed interests, aggregated wealth and capital, imperious, arrogant, compassionless . . . On the other side stand an unnumbered throng . . . Work-worn and dust-begrimed, they make their mute appeal, and too often find their cry for help beat in vain against the outer walls, while others, less deserving, gain ready access to legislative halls.[29]

Despite Bryan's rallying cry for the populist cause, thanks to heavy lobbying by Wall Street led by J. P. Morgan, the Silver Act was repealed.

The populist movement stood strong and struck fear into the minds of the Republicans and hard money Democrats. Populists were considered reckless in their economic ideologies and were even considered lawless and anarchistic by some of the more conservative political climbers. Theodore Roosevelt, New York City's police commissioner at the time accused the new political group of "plotting a social revolution" and proposed "lining twelve Populist leaders against a wall and shooting them dead". With William Jennings Bryan at the head of the Party, his bid for the 1896 presidential election was one to watch.[30]

On the heels of the election, a J. P. Morgan syndicate of bankers, led by the Rothschild family brokered a bond issue for a sale of gold to the US government, with a majority of it coming from the Rothschilds in Europe. Profits from the deal were estimated at between $5million and $18 million and Bryan used this to his advantage in the presidential race by pounding the deal and the bankers who were behind it. He demanded, "The Treasury shall be administered on behalf of the American people and not on behalf of the Rothschilds and other foreign bankers". This stance along with the endorsement of the populist movement secured the Democratic nomination for Bryan.[31]

It was at the Democratic national convention in Chicago where Bryan rode the wave of anti-Wall Street sentiment, pro-working class ideology, a dash of anti-Semitism, and a bimetallism economic plan, directly into a presidential nomination. The 1896 convention was the site of Bryan's famous "Cross of Gold" speech, wherein he moved the convention to tears, yawps, and a 35 minute standing ovation. His most stirring words rang out:

> Having behind us the producing masses of this nation and the world, supported by the commercial interests, the labouring interests, and the toilers everywhere, we will answer their demand for a gold standard by saying to them: You shall not press down upon the brow of labour this crown of thorns, you shall not crucify mankind upon a cross of gold.[32]

Bryan went on to lose the election to the "gold bug" William McKinley.

With the completion and the magnitude of America's railroad network, entrepreneurial America gave way to massive corporate consolidation, and the country's capital began to quickly concentrate into pools and trusts in order for the burgeoning investment banking community to tie itself to every region and sphere of enterprise even before the turn of the century.[33] Corporations began to control commodities and their production with their long and pecuniary scope of influence. Having broken the "craft unions" (skilled manual workers) after a prolonged battle between 1892 and 1902, new forms of working practices were installed: "the 'bureaucratization' and 'professionalization' of mental labor in the new central offices of large corporations", and a new labour system with "labor-saving machinery" and "centralized manufacturing".[34]

This age of excess brought the country the railroads, the telegraph, oil, shipping, and a host of other incredible technological advances of the time – as well as the solidification of the United States as a major economic competitor in the global market. However, when the goliaths of these industries straddled their constructions, they chose to exclude the workforce, guilds and the interests of consumers from participation, recognition and benefit, in the self-absorbed narcissism of securing a legacy. On the surface, this would be cause for outrage and directed at these men of greed. However, blaming these men for the conditions of waste and poverty in which they put much of the American citizenry is like blaming a compass for pointing north. These men would do anything they could to seal their names in the annals of business history. They could not be left to their own devices to self-govern. It was in their nature to dominate.

The Patriot days when, after the Panic of 1792, in the words of Fraser, "a group of brokers were alleged to have met under a buttonwood tree on Wall Street to enter into a formal agreement regarding the trading of securities . . ."[35] were long gone by the end of the nineteenth century. The politicians who were assigned to police these men, instead, joined them on their quest for riches. Representing themselves with no regard for the workers and businessmen who were caught in the wake of these giants, political appointees failed to take legislative action against monopolies and the consolidation of corporate and banking interests to the detriment of the American citizen. Without proper federal regulation of business practices, the Wild West of America reigned in the boardrooms with many more disastrous effects than that of the frontier. This precedent allowed a senator, an economist, and four Wall Street men to monopolize the banking industry, once and for all.

2

The System

Since the charter for the Second Bank of the United States expired in 1836, the country had been without a central banking organization. With the Civil War of the 1860s, the Long Depression of the late 1800s and two silver panics, the country was arguably in need of an economic upgrade. Although central banking was still seen as an unconstitutional taboo at this point, American citizens and most of their representatives in the Senate and Congress succumbed to a gradual and controlled redirection towards a central banking system early into the new century, carefully steered by Wall Street bankers.[1]

The idea for a central bank began early in the turn of the century. What would become of those ideas would be the Federal Reserve System, which was not federal in the least and barely a reserve. It was (and still is) a union of private banks that abandoned any scant gold reserve requirements they had originally set for themselves. Some historians, economists, sociologists, bankers and businessmen see the Federal Reserve as representative of the demise of free enterprise and the competition of businesses in the American marketplace. When the Federal Reserve was born, President Woodrow Wilson said about it, and the rise of immense corporations, "The old time of individual competition is probably gone by. It may come back; I don't know; it will not come back within our time, I dare say."[2]

Banking was not always like that. Before the Federal Reserve's existence, Clearing House Loan Certificates were the things that kept the country afloat during a panic. They were highly touted by bankers as an effective means of thwarting economic disaster in times of crisis. The loan certificates lightened the load of a plummeting money supply, "like the emptying of barrels of oil from a storm distressed ship".[3] During a panic, people hoard their money and bank reserves empty out rapidly. So the banks were issued, by the New York Clearing House Board of Directors, these certificates in lieu of actual money.[4] They had approximately a four-month redemption limit and enabled the banks to continue to give out money to panicked withdrawers, with the knowledge that they would be compensated through the redemption of these certificates.

The fear was that deposits would eventually run out and that the banks would simply run out of currency to give employers, workers and retailers. After all, these certificates only worked on credit. Gold still had to be purchased to support the printing of new currency for banks to dole out. Bankers, especially more successful ones who could survive shrinking reserves, began to split or sell their certificates for a profit, leading to counterfeiting and an increasing lack of confidence in the temporary currency. However, the Clearing House Loan Certificate System held its ground, and although the entire process was technically unconstitutional, the federal government knew that if such measures were not taken, a full-scale collapse of the monetary system could occur, and citizens could simply lose everything.[5]

Despite the effectiveness of the Loan Certificate programme, it remained a far greater power of the government's than of the bankers' or investment firms' of the time. Banking reform forces soon began to congeal and the 1902 Fowler Bill was proposed to centralize the country's banking system. This bill was strongly supported by then, US Treasury Secretary Leslie M. Shaw, mostly because it instituted provisions to use the US Treasury as a surrogate central bank. However, the bill was thwarted and never passed because many politicians and their constituents were fearful of a central banking system, and wary of how much power the US Treasury would have been given.

It was only a short time later that the bankers on Wall Street formed an alliance and envisioned a central bank for the country, with them at the helm, and they proved steadfast in their pursuit of making their idea a reality. In January 1906, Jacob H. Schiff, head of the Wall Street banking firm of Kuhn, Loeb & Co. gave a speech to the New York Chamber of Commerce in which he warned that the country "needed money" and a more "elastic currency" that could not be obtained from the US Treasury. He urged the chamber of commerce to draw up a comprehensive plan for a "new, modern banking system" – a central banking system.

The chamber of commerce proved reluctant to directly attach its name to such a concept, so James Stillman, head of the National City Bank of New York secured his bank's president, Frank A. Vanderlip, to create a five-man commission, set up through the offices of the New York Chamber of Commerce to draw up a report. The commission was composed of Wall Street heavy-hitters and New York businessmen in favour of a central banking system. They were Frank Vanderlip; Isidore Straus, director of R. H. Macy & Co., and close friend of Jacob Schiff; Dumont Clarke, president of the American Exchange National Bank, and a personal advisor to J. P. Morgan; Charles A. Conant, treasurer of Morton Trust Company, and also an advisor to J. P. Morgan; and John Claflin, head of the massive dry goods wholesaler, H. B. Claflin & Co.[6]

In October 1906 the commission presented its currency report to the New York Chamber of Commerce, calling forcefully for the creation of a central bank. The themes of the report began to pour into the ears of politicians and bankers across the country, and when the Panic of 1907 hit (an unexplainable US economic aberration) less than a year later, the iron for their new system was hot to strike. The political leader of the charge for centralized banking was Senator Nelson W. Aldrich, head of the Senate Finance Committee and also the father-in-law of John D. Rockefeller, Jr.[7]

The Clearing House Loan Certificate system was time-tested, reliable, carefully scrutinized and very successful in producing emergency funds in times of crisis. Unfortunately, with the effects of the Panic of 1907 still lingering, and thanks to a Herculean propaganda push from Wall Street, on 27 May 1908 the Aldrich–Vreeland Emergency Currency Act was passed, under considerable opposition.[8]

The Emergency Currency Act was penned as a means for issuing hundreds of millions of dollars in emergency currency, and designed as a temporary fix in times of financial stress. At the time, clearing house certificates had been issued to the value of $255,536,300 – a huge sum by turn of the century standards. The Aldrich–Vreeland Act could pump another $500 million into the economy; with many detractors claiming it would grossly inflate the currency if ever used.

The time period of the Act's effectiveness was from its approval date, 27 May 1908 to 30 June 1914. The future proved to be serendipitous for the Act, for when the Federal Reserve Act was passed in December 1913, it had not gone into full effect until 16 November 1914. With the outbreak of the First World War on 28 July 1914 the Aldrich–Vreeland Act was brought back and extended until 30 June 1915, and its emergency currency began to flow, with the newborn Federal Reserve opening the faucet.[9]

The act solidified Senator Aldrich's reputation as a politician with keen interest in the country's economy and currency issues, and with heavy ties to its private banking industry. Even more important than its later economic affects, the Aldrich–Vreeland Act's most influential and widely overlooked provision was its establishment of the National Monetary Commission (NMC), with Aldrich at its helm. This entity was set up to investigate the currency issues of the country and suggest proposals for comprehensive banking reform. It would prove be the conduit through which all Federal Reserve plans would flow.

The NMC consisted of an equal number of senators and representatives; however, it was the advisors to the Commission that had the country's brow collectively furrowed. Aldrich chose as his top advisor, Henry P. Davison, a partner of J. P. Morgan & Co. Urged by Jacob Schiff, Aldrich chose Harvard University president Charles Eliot for his technical economic expert and director of research. Then, Harvard University economist Abram Piatt Andrew was appointed, as well as Charles A. Conant for his public relations skills, along with Frank Vanderlip of James Stillman's National City Bank of New York, and Paul M. Warburg, Schiff's protégé at Kuhn, Loeb & Co. and head of the longstanding European family-banking dynasty of M. M. Warburg & Co. This would be the core of the brain trust that designed the Federal Reserve Act.

Long before Aldrich appointed Warburg as one of his personal advisors, he urged Warburg, because of his extensive knowledge of European central banking, to educate the public on central banking through speeches and interviews. By the time he began working as a member of the NMC, Warburg had been lecturing for several years. During his intensive campaign for a central bank, he gave a famous speech to the New York YMCA on 23 March 1910 on "A United Reserve Bank for the United States". It was during this speech that he outlined the first iteration of his central banking plan, mimicking the German, Reichsbank, and insisting it "not be controlled by Wall Street or any monopolistic interest".

Opposition to a central bank was ubiquitous. Uninfluenced by Wall Street, many bankers and economists of the time insisted upon a revamping of the Clearing House System instead, which would enable troubled banks to "meet a temporary paroxysm of credit by getting more reserves and by increasing their lending power through the deposit of first-class collateral".[10] Local and national boards were to be established within the banking community to act as mediation and communication centres for the smaller local banks and the larger national banks. This system, unlike the central banking system proposed by Senator Aldrich and the outspoken Paul

Warburg, "does not propose a money-making institution, or a financial 'octopus,' but a simple, direct method of enabling the borrowing public to get aid from banks in time of distress".[11]

Undiscouraged by the lack of popular support for their plan, the interests of top Wall Street bankers, Senator Aldrich, and his National Monetary Commission were represented in what proved to be an infamous, nine-day, secret meeting on Jekyll Island, Georgia, at the J. P. Morgan-owned, Jekyll Island Hunt Club in November 1910 in order to draft a plan that implemented their economic ideologies and financial motivations for Wall Street banking consolidation. Warburg wrote the bill, along with Senator Aldrich, Frank A. Vanderlip, Benjamin Strong, Jr, A. Piatt Andrew and Henry P. Davison, when they convened on the island. They all knew how difficult a task it would be to push this bill through, but they were determined to do so. No congressman would even consider a bill with the scent of Wall Street on it. So the real authors of the bill remained hidden, and the final plan was presented as a cogent response to the Panic of 1907 and Nelson W. Aldrich signed his name to it.

The Jekyll Islanders' final creation was the Aldrich Bill of 1911, and it was met with massive criticism, especially from the Midwestern bankers. Despite the smoke and mirrors used to disguise the bill's drafters and its private banking constructs, the bill seemed to blatantly favour Wall Street interests and the New York bankers who proposed its inception. Its main focus was on administration and control by the major banking and investment houses of Wall Street, rather than banking principles or economic and monetary protection and security. The Midwestern bankers felt left out of the fold, and recognized the bill for what it was – a lunging attempt by Wall Street to control the nation's currency. James B. Forgan, president of the First National Bank of Chicago, asked noted US economist J. Laurence Laughlin, after they were both asked to review the bill by Aldrich: "Laughlin, did you ever see such a mess for a banking bill?"[12]

Many western bankers and economists were invited to a banking conference, held in Washington, DC and asked by Senator Aldrich to review his bill. The famous *New York Commercial Bulletin* correspondent, H. Parker Willis, known for his columns on the banking and investment industry, noted: "The conference was so largely composed of Western men . . . Aldrich has shown a disposition to get the views of the most careful thinkers on the subject, and at the same time to avoid the criticism to which he has laid himself open in the past of working too closely with local financial interest."[13]

Willis crystalized not only the key features of the Aldrich Bill, but also the opinion of small bankers, small business, and the entire conference of non-Eastern bankers and economists of the simplistic aims of the bill when he further wrote: "It will be impossible to make the scheme successful if it simply consists of a plan for enabling one part of the country to throw its bonds and other securities into liquid form, and then lend the notes representing them to banks in other parts of the country with, of course, an additional rate of interest".[14] On the other hand, Paul Warburg was, not surprisingly, quoted as saying he was, "delighted with Senator Aldrich's plan as published today from Washington".[15] Warburg knew that the public would never get behind a bill so heavily weighted by eastern banking and investment interests. So he sought ways to "educate" the public in favour of the plan. He devised a scheme to appoint a committee, through the National Board of Trade and the National Monetary Commission with the political influence of Senator Aldrich, to organize a league for the purposes of swaying Representatives and the general public to support the bill through media propaganda and marketing.

He knew none of this could come from New York or Washington, so very skillfully, he and other Aldrich Bill supporters met with 30 hand-picked Chicago businessmen through the Chicago Association of Commerce and its chief, Harry A. Wheeler, on 26 April 1911 and formed the National Citizens' League for the Promotion of a Sound Banking System. Since the League was made up of Chicago business interests, it was adeptly veiled as an entity unattached to any one particular political interest group, or bill. However, promises were made and palms were pressed, and Chicago businessmen and bankers were convinced that what was good for New York was good for Chicago; and what was good for Chicago was good for the Midwest.[16]

However, the ruse didn't work for long. By January 1912 the American Bankers' Association (ABA) proved that the League was "engaged in enacting a banking law" and not "educating the country", therefore their aim was political in nature, and therefore, illegal. The ABA would not commit itself to the Aldrich Bill. What followed was a rift between those in favour of a purely centralized banking system, and those who supported a system of regional banks. The Aldrich Bill was put on hold.[17]

President Woodrow Wilson was then in office, and another year of arduous planning for banking reform continued. By January 1913, Democratic Congressman Carter Glass, then chairman of the House Banking and Currency Sub-Committee, and soon-to-be Secretary of the Treasury under President Wilson, submitted the first draft of the Glass Bill on Banking Reform to the president for review and polish before it was seen by the public or by Congress. By June, members of the Banking Committee had reviewed it and the partisan disagreements began.

Glass's bill was almost a carbon copy of the Aldrich plan. Minor changes included the implementation of a multi-regional reserve system, with many cities having their own reserve bank to regulate the progress of their own local banks. The Glass Bill read like the creation of a monopolistic oligarchy, made up of heads of a few large city banks making the decisions and structuring policy for countless smaller institutions, which was exactly what the Aldrich Bill was. The largest disparity in equality for the smaller banks was the fact that none of them would have representation on the Federal Reserve Board.[18] Wall Street's largest banks would have all the control, which was just the way the six men who went to Jekyll Island to draft the Aldrich Bill wanted it.

The secrecy of the Glass Bill remained of the utmost importance. No one outside the House Committee had seen the bill, so to obtain a copy, at this stage, became the first aim of the "conspirators" who wanted to control it. President Wilson obtained a digest of the bill, and although there is no proof he was in on the conspiracy, he put it in the hands of his top presidential advisor, Texan, "Colonel" Edward M. House (House awarded himself the title "Colonel" despite having no military background).

House, notorious for wanting to impress New York bankers with his influence over President Wilson, passed the digest of the bill on to Paul Warburg, and then expeditiously left for Europe. Warburg revealed the digest to his New York banking group, left for Switzerland, and then penned a harsh criticism of the bill to Secretary of the Treasury William Gibbs McAdoo (President Wilson's son-in-law) as well as to a number of bankers. Warburg was not in favour of the bill's multi-regional implementations; neither was Benjamin Strong, Jr, and the other New York bankers. Wall Street wanted total control. That is what made the covert publicity of the bill so important. Forewarned by Warburg's leaking of the bill, Wall Street was forearmed to fight for more control.[19]

The big bankers were not the only ones who scorned the bill. Secretary of the Treasury McAdoo penned his own plan for reform, backed by prominent lawyer, Samuel Untermeyer and Colonel House. The partisan battle lines were drawn and the special interests went full-bore for getting their own needs met. Each wanted to be immortalized as the one credited with the creation of central banking in the United States, and they all wanted it on their terms.

More liberal politicians such as Secretary of State William Jennings Bryan denigrated the bill on the basis of its prodigious credit system. Bryan had an army of followers in political circles and amongst the general public. He backed "Free Silver", "Trust Busting" and had a complete disdain for Wall Street "elitism", all of which he was very vocal about in his presidential campaigns. Bryan urged for a much stronger government influence over banking, its regulation, and the issuance of notes and credit. He also demanded that these new bills being drafted in favour of a central banking system for the country contain much more restriction and government regulation, and much less freedom for big bankers. Bryan stated with fervour: "You tell those gentlemen that no change whatever, not one jot or tittle, will be made in the provisions allowing the Government issues. The bankers have had too many privileges given to them in the past. The issue of notes by the Government has, for years, been pure Democratic doctrine."[20]

In July 1913 Paul Warburg announced to the Banking Committee, "Both parties are thus in agreement to the ends to be striven for; more than that, they are in agreement even as to the technical means by which they must be attained".[21] Obviously, this could not be further from the truth. However, despite the actual maelstrom of opposition and disagreement, President Wilson surprisingly supported the Glass Bill. The Democratic caucus made some minor changes. The Banking Committee modified it (this was the fourth draft of the bill thus far and only the first draft presented to the public). The bill passed the caucus by a party vote of 168–9. Despite major objections regarding the autonomous powers granted to the Federal Reserve Board, the mandatory and coercive membership of the national banks, and the transfer of reserves, the bill passed the House on 18 September 1913, by a vote of 287–85. Only 3 Democrats voted against it, 48 Republicans for it and 82 against.[22]

The framers of the Federal Reserve left the system's architecture in the hands of Paul Warburg. Since his ideologies on central banking were based on his experience with his native German central banking system, his concepts were quite literally foreign to many of the votes. It was this lack of understanding of Warburg's vision, coupled with the natural suspicion many voters of the bill had regarding Wall Street interests controlling the nation's banks that was the focus of much of the debate during this stage of the bill's reconstruction. Weighing the government's power with the bankers' power remained the battle throughout the process.

Senator Robert L. Owen structured a further bill, with the help of A. Piatt Andrew, one of the original framers of the Aldrich Bill and advisor to the NMC. Now, the Glass Bill, the McAdoo Bill and the Owen Bill were to be reviewed by the president for submission to the Senate for a vote. Wilson passed on the Owen Bill, decided against the McAdoo Bill, and went with the heavily Democratic Congressional-favoured Glass Bill. Since business and banking interests, especially in New York, had much influence in the Congress and the Senate, the Glass Bill was attacked on issues of ultimate control and its disposal was significant to its many detractors. Frank A. Vanderlip and Benjamin Strong, Jr prepared a central bank measure. The American Bankers' Association and the United States Chamber of Commerce were heard from in the Senate. Sixty-eight bankers and eight "experts" were heard supporting a central bank plan, and the nationwide campaign of propaganda began led by the still active, yet formerly deemed, illegal National Citizens' League for the Promotion of a Sound Banking System.

Senator Gilbert Hitchcock, Paul M. Warburg and the rest of Wall Street were now heard loud and clear. A strong central banking package, with regional reserve banks under it, and the ability for that central bank to use government notes as legal reserves for member banks were penned as amendments to the Owen Bill on 18 December 1913; the Senate passed it the next day by a vote of 54–34, with only three Republicans voting for the bill. Many members of Congress and the Senate had left for their allotted Christmas vacation. It was very suspect to many that the bill was being voted on at this time, with so many representatives and senators not in attendance.

After eight drafts, in record time, the Owen Bill and the Glass Bill were finally integrated, forming the Owen–Glass Bill, voted in by the House, 298–60 (16 not voting) and the Senate, 43–25 (27 not voting) and signed by President Wilson on 23 December 1913.[23] The bill was signed into law as the Federal Reserve Act, and went into full effect after almost a year of organization on 16 November 1914.

Wilson's signature of the bill proved to be quite the antithesis of his original stance on the concept of central banking. Many of his supporters and the public in general were dumbfounded by his decision. During his 1912 run for election, less than two years before he signed the Federal Reserve Act into law, on behalf of the Democratic Party's platform, Wilson proclaimed to the American people:

We oppose the so-called Aldrich Bill or the establishment of a central bank . . . Banks exist for the accommodation of the public . . . All legislation on the subject of banking and currency should have for its purpose of securing of these accommodations on terms of absolute security to the public and of complete protection from the misuse of power that wealth gives to those who possess it.[24]

A central bank would permit banks to realize their assets without delay by redis-counting[25] them, or lending banks money based on their forecasted assets. It would also give a "bank rate" that was supposed to protect the US gold supply and restrict speculation in the economy. Under a system of "modern banking paper" in which all banks were interested, the central bank's charge for rediscounting paper of individual banks would necessarily affect domestic and international economic behaviour in ways consistent to national requirements. Wall Street bankers contended that a central bank would make the United States a "modern and completely civilized nation". It also embodied the representation of complete control over all banking practices and business loans throughout the entire country.[26]

No one bothered to argue that the mere sight of the scramble of several thousand bankers for profitable alignment with this new system of American finance was, in itself, sufficient to cast doubt on the likely maintenance of banking integrity in the United States. Nor, that to embrace profit was to contain the business cycle with limits. Paul Warburg explained the dichotomy of the economic system he and other bankers wished to install: "Money making and the maintenance of a safe proportion between cash and cash obligations are at times distinctly opposed functions".[27]

The theory was that corporate leaders and the major Wall Street banks had proven themselves worthy of recognizing the difference between short-term profit and long-term financial growth and stability. They represented the economic structure of America, and now that they could obtain centralization, the banking system would be their domain, as a special interest group, unencumbered by any political or judicial barriers. The unpredictability of the American system of free enterprise would be thwarted by this corporatization of centralized banking, and the kingpins of American finance could now have both their short-term profits and their long-term financial growth and stability with minimal risk. Central banking put the "power in numbers" theory into effect for the small number of controlling interests.

The president would become a useful tool in administering and extending corporate policies – not the government's agendas, and not political capitalism. This period saw capitalism continue to be redefined in America, as it did with the railroads in the previous century. The Federal Reserve is a monument to its founders' commitment and their efforts. Large corporations consolidated, conglomerated, and worked cooperatively, despite their competition, to restructure industry in America, and left the smaller companies fighting for a tiny share of the same market. Many of the same men who controlled these industrial corporations – Rockefeller, Morgan, Harriman, Vanderbilt – controlled or influenced much of the banking industry as well. Since their monopolization efforts were so successful in the industrial sector, they took the next logical step and asked "Why not do the same with the banking industry?" They did.[28]

The Federal Reserve Act was a four-year grind from its controversial inception at Jekyll Island in November 1910 to the final signatures in December 1913 and its organization in November 1914 that created the first central banking system in the United States in almost 80 years. In the end, it was the original six men who drafted the first blueprint of the Federal Reserve Act who got their way. There was a change here, an adjustment there, but in the words of Frank Vanderlip regarding the outcome of the Wall Street bankers' original scheme, "Its essential points were all contained in the plan that was finally adopted".[29]

Supporters of the Federal Reserve Act recognized its advertised aim to sustain the original system of many independent banks working autonomously, but "federated" to unify them in a nationwide, democratic organization. They crowed that it was a system "dedicated to public service", and that it did not, contrary to popular belief, destroy the American banking system. It upheld the essential functions of the existing banks, and merely enhanced their operation and aided in protecting them, and the public.[30]

The Federal Reserve Act produced new legislation with some very innovative and striking provisions. Section 2 of the act stipulates the formation of "districts" in which the Federal Reserve banks would operate. However, the districts and their number were not established until months after the act began. It was finally agreed that there would be 12 Federal Reserve cities in 12 Federal Reserve districts, which remain to this day, although the borders have changed over the years.

The 12 districts of the Federal Reserve System, from an economic perspective, dissolved the traditional political boundaries of the 48 states of the time. No state law could supersede any provision of the Federal Reserve Act. This was exactly what Thomas Jefferson had warned against in 1791 when he battled Alexander Hamilton and the bankers of his time over the formation of a central bank. Years later, in 1816, in a letter he wrote to John Taylor from his home in Monticello, Jefferson proved that his views on banking and bankers had soured even further since the days of

Hamilton's bid for a central bank in the new Republic: "... And I sincerely believe, with you, that banking establishments are more dangerous than standing armies; and that the principle of spending money to be paid by posterity, under the name of funding, is but swindling futurity on a large scale".[31]

The districts made it easier to control the formation and distribution of the stock in the Federal Reserve as well. This stock, by the provisions of the act, legally formed a corporation (protected by the Fourteenth Amendment as an entity with human rights) of the new US banking system. The owners of this stock could then keep it in a line of succession of their choice, and wield enough power to legislate and regulate their own industry for generations. These tactics are considered by economists to be monopolization of an industry.[32] However, from a strictly banking perspective, the districts were evenly divided and convenient in their organization. They were large enough to provide the system with its requirement of $4 million of capital, and they were small enough so as not to be dominated or cannibalized by each other.[33]

Not only did the system centralize credit and concentrate control of the country's wealth into the hands of a few bankers, but the ratio of the amount of money a bank could loan, to the amount it could lend, was of equally grave concern to Federal Reserve detractors. Under the provisions of the act, only 12–18 per cent of reserves were required for demand deposits, and 3–5 per cent was required for time deposits. Approximately, for every 1 dollar accepted by a member bank in demand deposits, 7 dollars could be loaned out, and about 33 dollars for every dollar could be loaned out, based on time deposit requirements. The amount of money the banks could loan far outweighed the amount they actually had.[34]

As far as the gold that backed the reserves, its value was of great importance. The creators of the Fed favoured a "compensated dollar". That is, the gold equivalent to every dollar loaned out, or kept in reserve, would vary in order to keep things like the market price index, inflation, and the ratio to international currency relatively constant. Essentially, the dollar's weight in gold would change "to compensate for the change in purchasing power . . .".[35]

Every commercial bank in America must signify, in writing, its acceptance of the provisions of the Federal Reserve Act. If they fail to do so or fail to comply in any way with the Act's provisions, that bank would cease to exist as a reserve agent, and would forfeit its rights, privileges, stock and franchises, and would be dissolved.[36] Many banks deferred joining the Federal Reserve System at its inception. However, the First World War made private bankers face the scrutiny of patriots who believed it was their duty as Americans to join the system and work together to win the war and stave off the ongoing national emergency.[37]

All "participating" Federal Reserve Banks must buy stock in the Fed itself. Section 4 of the act states that once all the capital stock is purchased, banks may apply for Federal Reserve Bank status. If approved by the organization committee, these banks were issued with organization certificates giving them Federal Reserve Bank status and corporate body status, having the same powers and legal rights as any corporation. The capital stock of each Federal Reserve Bank had an Initial Private Offering of $100 per share, which made it one of the most expensive opening stocks in the world. The stock value increased as new banks became members or as member banks increased their stock.[38]

Any businessperson would agree that whoever owns the most stock in a corporation ultimately controls that corporation. About a decade after its formation, Democratic congressman from Texas, Wright Patman, one of the Federal Reserve System's leading critics, tried to find out who actually owned the stock in the original Federal Reserve banks. He found that most of the stock in the regional banks of the 12 districts was purchased by national banks in those corresponding regions. Patman knew that the Federal Reserve Bank of New York was the hub for the regional banks with its powers to set interest rates and direct open market operations, equivalent to controlling the daily supply and price of money throughout the country. Given this, the stockholders of the New York branch of the Federal Reserve Bank occupied the most powerful position of anyone in the entire banking system.

With Benjamin Strong, Jr (president of J. P. Morgan's Bankers Trust Company) as its first governor, the original organization certificates of the Federal Reserve Bank of New York, filed with the Comptroller of Currency on 19 May 1914, state that that branch issued 203,053 shares. Of those shares, the largest blocks were purchased by the National Bank of Commerce of New York City (later known as Morgan Guaranty Trust Company) which took 21,000 shares; Chase National Bank (6,000 shares); the Marine National Bank of Buffalo, later known as Marine Midland Bank (also 6,000 shares); the National City Bank of New York (headed by James Stillman, with Frank Vanderlip as its president) purchased 30,000 shares, and J. P. Morgan's First National Bank of New York (run by George F. Baker) held 15,000 shares.[39] In 1955, the National City Bank of New York and First National Bank merged to form the largest, most powerful and influential stockholding bank in the entire Federal Reserve System. Known as First National City Bank, its ultimate moniker became, Citigroup.[40]

Section 14 of the Federal Reserve Act stipulated that Federal Reserve Banks could execute business transactions in the open market with banks, firms, corporations, or individuals – foreign or domestic. They may deal in gold at home or abroad. They may also maintain bank accounts in foreign countries, appoint correspondents, and establish separate agencies in foreign countries for the purposes of transacting banking business. This section proved to be a major coup for the Wall Street banks, especially National City Bank, as will be explained in future chapters.

Sections 4 and 14 would prove extremely useful for the growth and global expansion of the System after the First World War, giving the Federal Reserve the opportunity to open branches all over Europe for the purposes of loans and gold exchange during a period of postwar foreign economic stimulation. But, the banks did not stop there. They were given the right to expand, internationally, under the provisions of Section 25, and they soon became global entities with more power than any other banks in the world.[41]

Section 15 gave the Federal Reserve ultimate power over the country's finances. It allowed money held in the general fund of the US Treasury to be deposited into a Federal Reserve Bank, making that bank a fiscal agent of the United States. It also stated, "Every Government fund, postal savings fund, or public fund of the Philippine Islands must be deposited into a Federal Reserve Bank".[42]

Sections 10 and 11 of the Federal Reserve Act are seemingly the most vague. They explain the formation, the power and the responsibilities of the Federal Reserve Board. Under the heading, "Federal Reserve Board", the act provides that the Board consists of seven members. One is the Secretary of the Treasury, another, the Comptroller of Currency, and the other five (at least two of which must be in the banking or investment field) are appointed by the US president.[43] Although this gave the act the appearance of existing without any one-sided or partisan motivation, the reality was a group of private bankers, operating privately-owned banks, which conduct their private business outside the parameters of public, government, and even minimal presidential regulation or oversight.[44]

Under the original terms of the Federal Reserve Act, each board member was paid a salary of $12,000 per month (which converts to $289,718 per month, or an annual salary of $3,507,883 in 2017),[45] which was to be levied, semi-annually upon member Federal Reserve Banks. This provision was of major significance because the Board's power to levy an assessment on other reserve banks to pay expenses and salaries made the Board "independent of the congressional appropriations process" and thus, could not be audited by any government agency. The power of the government, or any outside entity, to audit the Federal Reserve Board did not come until 1978, with the Federal Banking Agency Audit Act, which gave the General Accounting Office the ability to audit the Board. Although, they never have.[46]

The Fed's supporters saw the power of the Board as the essential centralizing cog in the new system's engine. It brought order to the system and it had the ability and the collective experience to develop the broad financial policies that would sustain the nation's wealth, as well as possessing the ability to carry out those policies swiftly and unencumbered by political bureaucracy. To pro-Fed drum-bangers, decentralization had become the "old evil" and the Federal Reserve was the remedy to the disorganized, randomly disseminated, immobile reserves the country had been mired in.[47]

The Board may look into the finances of any member bank at will, and write weekly reports on such affairs. Reserve banks may rediscount the discounted paper from other banks at a fixed interest rate. Any reserve requirements may be suspended for a maximum of 45 days. The Board can suspend or remove any officer of any member bank. Finally, the board may suspend the operations of any bank and may liquidate or reorganize said bank at the Board's discretion.[48] This power proved to be contrary to the original responsibilities of the Comptroller of the Currency. An extensive power struggle ensued for years between the five members of the Board who were bankers, and the two ex officio members: the Comptroller of the Currency and the Secretary of the Treasury. These two government officials had authority over state banks and holding companies in the past. The Comptroller of Currency chartered all the national banks, which were required to become members of the Fed. The question quickly arose as to who had ultimate regulatory control over member banks. This battle raged quietly but consistently for many years after the formation of the Board, until finally, under the Banking Act of 1935, the Secretary of the Treasury and the Comptroller of the Currency were removed from the Federal Reserve Board completely, and sole responsibility for US monetary policy was placed in the hands of the bankers, or the economists who were employed by them, of the Federal Reserve Board.

The original 1914 Federal Reserve Board members were Secretary of the Treasury, William Gibbs McAdoo; Comptroller of Currency, John Skelton Williams; president of the Seaboard Air Line Railway and uncle of President Franklin Delano Roosevelt, Frederic Adrian Delano; Boston attorney, former Governor of

Massachusetts, and, at the time, Assistant Secretary of the Treasury, Charles Sumner Hamlin; president of Birmingham, Alabama's First National Bank and the managing director of the War Finance Corporation, William Proctor Gould Harding; economist, professor at the University of California, Berkeley, and, at the time, Assistant Secretary of the Interior, Adolph C. Miller; and Paul M. Warburg, whose appointment to the Board fell under the most suspicion because of his employment at Kuhn, Loeb & Co., his close ties to "money interests", his drafting of the Aldrich Bill, his German and Jewish heritage, and his opposition to the final draft of the Federal Reserve Act because of its "limited powers".

Despite controversy over many of the appointments to the Board, once appointed, no member would ever be directly responsible to the government, who possessed no legal powers over Fed policy and, at the Board's discretion, may have no means of communication with board members at all. The president of the United States is not permitted to sit in on a meeting of the Board of the Federal Reserve.[49]

At the Board's inception in 1914, US Attorney General T. W. Gregory commented on the extent of the reach and autonomy of the Board as being "not merely supervisory, but . . . a distinctly administrative board with extensive powers." President Wilson described the breadth of the Board's authority when he called it "the Supreme Court of Finance".[50] The power the Board came to possess over time didn't go unnoticed. Karl Gustav Cassel, Swedish economist, professor of economics at Stockholm University, and founding member of the Swedish school of economics wrote in 1928: "The American dollar, not the gold standard, is the world's monetary standard. The American Federal Reserve Board has the power to determine the purchasing power of the dollar by making changes in the rate of discount, and thus, controls the monetary standard of the world."[51]

The Federal Reserve is the most powerful influence on the status and health of the US economy. But exactly what does the Federal Reserve do to help the economy? In simple and accessible language (if that's actually possible), the basic functions and powers of the Federal Reserve are as follows:

The Open Market Committee. This committee of Fed members controls the purchase and/or sale of government securities on the open market. When the Fed orders the purchase of securities (like Treasury Bills), the byproduct is an increase of money into the economy, which increases inflation. When securities are sold, the opposite effect is felt, and money becomes tighter.

Setting Interest Rates. The Federal Reserve determines the interest rates a bank charges a customer for a loan, and the corresponding interest rates a customer's money earns while in the bank. The lower the interest rate, the higher the amount of credit a customer can receive.

Setting the Discount Rate. The discount rate is the interest rate charged to member banks to take out short-term loans from the US Federal Reserve Bank. The lower the Fed sets these discounted interest rates, the more the banks can borrow, and the more money they can lend out to customers, which leads to cheaper credit and economic stimulation. If the discount rate is set high, the opposite effect occurs.

Setting the Reserve Requirement. The reserve requirement is the amount of assets (or gold, before President Roosevelt, in 1933, abandoned the gold standard and confiscated every American citizen's gold, making its private ownership punishable by ten years in prison) banks had to keep in reserve to back up the loans they had outstanding. For example, Benjamin Strong, Jr cut reserve requirements from his office as governor of the New York Federal Reserve by more than half over the first four years of the creation of his post. This single act doubled the US money supply by the end of the First World War.

Fractional Reserve Banking. This describes the amount of cash reserves a bank must have to back up its outstanding loans. For example, today a Federal Reserve member bank can lend out $10,000 for every $1,000 it keeps in deposits. It must have only 10 per cent of all "demand deposits" in reserve.

Creating Money. The Federal Reserve determines the printing and minting of all the money in circulation. The more money that is in circulation, the more accessible it is, and the more its worth diminishes; and vice versa.[52]

With fractional demand deposits and the adjustments of reserve requirements, the actual value of money is, in practice, based on how much of it there is. Since a very small portion of gold backs it, and given the drastically unbalanced ratio between how much the Fed and its reserve banks can lend to the amount they actually possess, the ability to create money has always been synchronous with the ability to control its value, and the Federal Reserve Board controls that entire process.

If all this seems confusing, that's because it is. But the basic, obvious progression is very simple: the Federal Reserve prints money and lends it out to banks, with interest (the discount rate), which the Fed sets. The banks then loan that money to their customers at a higher interest rate (the interest rate), which the Fed also sets. So the second the Fed prints a dollar bill, that dollar carries the discount rate and the interest rate with it at its inception. So at all times, there is more money owed than money that exists. The cycle is never-ending and debt is always owed to the Federal Reserve.

These rights the Federal Reserve possesses are enormous in power and responsibility. From the average citizen, to the global corporation, to the economies of entire nations, these functions affect everyone who is under the umbrella of the US monetary system – which extends to the entire world. The slightest adjustment in any aspect of the Federal Reserve's domain is shockingly felt domestically, and its economic ripple-effect reaches across the globe; and the Federal Reserve protects its power by any and all means necessary to maintain its quiet yet immense control over American and foreign finance. As William Greider writes:

> The Federal Reserve quite literally protected money's illusions. The complex bundle of psychological meanings, the social consent, and the fantastic implications attached to money – all were sustained by concealment, an austere distance from popular examination. The Fed proved that; with its secrecy and its obscure language, with its tradition of mystery and unknowable processes. [The public's] ignorance was comforting, perhaps even necessary for belief, and the Federal Reserve's mystique allowed people not to look directly upon these questions.[53]

3

The Island

Jekyll Island is a small, narrow island off the coast of the state of Georgia. Today it has golf courses, small hotels and B&Bs, a quaint village district, and a historical society. People from both north and south go there to vacation and relax. At about the turn of the nineteenth century, East-coast Americans did the same things on Jekyll Island as they do now. However, back then, another attraction of the island existed, and it accommodated some of the richest men in the world.

In 1733, General James Oglethorpe founded Georgia as a British colony and named the island after his financier, Sir Joseph Jekyll. Decades later, Cristophe DuBignon fled the French Revolution and landed on Jekyll Island, purchasing much of the property. In 1879, DuBignon's descendant, John Eugene DuBignon and his brother-in-law Newton Finney turned Jekyll Island into a private hunting club for the wealthiest men in America. *Munsey's Magazine* called it "the richest, the most exclusive, the most inaccessible club in the world". In 1888, the club officially opened its doors, and by 1896, J. P. Morgan owned much of it – building the six-unit, "Sans Souci", which would be one of the first condominiums in the United States.[1]

Future membership was by inheritance only and the only non-members allowed were servants. The club comprised splendid mansions called "cottages" where the members would stay, dine, socialize and conduct business. The club's membership was so exclusive and steeped in such astounding amounts of international wealth, that after one of its members, George F. Baker, founder of the First National Bank of New York, and very close associate of Morgan's, died in 1931, The *New York Times* noted, ". . . the Jekyll Island Club has lost one of its most distinguished members. One-sixth of the total wealth of the world is represented by the members of the Jekyll Island Club".[2]

Jekyll Island Club, circa 1900.

It was on this island at the Hunt Club where six men – four Wall Street bankers, an economist and one politician – would plan and draft the first blueprint for the United States Federal Reserve System: an all-controlling central bank that has overseen the currency, monetary system, and economic policy for the United States for over a century. All accomplished from a tiny island in Georgia. Nelson W. Aldrich, Republican Rhode Island senator and multimillionaire was the political representative on this cloak and dagger episode. Accompanying him at this most enigmatic meeting were A. Piatt Andrew, Assistant Secretary of the Treasury; Frank A. Vanderlip, President of the National City Bank of New York (headed by James Stillman); Henry P. Davison, senior partner of J. P. Morgan & Co. (regarded as Morgan's personal emissary); Benjamin Strong, Jr, known as Morgan's "lieutenant"; Paul M. Warburg, partner in the Jacob Schiff-run banking house of Kuhn, Loeb & Co.; and senator Aldrich's personal secretary, Mr Arthur Shelton.

By November 1910, the secret meeting on J. P. Morgan's Jekyll Island was only days away. Harvard economist and Assistant Secretary of the Treasury, A. Piatt Andrew kept Aldrich abreast of the goings on of Western banks and businesses on the side of central banking through vast and regular correspondence. However, Frank Vanderlip, wrote to Senator Aldrich that month about a completely separate issue but one that would become of grave importance for those in control of the soon to be Federal Reserve: foreign branches of national banks. "We deem it extremely desirable so to extend the powers of national banks as either to permit foreign branches or permit the organization of banks to conduct foreign business. We believe it will be an important factor in furthering the development of our foreign trade if this enlargement of privilege is authorized."[3] This, and many other issues would be discussed and mapped during the meeting.

Paul Warburg's blueprint for the central bank was also ready for the meeting on the island. Aldrich, however, needed to convey the appearance of impartiality and appear to consider many sides of the argument on central banking and certainly not entertain the demands of Wall Street barons like Warburg. So on 6 November 1910, just days before the Jekyll Island meeting, Warburg pretended to send the plan to Dr A. Piatt Andrew, headed, "My Dear 'Doc'" but actually sent it to Aldrich: "For reasons that you will readily understand I have given my letter the appearance of being addressed to Dr. Andrew, with whom I have often exchanged letters of this kind, and I refer, for safety's sake, to a discussion at Columbia [University] concerning my plan, while, of course, the more recent scheme is meant." Enclosed with that letter was a document that explained the entire first draft of the Federal Reserve Act, all done in secret.[4]

Very little has been written about the Jekyll Island meeting. Even the men who attended the meeting are in question. We know that Senator Aldrich and his personal secretary, Arthur Shelton were on the trip, along with Warburg, Andrew, Davison and Vanderlip. However, questions surround Benjamin Strong, Jr's presence. Vanderlip's archives mention that Strong was there. But no one else who attended the meeting corroborates this. Even Benjamin Strong's biography makes no mention of his attendance. All this would easily be put to rest by reviewing the minutes and recorded proceedings of the Jekyll Island meetings. This is impossible, however, because Aldrich's private secretary, Mr Shelton, destroyed all the notes from the trip.[5] The fact that Strong is mentioned in Vanderlip's papers, his extensive work on the Aldrich Bill after the trip, his deep friendship with Henry Davison, and the fact that he was chosen by all of the men to be the first governor of the New York Federal Reserve is reason enough to at least suspect his presence on the island and include him in this book with the others.

The preparations for the meeting were so clandestine that the men could not speak to or acknowledge each other on the train. They could not meet or dine together for days before the trip, and as an added precaution, they were only to address each other by their first names. Strong was "Mr Benjamin", Warburg was "Mr Paul", Abram Piatt Andrew was "Mr Abram", and Davison and Vanderlip adopted the pseudonyms "Wilber" and "Orville" in honour of the Wright brothers' first engine-powered flight a few years earlier in late 1903. Many years later the group would jokingly refer to themselves as the "First Name Club".[6] The meeting was cloaked in such secrecy so that the press and the public would not surmise that the central banking scheme was an instrument of Wall Street, and if passed, the organization would be in their ultimate control.[7]

The fact that Senator Aldrich's National Monetary Commission had no idea of the meeting, as well as Secretary of the Treasury, Franklin MacVeagh's ignorance of where his employee, A. Piatt Andrew had gone, made it clear that President Taft himself was most likely in the dark about the events that took place that week as well. This is rather remarkable considering members of the Taft administration were directly responsible for the drafting of the most important banking reform bill in US history, and to do so without the knowledge of the president was without precedent. The level of secrecy was akin to a spy novel.[8]

A few investigative reporters were there at the Hoboken, New Jersey train station to try to find out why some of the mightiest financial titans of New York City were gathering on Nelson Aldrich's private train car and secretly heading off together. Financial writer Bertie Charles Forbes (founder of *Forbes Magazine*) described the scene when he wrote:

> Picture a party of the nation's greatest bankers stealing out of New York on a private railroad car, in the cover of darkness, stealthily hoeing hundreds of miles South, embarking on a mysterious launch, sneaking onto an island deserted by all but a few servants, living there for two weeks under such ridged secrecy that the names of not one of them was once mentioned, lest the servants learned the identity, and disclosed to the world this strangest, most secret expedition in the history of American finance.[9]

Paul Warburg even borrowed a shotgun in order to make it look as if the men were on a duck-hunting trip. The men took the two-day journey down to the Brunswick,

Georgia railroad station, before boarding a boat to the island for the final leg of their trip.[10]

They left New York in Aldrich's private railcar, and Davison made all the arrangements for the men's stay. As he worked for J. P. Morgan and it was Morgan's club, he made sure that the Hunt Club would be empty, except for a few servants. According to Lowenstein, the men worked day and night trying to hammer out what could pass as a political draft of a bill for a central banking program. Free time was sparse, so the men walked among the trees and sand of the island for any fresh air they could enjoy. Davison and Andrew would rise early and swim or ride. They worked feverishly, but took the time to dine on turkey with oyster stuffing on Thanksgiving Day.[11]

Paul Warburg was the mastermind behind the plan. He was the most technically proficient in the ways of banking, and with his experience as a banker in Europe, where most major countries had a central banking system, he did most of the drafting of the plan. Warburg was familiar with the politics and the social ramifications of the system he and his colleagues were trying to construct. He argued that the name of the plan was as important as the plan itself for it to be accepted by the public and by Congress.[12] He was clever enough to name the system the "Federal Reserve System" and not a "central bank" so as to falsely suggest to naysayers that it would be government-run and government-controlled.[13] Of course, it was not and remains to this day, completely private.

The exact nature of the meeting had to be kept secret from many eyes and ears. Politicians could not find out that Wall Street men were drafting a banking bill. Otherwise, its failure would be imminent. Similarly, it would be better that the wider public did not know given the country still had a bad taste in its mouth from the bitter Panic of 1907, which was blamed on Wall Street bankers and speculators. Also, the international community of bankers could not hear of this either. Forewarning is forearming, and Wall Street knew this. The less prepared some European banking rivals were, the better for everyone involved in the scheme.

As the American Revolution was born of distrust of central authority, a political revolution could have brewed if news of the motives for this meeting became widely known. After all, it was this same distrust of the rich elite and powerful banks that the Revolution ensured that a central bank would not be a permanent part of the nation for 130 years. As Irwin writes: "The men on Jekyll Island weren't just trying to solve an economic problem – they were trying to solve a political problem as old as their republic".[14]

4

The Politician: Nelson W. Aldrich

If Alexander Hamilton, Richard Nixon and Al Capone had a love child, he would be Senator Nelson W. Aldrich. The London *Times* called him, "the general manager of the United States".[1] Writer for *The Cosmopolitan*, David Graham Philips, described him as, "the organizer of treason". The *New York Times* called him, ". . . pretty close to being the most powerful man in the United States" and "a disgusting hypocrite".[2] And author Ron Chernow described him as "the Czar of the Republican party and the maestro of the smoked-filled room".[3] Probably guilty of all these dubious distinctions, Nelson Aldrich's political power, banking and economic erudition, spectrum of friends that included the most powerful men in the world, and predilection for corruption made him the perfect political representative for the enclave of financial demigods who christened the US Federal Reserve System.

Born in 1841, Nelson Wilmarth Aldrich grew up in East Killingly, Rhode Island. He attended the local elementary school and went on to East Greenwich Academy for a year. Aldrich family lore tells of a time when Nelson was nine years old and his mother gave him money to buy lunch and go to the circus. He went to the circus, but skipped lunch and used that money to buy a copy of *The Tinker's Son, or I'll Be Somebody Yet*, a kind of self-help book, but not one for a nine year old.

He was fascinated with the preachers in his East Killingly church. He noted the influence that oration commanded over people. A young Aldrich ". . . felt an uncontrollable yearning to become at some time a public speaker, to wield myself this wonderful power."[4] His Calvinist upbringing was no doubt a part of his license for control and privilege. John Calvin preached that every man's goodness or evil is predestined, and the more successful he is – the more God has favoured him. The poor are obviously sinners, doomed to hell and the rich are obviously deemed by God to be good, as their status and class in life on earth attest.

Aldrich's father, Anan, was a mill worker and farmer with no illustrious lineage to speak of. However, Aldrich's mother, Abby Burgess, daughter of Major Gideon Burgess, and great-granddaughter of Peleg Williams (a member of the General Assembly that passed the 3 May 1776 Rhode Island Declaration of Independence) could trace her ancestry back to Roger Williams himself, the Puritan minister who founded Rhode Island. Nelson and his brother, Clarence listened to their father discuss politics with neighbours at the local store and heard the praises of the Democratic Party from both parents at the dinner table, by the light of Anan's quiet-natured demeanor and Abby's violent head shaking and eye twitching.

In 1858, at the age of 17, Aldrich entered the business world at the bottom rungs of a Providence wholesale grocery store called Waldron and Wightman. He worked hard and adroitly, and moved up the back office ladder quickly for four years. This early experience in business would provide later rewards in the prodigious fortune Aldrich would amass over his political and business career.

By 1862 the country was in the midst of the Civil War and Aldrich joined the Rhode Island National Guard. As a private in Company D, Aldrich was dispatched to Washington DC to help guard the capital. Aldrich was there for four months until his lack of hydration and "sentry duty amid driving rains"[5] led to a bout of typhoid fever. He was immediately relieved of his duty, returned to Providence, and resumed his climb up the grocer's ladder.

Mr and Mrs Duty Greene couldn't have children, so they took in their niece, Abby Chapman. It is undocumented why her parents gave her up at infancy, but she grew up in the arms of wealth and privilege, so a clerk at a grocery store would have had to compete with many suitors for her hand. Despite a long line of men vying for Abby, in 1865 Nelson Aldrich married money in Abby Greene, but he sought a career in politics to make his own fortune.

Aldrich attended Brown University and graduated from law school. Soon politics began to call him, yet he held a firm hand on the business of which he vested himself in Waldron and Wightman. He started debating at the lyceums of Providence and soon learned he had the gifts of intelligence, persuasion and intimidation. His friends and debating foes, who recognized his strength in oration, urged him to pursue politics. In 1869 Aldrich stood for the Common Council of the Fifth Ward of Providence and won a convincing election. Aldrich's political career is as follows:

member of the city council 1869–74, serving as president in 1872–73; member of the state house of representatives in 1875–76, elected speaker in 1876; elected as a Republican to the Forty-sixth and Forty-seventh Congresses, serving from 4 March 1879 to 4 October 1881, when he resigned to become senator; elected as a Republican to the United States Senate to fill the vacancy caused by the death of Ambrose E. Burnside; re-elected in 1886, 1892, 1898 and 1904, having served from 5 October 1881 to 3 March 1911; he was not a candidate for re-election in 1911. He was chairman of the Committee on Transportation Routes to the Seaboard (Forty-eighth and Forty-ninth Congresses), Committee on Rules (Fiftieth through Fifty-second, Fifty-fourth and Fifty-fifth Congresses), Select Committee on Corporations Organized in the District of Columbia (Fifty-third Congress), Committee on Finance (Fifty-fifth through Sixty-first Congresses) and chairman of the National Monetary Commission (1908–12), retiring to Providence, RI in 1912.[6]

Nelson W. Aldrich

Higher platforms of the political structure were there for the taking, and Aldrich's ambition led him to not only the top rungs of the wholesale grocery business, but into the eagle's nest of Rhode Island politics – the offices of Senator

Henry B. Anthony and his enforcer, General Charles R. Brayton. Lessons in cunning and political chicanery were soon to follow. His biographer: "Altogether (Aldrich) was an unknown quantity from the Brayton point of view, and perhaps (Aldrich) was worth purchasing."[7] Aldrich had been in Congress for a few years when Brayton locked onto him and began to show him the "finer points" of politics. The canals Aldrich dug between his business interests and political career began to flow together. He became involved with many businessmen, and Freemason, General Brayton taught him how to use those interests to his benefit, leading Aldrich to the US Senate, and amassing formidable political power and millions of dollars.

Rhode Island was known as the most politically corrupt state in the United States at the time, and Aldrich's mentor "Boss" Brayton ran the state as the Republican High Sheriff, with governors coming and going at his behest. In a 1905 interview with *McClure's Magazine*, Brayton's candid philosophies on bribery and vote-fixing is astounding to a naïve eye: "I have had connections, not permanent, with various companies desiring franchises, charters, and things of that sort from, the Legislature. I never solicit any business. It all comes to me unsought, and if I can handle it I accept the retainer." The reporter then asked, "What is your power in the Legislature that enables you to serve your clients?" General Brayton replied, "Well, you see, in managing the campaign every year I am in a position to be of service to men all over the state. I help them to get elected, and, naturally, many warm friendships result, then when they are in a position to repay me they are glad to do it."[8]

Brayton continued to expound on how he controlled the purse strings and the leadership of the state. When the time for local caucuses approached, the party leaders came down to Providence to get money for expenses from Brayton. The article recounted the process: "How much do you think you'll need?" Brayton would ask. "Oh, say $500" would come the reply. "Five hundred dollars to carry that town! Who's your man for senator?" The leader would tell him. If the local candidate suited Brayton a bargain was struck as to the amount; if not, he would say pointedly: "I guess there isn't any money for you this year". The leader then had to pick out another candidate, or, perhaps, Brayton would give him a suggestion, which the "other fellows" would have to "agree upon". The bottom line was that Brayton had to be satisfied with the candidate, or the party got no money for expenses.[9]

Even the Governors themselves recognized and admitted the rampant corruption of Rhode Island politics. In a speech given by Governor Lucius F. C. Garvin, he states:

Gentlemen. That bribery exists to a great extent in the elections of this state is a matter of common knowledge. No general election passes without, in some sections of the state, the purchase of votes by one or both of the great political parties. It is true that the results of the election may not often be changed, so far as the candidates on the state ticket are concerned, but many assemblymen occupy the seats they do by means of purchased votes.[10]

This was the home and the political and business origins of Senator Nelson W. Aldrich. As lurid and unscrupulous as it all seems, perhaps Aldrich was not influenced by his surroundings and chose a higher, more righteous path through his career. Unfortunately, it can be argued that the political face of America's central banking act was truly a product of his environment, and once in a position of national power, Aldrich ratcheted up his thirst for success by any means necessary.

By 1881 Aldrich was both a senator and a partner in Waldron and Wightman, which had become one of the largest wholesale grocery firms in New England. One of the specialities of such a firm would be the buying and selling of sugar. His familiarity with the business and tariff system concerning the sugar business soon allowed him to mix his business with his politics to aid his associates in the sugar industry.

The mid-nineteenth century saw prevailing overproduction of sugar, which lead to fierce competition between large and small sugar companies and refineries. The largest points of contention were the tax on sugar and the grading process by which the tax was implemented. Politicians tried to figure out what was fair for all parties concerned so as not to disrupt American business interests.The smaller firms lobbied for a uniformed tax on all sugars, regardless of their grade of quality, and a revamping of the grading process. The larger firms wanted no change in the existing grading process (the Dutch Standard System of polariscoping), along with much lower taxes on lower grades of sugar. The incentive for the bigger sugar companies to adopt these views was the fact that lower taxes on low-grade sugar meant it would cost less money to import it. Therefore, the larger companies could monopolize the importation of the poor sugar, save massive amounts of money on tariffs, and then squeeze out the smaller firms. Furthermore, the polariscope grading system could, and did, lead to huge amounts of grading fraud, and according to the Treasury Department the existing system also undervalued the good sugar, which was mostly imported and sold by the smaller firms.

Enter, Senator Nelson W. Aldrich. In 1882 Aldrich was appointed to the Senate Finance Committee, so he was in an advantageous spot to influence or control tariffs. He, along with other like-minded senators and "Big Sugar" lobbyists, hammered congress and the tariffs and sugar grading systems stayed the same. Sternstein writes:

> Although no sugar refiners operated in Rhode Island, Nelson Aldrich was suited ideally to take up their cause in Congress. Not only was he committed to the principle of utilizing the resources of government to foster the growth and development of American business enterprise in general but, as a banker and partner in one of southern New England's largest wholesale grocery firms, which specialized in buying and selling sugar . . . he had a functional interest in promoting the economic wellbeing of the eastern sugar trade.[11]

Sugar duties were a very big deal at that time, representing one-sixth of the US government's income through taxes. Aldrich took full advantage of the importance of the tariffs by suggesting new, lower taxes every time the house heard the sugar schedule. Through his Finance Committee, Aldrich pushed Chester A. Arthur's Tariff Commission to lower taxes on low-grade sugar by 20–25 per cent across the board, and made sure the polariscope grading system was kept in place. The small refiners were outraged, as well as many industrialists from other walks of business life, wondering how and why these big sugar companies were getting such special treatment.

Aldrich moved to cut the sugar tariff to $1.85 per pound. It settled at $2 per pound, but even that that was a considerable reduction from the existing tax of $2.25 per pound. The smaller refiners denounced the rates whereas the large ones were satisfied both with the cut and that the schedule included the polariscoping method of grading. Also, the big firms were granted their request of even lower tariffs on lower grades of sugar. Soon even the Finance Committee could not support the painfully obvious feathering of the "Big Sugar" nests, which was costing the federal government millions of dollars in lost tax revenue. The Senate floor had to vote on supporting large eastern sugar refiners, or the recommendations of the Finance Committee to halt further tax breaks. Aldrich broke from his own committee and voted to support the sugar companies. He voted to cut the tax on raw sugar and raise the one on refined sugar, further squeezing the interests of the smaller refining companies.

Aldrich was working alongside the sugar lobbyist and managing partner of one of the largest sugar companies, John E. Searles. Searles partnered with the largest sugar refiners in the country, Theodore and Henry Havermeyer, and cut a deal with the Louisiana Sugar Planters Association under which the growers would help the Havermeyer brothers ensure that the Tariff Commission would adopt the polariscope even if they wouldn't advocate a lower tax. Aldrich knew this going into the final voting process, and told no one in the senate or the Finance Committee about it.

Aldrich's vast knowledge of the subject swayed voters to agree with a comprehensive bill that included lower rates on raw sugar, the polariscope system, and a small reduction on refined sugar rates. Then, at the eleventh hour before the vote, he changed the bill to a much higher rate for refined sugar. Known as the Mongrel Tariff, the lower rates stimulated manufacturing. However, what the country did not need more of was sugar. When any given market is saturated, and production increases, prices drop because supply outweighs demand. The market gets much more competitive and only the largest companies can survive. This was exactly what Aldrich and his sugar friends were anticipating. A vast amount of the smaller refiners were forced to shut down or were bought out by the larger ones, and a Sugar Trust was formed with Searles and the Havermeyer brothers at the helm; all indebted to Aldrich.

The Sugar Trust grew to 24 refiners, all east of the Rocky Mountains. This also squeezed out the western refiners as well as the smaller ones. With Senator Aldrich drawing up the sugar schedules every season to benefit the Trust, the relationship between him and "Big Sugar" continued through to the mid 1890s, with his Finance Committee becoming known as a "sugar shop".[12] Tariffs passed to enhance the financial standing of the Trust included the Mills Bill, the Senate Substinate Bill, the Wilson–Gorman Tariff and the McKinley Tariff. Years later, author and reporter Lincoln Stephens wrote to Theodore Roosevelt, regarding Aldrich, "What I really object to in him is what he probably does honestly, out of general conviction . . . he represents Wall Street; corrupt and corrupting business; men and Trusts that are forever seeking help, subsidies, and privileges from the government".[13]

In 1894, the Sugar Trust was brought up on non-disclosure charges for not reporting its profit information on its 1890 census report. During these hearings, when one of the Havermeyer brothers was asked if he gave campaign contributions to Aldrich or other members of the Finance Committee, his response was, "Under advice of council I decline to answer".[14] When the New York Times grabbed ahold of the story, they uncovered corruption. To begin, Senator Aldrich lied about the existence of a Sugar Trust in 1890, and continued to deny its existence even though Trust shares existed on the market during the 1890 tariff debates, and in the opinion of the newspaper, "what a stupid lie it was".[15] The *New York Times* reported the next day that the McKinley Tariff "was constructed to satisfy the greed of every Trust combination in the land" and was supported by every Republican member of Aldrich's Finance Committee.[16]

On 20 June the true nature of the relationship between Aldrich and the Sugar Trust was revealed. While Aldrich was aiding the Sugar Trust, he had been accumulating stock in the Union Railway Company in his home state of Rhode Island. When he established his relationship with Searles, the Trust's secretary and treasurer, it was not limited to the workings and favourability of the Trust. Searles and Aldrich went into business together to purchase the remaining stock in the railway system, with the intention of forming a monopoly and cornering the market on Providence transportation.

During Havermeyer's deposition before the Senate, he stated that the Trust earned an estimated $35 million over the previous three years, of which $1,500,000 was funnelled to Senator Nelson W. Aldrich for the purposes of buying railway stock and revitalizing the railway system. Searles, personally, gave Aldrich $100,000 and Searles & Associates invested between $5.5 million and $7 million dollars to purchase and modernize the railroad. Aldrich formed the New Jersey Holding Company and the United Traction & Electric Company to own the railways as the companies' president, with John Searles as the director.[17]

The *New York Times* did the maths and thought Havermeyer's original estimate of $35 million in profits for the Trust was conservative at best. With each strategic drop or hike in taxes through each bill that was passed, each favourable polarization grade of sugar, and each generous sugar schedule that Aldrich drew up, all told the Sugar Trust made an estimated $51 million, "robbing the working man" and making Senator Aldrich a millionaire.[18]

Sugar wasn't the only thing in which Senator Aldrich was interested. Aldrich made many friends in industry and on Wall Street. In October 1901 his daughter Abby married into one of the wealthiest families in the world when she wed John D. Rockefeller, Jr. With Aldrich now in the Rockefeller family, he could manipulate many business interests, and his political power only strengthened his influence and impregnability.

For an idea of the amount of wealth Senator Aldrich was then related to, by 1910, John D. Rockefeller, Sr's Standard Oil Company, the most controversial and most powerful of the great American trusts, was worth at least $660 million. Dwarfing the Sugar Trust, Standard Oil was able to produce 40,000 barrels of refined oil a day, had ownership of hundreds of thousands of miles of pipeline and a fleet of one hundred tankers.[19]

In May 1911, the Supreme Court decided that Standard Oil had a corporate structure that violated the Sherman Antitrust Act. Rockefeller was given six months to divest the company of all its subsidiary companies. Once the trust was dissolved and stock had been issued for thirty new companies, Wall Street went berserk, and in the biggest bull rally in American history, Rockefeller's IPOs went through the roof. As the major stockholder in all the new companies, John D. Rockefeller, Sr's personal wealth increased by an estimated $200 million, and by the summer of 1911, he became the country's first billionaire.[20]

In 1901, another marriage occurred – Aldrich used his friends on Wall Street to invest in the new Continental Rubber Company, of which he immediately became president. The CRC harvested valuable Guayule rubber from Mexico. This type of rubber gave access to contracts with tyre companies throughout North America, Europe and South America, which quickly vaulted the CRC into the largest producer of Guayule rubber in the world.

However, due to aggressive over-harvesting, guayule rubber was becoming scarce in Mexico. In addition, its location in very remote parts of Mexico's jungles, and the lack of patent protection inhibiting international cooperation, meant that business began to taper for Aldrich and his Wall Street investors.[21] Then, the King of Belgium, Leopold II entered the American business and political scene.

During the Great Scramble of the 1850s, when every major European country was inflicting imperialistic, industrial mercantilism upon the entire continent of Africa and most of Asia, the country of Belgium was able to form a protectorate for the Congo. Soon the Congo became an official colony of Belgium and it was sought after by many business interests from all over the world, due to its huge reserves of timber, copper, gold, silver, ivory and rubber. At the turn of the century, Leopold II began a push towards attracting American money to his colony. He wished US business, ". . . to invest money . . . to plant rubber forests on modern principles so that they can be easily worked by the natives . . . There is fabulous wealth in this country".[22]

King Leopold sought to induce US politicians to aid him in his quest for opening business interests in the Congo. The problem was his reputation as a maniac and utterly ruthless ruler in the Congo. The rest of Europe was vehemently opposed to Leopold's methods in the Congo, so much so that the British government formed the Congo Reform Association and spread branches of it throughout the continent and in America. Of course, much of this opposition was due to the fact that Liverpool and Manchester trading interests were coveting the Congo for themselves, and not only the fact that Leopold was mistreating the people of Africa.

Leopold was an international pariah among even the most conservative European political parties. He even formed an organization in Germany called, "The Free State", to spread pro-Belgian Congo propaganda that refuted any accusations that Leopold was anything less than virtuous.[23] The true scale of the brutality of the regime was documented by the British Foreign Office's consul at Boma, Roger Casement and has been recounted by Wuliger:

> Casement described the forced labor by which European fortunes were being made. The grandfathers of the Africans who today swing picks, operate Bucyrus-Erie buckets, handle air hammers, and drive trucks in the Congo mines had to gather their quotas of rubber from the wild vines or have their hands chopped off, their genitals severed, their villages burned down, their children murdered . . . Roger Casement, who knew Africa from twenty years earlier, estimated a decline in population of three million by 1904. During the next eight years there was an estimated loss of at least another three million.[24]

Although the Free State spread to Italy and even parts of Great Britain, Leopold could not escape the demons of his reputation or the influence of the British government. His only option was America. If he could get US business interests involved in the Congo, with kickbacks going to him and the Belgian government, his troubles would be solved. His first effort was to convince President Theodore Roosevelt to turn a blind eye to the ravages he placed on the natives of his colony.

Leopold's charm and power coaxed the American ambassador to Austria, Bellamy Storer, to speak with the president. Storer was in the Leopold camp and was anything but hypocritical when he wrote to President Roosevelt, "cruelty there certainly might have been . . . [but], when did mankind spread the civilizing sway of a superior race without ruthlessness?" He continued, "and it would be indeed a pity if public opinion with us should be so misled as always to run, without exception, in the lines . . . [to which] Great Britain would like to confine it."[25] Despite this frank attempt to convince him, Roosevelt felt the pressure of the media and his constituency, and closed the book on the Congo, but made no mention of any intervention in Congolese affairs.

By now, the Continental Rubber Company was a $30 million business. King Leopold sought out the master technician, Senator Nelson W. Aldrich for dealings in the Congo, which was blanketed in the valuable guayule rubber that Aldrich's company was tearing through in Mexico. Aldrich, along with his partner Thomas Fortune Ryan, the converted Catholic railway man and tobacco company owner; financial backer Bernard Baruch; and smelting and mining kings, the Guggenheim brothers, began the process of entering the Congo through the purchase of stock, despite the Senate Foreign Relations Committee calling for congressional action for reform in the Congo. This blatant disregard for his own government's opinion of the tyrannical Leopold, the strength of his political standing as the head of the Republican Steering Committee, and the fortune he amassed helped to build Aldrich's reputation as ". . . pretty close to being the most powerful man in the United States".[26]

Leopold knew that business interests could outmanoeuvre political interest. So to bypass the political pressure he was receiving, Leopold's plan was to involve US business interests to quell the Congo reformers. With Senator Aldrich as the political gatekeeper to major US business interest, Leopold knew he would have to recruit Aldrich first and foremost. So Leopold ordered his Belgian Baron Moncheur and Consul General, Mr James Augustus Napoleon Tallyrand Whitley (yes, his real name) to draft a letter to Aldrich, explaining that, "every facility and encouragement would be given to a properly organized American company that means business".[27]

Aldrich met many times with Whitley, and Fortune Ryan met with his confidant, the Catholic Cardinal James Gibbons of Baltimore. Leopold had asked Cardinal Gibbons for support when the US and British governments were considering revoking his status as the King of Belgium (granted to him and his family by the Treaty of Berlin). Gibbons petitioned the US government on behalf of Leopold, explaining that, "in his opinion the reports of abuse and tyranny by the Belgian government reported to him by his own missionaries were probably exaggerated".[28] Soon after, two new American backed rubber companies were started in the Congo – the Intercontinental Rubber Company and the Société internacianale forestière et minière du Congo (Forminière), with Nelson Aldrich at the helm of both.

Despite the blueprint for their opportunity having been drafted, the secrecy of their enterprise was evanescent. When the American media involved itself in these unscrupulous inner workings of Aldrich's business and political actions, the scheme came crashing down. In a four day, page one exclusive, The *New York American* newspaper covered an expose on the amoral dealings of Aldrich, his American financial backers, the Belgian government, King Leopold II, US lobbyists, and the US military.

The paper uncovered letters, such as one written by lobbyist Henry Wellington Wack to King Leopold, urging him to, "open up a strip of territory clear across the Congo State from east to west for the benefit of American capital . . . In this manner, you will create an American vested interest in the Congo which will render the yelping of the English agitators and Belgian Socialists futile".[29] A contract was drawn up for rights to 4,000 square miles of Congo land going to the American Intercontinental Rubber Company, which had been created for the sole purpose of merging with Aldrich's Continental Rubber Company, and Forminière, both separate entities but under the control and ownership of Aldrich and his cohort.

By 1909, the combined capital of both companies was $70 million and a spokesman for the company explained to the *Wall Street Journal* that it was:

> in no way a competitor of the United States Rubber Company as we are not engaged in manufacturing in any way. The United States Rubber Co. is a customer, and buys crude rubber largely from us. We are engaged in only the plantation, production, and sale of the raw material and [their] business does not conflict in any way with that of the 'trust' as the United States Rubber Co. is called.[30]

By this point the company owned and controlled massive plantations of valuable guayule rubber in Mexico, Brazil and the Belgian Congo. They had become too big to be stopped by their reputation.

The *American* also uncovered that through General Consul Whitley, Leopold and American bankers paid US Colonel Henry Kowalsky $45,000 to work with lobbyists to convince Congress to support Leopold, and not the political reformers of the Free State and the Congo Reform Movement. Kowalsky was apparently not discrete in his attempts to solicit favours, and when the deal collapsed, he was said to have turned down his next assignment, a base in Nigeria, in fear that it would lead to an attempt on his life.

The *New York American* went on to detail Belgian bribes to representatives and senators and named the stockholders of the rubber companies as Nelson W. Aldrich, Thomas Fortune Ryan, Edward B. Aldrich (son of Nelson), the Guggenheim brothers, J. P. Morgan, James J. Stillman and John D. Rockefeller, Sr. By the end of their report, the newspaper determined that "Ryan and his associates, by the mere purchase of stock . . . became part rulers over an empire larger than all of New England, New York, New Jersey, Delaware, and half of Pennsylvania".[31]

By 1910, Aldrich owned 25,000 shares of stock (after Edward Brush and Fortune Ryan, the largest share of equity held by the private stockholders) in a company that earned $400,000–$500,000 per month.[32] Conveniently in charge of the tariffs on the country's rubber schedule, Aldrich made his last adjustments to benefit his company and announced that he would not run for Senate again, just before he responded to "malicious and unjust attacks" of Senator Bristow of Kansas for rigging the rubber schedule.[33]

Nelson Aldrich embodied the phase, "The rich get richer". From 1907 to 1909 Forminière hired a geologist, Sydney Ball, to head the Mohun-Ball expedition through the portion of the Congo owned by the rubber company. It took two years to prospect only one third of the land, and in that time Ball found two gold fields. The first one, the Tele, was worth an estimated $500,000 in gold as well as high-grade gravel, worth $6 per cubic yard. The second gold field of Mai Munene also had massive iron ore deposits, and diamonds.[34]

Before the Panic of 1907 and the formation of the Aldrich–Vreeland Emergency Currency Act, which gave birth to the National Monetary Commission, Senator Aldrich and his Wall Street friends began the push for central banking and banking deregulation in the United States. As early as the first years of the 1900s, Aldrich began to meet with presidents and directors of banks and trust companies for the purposes of revamping the entire US monetary system. In July 1903 he was first introduced to some of the men behind the central banking scheme that would change America forever. He accepted an invitation to board *The Corsair*, J. P. Morgan's yacht, where he met with directors including James Stillman, George F. Baker, Samuel P. Colt, George Peabody Wetmore and Jacob H. Schiff.[35]

Aldrich and his Finance Committee, which years earlier aided the Sugar Trust, began to get the word out in support of banking deregulation and greater "elasticity" of the currency. Reports of the Finance Committee's meetings and their suggestions to free banks by lightening their reserve requirements and further their ability to loan money based on the interest of existing loans, were sent to banks all over the country in order to test the waters for these new ideas. Some bankers, such as the president of Waukesha National Bank in Wisconsin wrote his concerns to Aldrich:

> In these days when the country is filled with soft money the idea that a bank can extend its loans by taking notes of a customer with interests and ask them to take an asset currency issued by the bank without interest in exchange therefor, whether their own assets, including their deposits, will allow an expansion of loans or not, strikes me very forcibly as being what bankers term if customers attempted to do such a thing, "kiting."[36]

The "Trust Buster" President Theodore Roosevelt had a close eye on the intentions of the banking world, and it was up to Aldrich and other politicians like powerhouse New York Senator Thomas C. Platt to sway the president towards banking reform. Platt wrote to Aldrich regarding the president of the United States:

> He is not helping the situation very much. When we were there, he seemed to fall in with our opinions. But when Shaw [the Secretary of the Treasury], Carlisle and Cullom ventilate their ideas, he is just as apt to side with them. He will mix and muddle this thing all up I fear . . . I believe you ought to keep in pretty close touch with him. If you do this, he will accept your ideas as his own, and push them . . . I am convinced that it is pretty important that in some way there should be a meeting with [J. P.] Morgan, and that you ought to arrange it very soon. If we are to get our idea as to the necessary kind of legislation accepted, a good deal must be done by way of educating the public mind.[37]

Of course, banking regulations were loosened, and the Panic of 1907 brought about a central banking propaganda machine that was unmatched by any before it. The Aldrich–Vreeland Bill was passed the next year, and Aldrich became the political spearhead for a central bank in America to be controlled by his Wall Street friends. Even the press was under control with the Associated Press's John Gavit oiling the central banking cogs by tearing up critical reviews of publications that supported central banking.[38]

As we know, Aldrich was among the caravan of Wall Streeters that went off to

Jekyll Island. Upon his return, he received two death threats on 19 December 1910. Both came from 149 Union Street in Chicago, one from "The Red Circle" that read "Sir, Can you offer any valid excuse or defense why you should not be assassinated?" and another (in what looks like the same hand writing) from the "Committee for Execution" which urges Aldrich to "Read the article published in Wilbur's Magazine: 'What will the country lose if such creatures as Nelson W. Aldrich were assassinated?'".[39]

Upon Aldrich's return, two interesting things happened. The first had to do with the request of Frank Vanderlip to open foreign branches of US banks in other countries. For decades US banks had been prevented from opening branches in foreign countries. The following inquiries were the first steps in the provision of the Federal Reserve Act, which allowed US banks to open foreign branches. This scaled Wall Street from national dominance to a global powerhouse. From 20 December 1910 to 24 January 1911 a deluge of letters came in to Aldrich's office. These letters were all addressed to the Secretary of State, Philander Chase Knox. It appears that Knox forwarded them to California Senator Frank P. Flint, and then Flint forwarded them to Aldrich. Every letter concerned a given country's regulations on the founding of foreign banks on that country's soil. In every case, the option was affirmative, and every letter was signed, "Your Obedient Servant", followed by signors, M. Beaupre, Charles Campbell, Jr, William Lawrence Merry, Charles Paige Bryan, Ronald B. Harvey, Henry Lane Wilson, and many more. Within five weeks after the return of the members of the Jekyll Island summit, inquiries regarding the possibilities of opening US bank branches in foreign countries came in from Spain, Greece, the Netherlands, Switzerland, the Dominican Republic, Belgium, Mexico, Turkey, Serbia, Brazil, Honduras, Venezuela, Romania, Haiti and Cuba. With all these counties confirming that foreign branches were not restricted, Vanderlip and Aldrich made certain that the Aldrich Bill would include the international expansion of the US banking system.[40]

The other occasion worth noting that happened after the meeting was the fact that Aldrich returned to Jekyll Island with J. P. Morgan just weeks later. Morgan and Aldrich were close. The two had sailed together a few months before the Jekyll Island meeting on Aldrich's boat during a "purely social" meeting with Charles D. Norton, of George F. Baker's First National Bank of New York, and George Peabody Wetmore.[41] In August 1914, just before the organization date of the US Federal Reserve, Morgan and Aldrich's son-in-law, John D. Rockefeller, Jr both visited

Aldrich at his summer home in Rhode Island. The *Wall Street Journal* documented the meeting and wrote of the three men:

> One represents the largest personal fortune that was ever accumulated in the history of the world; one represents the leading American banking house allied with more transportation and industry than probably any other house in the world; and one represents more knowledge concerning the moneys of the world and the banking, business and industry of the world than is possessed by any other man.[42]

In January 1911 Aldrich reported to much of his cohort that he had a bout with the flu and his doctor had ordered him to go to the southern states and seek a warmer and more relaxing climate. He received "get well" notes from many politicians and businessmen, including President Taft, Frank Vanderlip, Henry P. Davison (of J. P. Morgan & Co.) and Paul Warburg.

However, it was a letter from his son-in-law that proved he went back to Jekyll Island. John D. Rockefeller, Jr wrote to Aldrich that he had enclosed a copy of the periodical, SURVEY of 14 January which contained an editorial by Dr Edward Devine on the Rockefeller Foundation, also one by Mr Robert W. DeForest (director of the Metropolitan Museum of Art), and that he and his wife Abby were ". . . happy to think of you and Mrs. Aldrich in such a charming and restful place." The letter was dated 17 January 1911 and addressed to "Hon. N. W. Aldrich, Care Mr. J. Pierpont Morgan, Jekyll Island, Georgia".[43]

What makes this second trip significant is that when Aldrich and Morgan returned from the island, Aldrich's secretary, Arthur B. Shelton, sent out the following letter, on 31 January 1911, to the heaviest hitters of the entire US banking community, covering all corners of the country, via telegram, postal and Western Union:

> Senator Aldrich requests me to ask if you can meet with a few other prominent bankers at the Marlborough-Blenheim Hotel, Atlantic City, on the afternoon of February tenth next, to consider his outline for a plan for monetary reform. Probably two or three days will be required for the purpose. He regards it as essential that you should be there, and very much hopes you will be able to do so. It is desirable that no publicity be given this meeting; and he therefor

suggests that for the present it be treated as confidential. Please wire reply to me at the Senate Office Building, Washington, D.C.

The letter went out to: Hon. Edward B. Vreeland, Hon. A. Piatt Andrew, F. A. Vanderlip, Esq., President National City Bank, New York City, A. Barton Hepburn, Esq., Chase National Bank, New York City, Paul M. Warburg, Esq., William and Pine Streets, New York City, H. P. Davison, Esq., 23 Wall Street, New York City, D. G. Wing, Esq., First National Bank, Boston, W. A. Gaston, Esq., National Shawmut Bank, Boston, C. Stewart Patterson, 1000 Walnut Street, Philadelphia, S. Wexler, Esq., Whitney-Central National Bank, New Orleans, James B. Forgan, Esq., First National Bank, Chicago, George M. Reynolds Esq., Continental and Commercial National Bank, Chicago, J. J. Mitchell, Esq., Illinois Trust and Savings Bank, Chicago, Charles H. Hutting, Third National Bank, St. Louis, F. J. Wade, Mercantile National Bank, St. Louis, E. F. Swinney, First National Bank, Kansas City, F. O. Watts, First National Bank, Nashville, Stoddard Jers, First National Bank, Los Angeles, Judge J. W. Lusk, National German-American Bank, St. Paul, F. M. Prince, First National Bank, Minneapolis, A. L. Ordean, First National Bank, Duluth, J. T. Scott, First National Bank, Houston, N. H. Latimer, Dexter-Horton and Company, Seattle, J. W. Hellman, Wells Fargo Nevada National Bank, San Francisco, Joseph A. McCord, Third National Bank, Atlanta and Luther Drake, Merchant's National Bank, Omaha.[44]

By the time Aldrich died, he had amassed an estate worth about $30 million.[45] Despite the corruption and scandal surrounding his career, perhaps he still stood as a man of the people? He obviously represented himself and his wealthy Wall Street and industrialist friends while a US senator, but maybe he also had the interests of his voting public in mind? It is, of course, possible to gain enormous wealth, and still do the right thing as a public servant.

He used his political career to make himself a multimillionaire and make his mega-wealthy puppeteers the financial rulers of the country. But, what of the working classes? Did Aldrich represent the vast majority of his Rhode Island constituency? Did he do what was best for the middle-class citizens of the United States of America as an elected official, despite his relationships with the corporate and banking elite? An examination of his voting record may shine some light on these questions: between October 1881 and March 1911, Senator Nelson Willmarth Aldrich missed 2,121 of 4,807 roll-call votes (41.1% of all the voting that took place during his time in office). The median of votes missed among the lifetime records of senators serving while Aldrich was in politics was 26.1 per cent. How does that compare to today? At the time of writing, the current US senator with the worst voting record of acting senators is Republican Mark Kirk of Illinois at 32.1 per cent votes missed. Most of them due to illness.[46] *The Cosmopolitan* in 1906:

> Various senators represent various divisions and subdivisions of the colossus. But Aldrich, rich through franchise grabbing, the intimate of Wall Street's great robber barons, the father-in-law of the only son of the Rockefeller; Aldrich represents the colossus. Your first impression of many and conflicting interests has disappeared. You now see a single interest, with a single agent-in-chief to execute its single purpose – getting rich at the expense of the labour and the independence of the American people.[47]

5

The Architect: Paul M. Warburg

The name Paul Moritz Warburg is synonymous with the founding of the Federal Reserve System. Warburg's impact on American banking is a parallel to his family's impact on European banking. The epic story of the Warburg family of European bankers can be traced back to the early 1500s when Simon von Cassel settled in the German Westphalia town of Warburg (originally founded by Charlemagne in 778 and was then known as Warburgum) and began the family's quest for money and financial power. Although the Warburgs excelled in many other occupations throughout Europe, it was this lineage that produced some of the most successful bankers in the world. Blessed with sharp minds and good business sense, the generations of the Warburg clan gained seemingly boundless money and power.[1]

In the eighteenth century the family splintered into two groups. Some went to Altona, Denmark and others to Hamburg, Germany. Despite being relegated to Jewish ghettos and, by law, referred to as "moneylenders" and not bankers, in 1774 a Warburg established the merchant-banking firm of S. G. Warburg. It soon became W. S. Warburg as the family grew and sons and grandsons began to contribute to the family business. In 1807 the Altona Warburgs sold to the Hamburg Warburgs of M. M. Warburg & Co., founded by Moses and Gerson Warburg in 1798.[2]

When Napoleon invaded Germany, Hamburg was captured by the French army in 1804, as was Moses's brother Gerson. Napoleon himself held Gerson hostage and demanded a ransom from the entire Hamburg Jewish community for his release. However, Gerson's own brother Moses wouldn't pay it. Only after prodigious pressure from their community did Moses finally put up the money, which was still a sum much lower than what was expected of him. Despite this lack of loyalty, the two brothers signed a partnership in 1810, and expanded M. M. Warburg together.

The end of the Napoleonic war marked the beginning of economic rebuilding for Germany. When the French withdrew in 1814, Moses and Gerson saw the need for replenishment of the country's stock of silver currency to boost the German economy. They wrote to the massive London banking firm of N. M. Rothschild & Sons requesting the opportunity to handle bills of exchange of silver stock on their behalf.[3] To put the Rothschild's empire into perspective, the family's biographer, Fredric Morton described the Rothschild dynasty as having, ". . . conquered the world more thoroughly, more cunningly, and much more lasting than all the Caesars before or all the Hitlers after them".[4] The Rothschilds and the Warburgs shared business ever since, and throughout the nineteenth century the firm of M. M. Warburg & Co. grew slowly and steadily. The century brought the Warburgs prosperity, and new relationships with very important people.

In 1857, 150 banks collapsed in the United States and the contagion spread to Germany. In Germany, banks were overleveraged and 10 million marks was needed to ensure the survival of German, particularly Hamburg, banks. When Prussian bankers refused to aid them, an attempt was made to sway the director of Austria's largest bank, the Kreditanstalt, who happened to be married to a Warburg daughter. A man named Paul Schiff applied pressure to the Austrian Minister of Finance, which resulted in the Emperor Franz Joseph sending to Hamburg a train loaded with silver ingots. In six months it was repaid to Vienna, with interest.[5]

After the Franco-Prussian War of 1870–1, Otto von Bismarck imposed reparations on the French in the form of merchandise, precious metals, commercial and financial bills, and myriad investments. M. M. Warburg & Co. once again joined the Rothschilds in loaning the French government the capital to pay the reparations. This act of association, and many others over the years, with the largest banking family in the world marked the arrival of the Warburg family in the global banking field, and their slow assent gave way to their amassing significant wealth and reputation.[6]

Moritz Warburg, Paul's father, was born in 1838. As a young man he was apprenticed to the Rothschilds in Paris and Italy. He was a practicing orthodox Jew and he married Charlotte, a member of the Frankfurt diamond merchant family of the Oppenheims, and she too was notably devout in her Jewish faith. They had five sons: Aby, Max, Paul, Felix and Fritz. They were so famed for their success, rebellion, and progressive attitudes among their descendants that future Warburgs referred to the brothers as the "Famous Five".[7] Aby, being the eldest son was in line to head the family banking business. However, his passion was art history, so he sold his birthright to his brothers, Max and Paul, who ran M. M. Warburg jointly.

In 1894 Jacob Schiff entered the lives of the Warburg family. Described as "the most famous Jew in New York" he was one of the richest men in America, and a man who J. P. Morgan admitted was "his only equal".[8] As a young man, in his late teens, Jacob ventured to America and met Abraham Kuhn. After writing a cogent letter to Kuhn's partner Solomon Loeb, he convinced the two men to bring him in to join the firm of Kuhn, Loeb & Co. in 1873. By 1875 he was a full partner and in 1894 he married Solomon Loeb's eldest daughter. Jacob's daughter Frieda married Felix Warburg in New York and when Paul went to America to be the best man at their wedding, he met Frieda's young aunt, and maid of honour, Nina Loeb – Jacob's sister-in-law – and Paul's future wife. The two Warburg brothers settled in New York to work for Jacob Schiff at Kuhn, Loeb & Co. The borderline-incestuous familial interweaving of the banking firm of Kuhn, Loeb & Co. has been described as follows:[9]

> ... [Abraham] Kuhn and [Solomon] Loeb (who were brothers-in-law) both related to Abraham Wolff, another K-L partner whose daughter married yet another partner, Otto Kahn. A Loeb son married a Kuhn daughter, and another Loeb daughter married another partner, Paul Warburg, while Jacob Schiff's daughter Frieda married Paul Warburg's brother Felix (a partner too). This turned an aunt and her niece into sisters-in-law, and made Paul his brother's uncle.[10]

The young Paul M. Warburg was a charmer, a playboy, a ladies' man, and as a young man, a terrible student. The future Harvard professor failed most of his high school exams back in Germany and never went to college. He divorced his first two wives and not until the 1920s did he, as his family put it, "begin to settle down". In the summer, he and his brother Felix would retreat from the city and retire to their 200-acre property in the Woodlands in White Plains, New York.[11]

Despite his many struggles in school, Paul was arguably the most brilliant of all the Warburgs. While at Kuhn & Loeb, he was on the boards of directors of many corporations, including the Oregon Short Line and the Pacific Mail Railroads,[12] the Carnegie Trust Co., of which the former Secretary of the Treasury Leslie M. Shaw was president,[13] and a leather company which, after a year of Warburg sitting on its board, made $2 million more profit than the year before.[14]

He spent six months each year in New York, and the other six months back in Germany to help run the Warburg family bank. He acted as a "financial liaison officer" between Germany and America, all the while frustrated with what he scoffed at as the primitive, disorganized, and decentralized US banking system.[15] Thus, his efforts began to change the system he thought so little of, and in doing so he changed the system, the country and the banking world, forever. Harold Kellock wrote in the *Century Magazine* in 1915: "Paul M. Warburg is probably the mildest-mannered man that ever personally conducted a revolution . . . He stepped forth simply armed with an idea. And he conquered. That is the amazing thing. A shy, sensitive man, he imposed his idea on a nation of a hundred million people."[16]

Paul M. Warburg

Warburg did start a revolution, but he was far from shy and was not an innovator by any means. He merely imported the central banking systems from the many European countries with which he was accustomed and had dealings with through M. M. Warburg. The reforms were adeptly advertised as simple adjustments to procure help to banks in times of emergency. Warburg said he wanted a central bank that could: 1) issue currency backed by less gold reserves; 2) institute a discount and a rediscount policy; and 3) dismantle stock and call loans as bank collateral.[17]

It is unclear, however, how helpful Warburg planned the banks to be. These three practices, along with others that Warburg wanted to enlist in his central banking scheme, favoured much larger banks and investment firms with massive capital at their disposal. The plan left out the smaller firms and country banks. Unfazed at the disparity, he acknowledged the favouritism as is clear from a letter he wrote to Samuel Sachs, who's lifetime friend was Philip Lehman of Lehman Brothers, and in 1904 joined his father-in-law Marcus Goldman to form the giant investment firm of Goldman Sachs:

> I doubt very much whether it would be wise for the Central Bank to deal with these people [small banks] . . . Private banking houses of good standing should have the privilege of dealing with the Central Bank in foreign exchange. I believe, however, that the 'proper restrictions,' which we provide in our resolution, will have to cover that. My own view is – as I said yesterday – that it would be better not to open the door for the criticism that private interests might enjoy favoritism with the Central Bank . . .[18]

Warburg's public theory was that the issuance of currency would make currency itself more "elastic". In times of crisis, banks and depositors would hoard their reserves, and money became very scarce and tight. A central banking system would enable money to circulate more freely, even in tumultuous economic times. This elastic currency that Warburg was trying to create could not exist under the constrictions of the existing US monetary system that depended on gold and government bonds. His system could expand and contract (hence, the term "elasticity") to accommodate fluctuations of the needs of the market. For this to happen, Warburg had to convince the United States banking community, the politicians, and the public, to adopt a currency based on "commercial paper", which is "banker-speak" for corporate IOUs.[19]

The discount policy he proposed would enable banks to receive liquid assets from the central bank through the rediscounting of commercial paper. Corporate loans were always frozen: money lent to corporations could not be resold as liquid assets. The central bank could rediscount those loans as assets so banks could pay depositors in times of need.[20] To put it a little simpler, when banks "discount" a security or loan, they are basically converting it into cash. When banks "rediscount" the discount, they are pooling their resources to pour more money into a market that has a higher demand for funding. This can be done in times of great opportunity, or desperate need. Warburg wanted a central bank to control this process, with him and his Wall Street and European banking interests in control of the central bank.

This would enable Warburg's third adjustment to take place. Since the central bank would be overseeing all banking bailouts, banks would no longer need to back their deposits with call loans and stock exchange collateral, as they had been. Warburg insisted that this system would ensure no more panics and stock market crashes.[21] That boast would quickly prove to be outrageously untrue. Warburg explained, "Banks issuing unsecured notes which are to pass as the people's money should be restricted to buying paper that is endorsed by other banks or banking firms . . . They should be restricted also as to the kinds of loans to be made by them." He favoured a central bank to oversee all of this. Warburg's worry was that these unsecured notes, mostly through short-term loans, would become viewed as fixed capital investments.

Warburg wanted to separate the loans from the capital by instituting a central bank to redefine acceptable bank assets so as to eliminate small business entrepreneurs from undertaking what he called "unproductive enterprises". Some bankers and economists took a different perspective and believed this was an illegal filtration process to weed out undesirable bankers and businesses from the capitalist marketplace. Others thought that this "Big Brother"-like monitoring of banking practices dismantled the financial foundations of the entrepreneurial, individualistic, free-market economic system of production and distribution that the American industrial revolution of the late eighteenth century was founded on. Still, others believed it was purely and simply unconstitutional.[22]

Warburg began by running the idea past his boss at Kuhn, Loeb & Co., Jacob Schiff. Schiff loved it, and encouraged Warburg to make his ideas public. The *New York Times* asked Warburg to write an article about his banking reform ideas. Oddly, while barely being able to speak English, no less read and write it, "Defects and Needs of Our Banking System" by Paul M. Warburg was published in the 6 January 1907 issue of the *New York Times*.[23]

Warburg came to publish regularly for the *New York Times*, including his "Letter to the Editor" that proved to be the entire outline for what would become the Federal Reserve Act. It was just after the Panic of 1907 so everyone in banking and industry, as well as the thousands of Americans who lost their life savings, were on high alert. Warburg presented his blueprint for a central banking system:

A plan, which does not purport to cover the situation fully, but embodies a general sketch of what might possibly be tried . . . It is proposed to create at Washington a bank to be called hereafter the Government Bank . . . the share capital to be owned, if feasible, half by the Government and half by the National banks. And [sic] the management to be in the hands of a salaried President or Presidents, who are to be appointed for an indefinite period by the Board of Directors. The Board of Directors is to consist of delegates of the various Clearing Houses of the central reserve and reserve cities; the Secretary of Treasury and the Comptroller of Currency are to be members ex officio . . .[24]

Everything he wrote came true, along with his explanation of the strengthening of the clearing-houses, the expediency of rediscounting bank notes, the central bank as an alternative to emergency currency, and how the Treasurer and Comptroller would be board members – and he wrote it almost seven years before its final draft, the Federal Reserve Act, was signed into law in December 1913. Except, of course, the part about relieving future panics. And the part about the government and the national banks co-owning the central bank together – the banks actually owned every share of it.

In December 1907, Warburg met the man who could, and did, make his plan a reality: Senator Nelson W. Aldrich of Rhode Island. The two men made each other's acquaintance when Aldrich visited Jacob Schiff at the Kuhn & Loeb offices, to inquire about the activities of the German Reichsbank, which was the German central bank. There, Schiff referred him to Warburg and the two formed an unmitigated alliance.

On New Year's Eve 1907, Warburg sent Aldrich his proposal on uniform currency and a central banking system. For months after the Panic of 1907, Warburg gave speeches on reform, testified at hearings set up by Senator Aldrich at the Metropolitan Club in New York, and by May 1908 the Aldrich–Vreeland Emergency Currency Act was passed. Then the central banking dogma seeped into Wall Street, and soon the banking kings were praising Warburg and clamouring for a change in the banking regime. It was then that Warburg, on the advice of Aldrich, applied for United States citizenship, and became one of Senator Aldrich's closest advisors.[25]

Warburg and Aldrich had been in agreement on a central bank, but Warburg knew that Aldrich's emergency currency could get in the way of it. When the Aldrich–Vreeland Emergency Currency Act was passed and was about to institute an influx of currency into the market in late 1909, Warburg wrote to Aldrich on Christmas Eve of that year that there was, "No need for additional currency" because, "this would increase the credit power of the banks and . . . cause additional expansion." Warburg knew that if the banks got back on their feet too quickly after the Panic of 1907, there would be no need for their intended privately-run central banking system: "It would render the problem of thorough reform so much more difficult".[26] Warburg and his Wall Street cohort who wanted to control the currency of the country knew they had to keep the economy in a weakened state for their scheme to work most effectively.

By December 1910, the clandestine meeting between Senator Aldrich, Paul Warburg, and the four other banking moguls on Jekyll Island had taken place, the Aldrich Bill had been drafted, and Warburg was on his way to becoming the "Father of the Federal Reserve". The *New York Times* agreed with that distinction when they wrote about Warburg, "In actual fact, he [Warburg] had a more legitimate distinction to that title ['Father of the Federal Reserve'] than any other American citizen".[27]

Warburg continued to speak and write extensively on central banking and express his views on the troubles concerning the existing banking system. He was a co-founder of the Economic Club of New York, in 1907, and used it, along with many other vehicles, to spread his word about the need for a central bank in America. Warburg's writings were extensive. In the beginning, he mocked the obsolescence of the current system: "The United States is in fact at about the same point that had been reached by Europe at the time of the Medicis, and by Asia, in all likelihood, at the time of Hammurabi".[28] Amid the Panic of 1907, Warburg referred to the financial crisis as "appalling" and wrote in November of that year, that it was "the absolute necessity of a change in our present banking and currency system than all the efforts that have hitherto been made to warn the nation of the imminent danger".[29] Warburg wrote further, describing a central bank as a God-like, omnipotent entity that would quell all economic fears:

> We need some centralized power to protect us against others and to protect us against ourselves, some power able to provide for the legitimate needs of the country and able at the same time to apply the brakes when the car is moving too fast. Whatever causes that may have precipitated the present crisis, it is certain that they never could have brought about the existing outrageous conditions, which fill us with horror and shame, if we had had a modern banking and currency system.[30]

By 1911, Warburg had become a seasoned writer and speaker; however the subject matter and scare-tactics remained the same for his audiences, despite the markedly improved economy over the four years since the Panic of 1907. He continued to convey his belief in the necessity for banking reform and continued to evoke images of economic disaster for America if changes were not made. He used the European banking model as a lifeboat in the white-capped sea of US banking upheaval. It was this European model that he sold as the template for his Federal Reserve System:

> Why has our building proved a firetrap and why is Europe's structure so safe? Why does Europe's system guarantee the avoidance of panics and why does ours inevitably insure their recurrence from time to time? . . . It is from this point of view that the final question of monetary reform must be approached . . . It is of no avail to patch up a theoretically wrong system and to strengthen it by some practical measures, which give a false assurance of safety. When the storm comes, fear and doubt will begin to creep in through the loophole which logic, then wide awake, will drill, and once well-founded distrust begins, the system loses its basis, which is confidence, and must collapse.[31]

The years preceding the formation of the Federal Reserve saw Warburg write many essays and give many public addresses on banking reform.[32]

Senator Aldrich did his speaking and public relations too. In an address before the American Bankers Association he said with both great clarity and great obtuseness, "The organization proposed is not a bank, but a cooperative union of all the banks of the country for definite purposes."[33] Very few men knew what those "definite purposes" were, and to many, even in the wake of the aftermath of the 1907 panic, believed that idea sounded like something much too large and much too powerful.

Paul Warburg mapped out the scope of the central banking plan in a 13-page letter he addressed to Dr A. Piatt Andrew, Harvard economist and fellow attendee of Jekyll Island. The contents of that letter described a national monetary power and a control that is almost unimaginable, until one glances at the finished product that is the Federal Reserve System. Warburg sent this letter to Andrew and sent copies to the other five men, who joined him during that secret meeting, only a week after the meeting took place in November 1910. In it, Warburg gave his impressions on how the central bank should embark on its journey to control US currency. The letter benignly opens, "Dear Doc".

He begins hypothetically, with a proposed "opening balance sheet" that lists capital at $125 million, deposits at $1 billion, a treasury balance of $100 million, bond circulation of $700 million, and discounts and foreign exchange at $125 million. He explains that since they cannot withdraw everything from the start, "The bank will have to do some business in order to set the machinery going". He also points out that state banks would have to immediately increase their reserves to the levels of the national banks, so that "would give to the bank a hold on the situation from the beginning".

Warburg then continues on to liabilities with an anticipated $1.225 billion in cash, $825 million in circulation, and $1.1 billion in reserves, deposited by the banks and the Treasury:

> Without adding to it any additional gold that the bank might secure . . . [referring to a Table in the letter] we find that the discounts purchased by the bank have increased from $125 million to $525 million or deposits from $1 billion to $1.4 billion, the liability of the bank has already gone down to 50% . . . On the basis of the plan as we discussed it, if holdings increase to $1.625 billion and discounts increase to $2.725 billion, the liabilities go down to 25%.

"In establishing the new bank, we have to bear in mind that, in cutting the cost, we shall have to be prepared for a continued growth in the business of the country", and the First World War certainly justified that preparation.

His most important point was then made when he explained the effect gold deposits would have on the success of the bank: "As the deposits of the bank increase, the gold holdings of the bank must increase too". But, how would they get more gold? Warburg explained that this could be done in two ways: 1) The exchange of United States lawful money into Federal Reserve bank notes; 2) The acquisition of new gold against the issue of new bank notes. "Both can only be done if the issue of *new* bank notes against gold be left tax free. It can also only be achieved if the bank notes gradually become the only circulating medium." That was Warburg's plan for total and exacting control over the entire country's currency.

There was still the issue of obtaining the gold. Warburg suggested that the US Government buy $700 million in bonds from the bank, and pay for it in gold, at

$50 million each year, and "At the end of 10 years one would have an almost uniform note issue in the United States".

Warburg then addressed the issue of inflation and tax. If the accumulation of gold reserves were taxed, that would cause inflation. With all this power (in terms of currency and gold) being transferred from the government to the central bank, the US economy would surely be affected. If not immediately, then at some point. Warburg debunked that contingency because "The forced and encouraged accumulation of gold by the bank be handicapped by a tax, it would have the reverse effect." So, any profit the bank would make would be tax free, but the bank would pay a tax on the gold it would receive from the sale of the bonds. That doesn't seem exactly fair to the Government, but would this at least be a mandatory tax? Apparently not:

> A conservative management will be willing to forego the additional income for the sake of the general safety of the country; But it would be asking too much to force them to not only to sacrifice a possible profit, but to incur an actual out-of-pocket loss for increase gold holdings . . . If it be taken for granted that the management composed of the best elements of the whole banking community should either be blind, or willing, with open eyes, to wreck the country.

According to Warburg, "The present plan makes the new bank the largest holder of lawful money and enables it, only through this ownership, to become the actual owner of so large a portion of the Treasury's gold". Warburg's Federal Reserve plan was designed to take a substantial amount of monetary power away from the US government and its citizens, with the representatives of Wall Street planning and executing that plan with a few adept strokes of a pen. Because of this he urged secrecy and distraction:

> However, it is not necessary to show the ulterior aims of the plan to any larger degree than it will be deemed advisable. If there be apprehension that the larger scheme might arouse too much discussion, no attention need be drawn to it now. All that will be necessary will be to insert a clause . . . 'That National Banks may pay each other in these notes and count the same as reserve money' (which will not arouse criticism unless the whole scheme, of counting balances with the new Bank as cash, be attacked) and furthermore a tax clause, carefully worded, which I believe can be worked out to everybody's satisfaction.[34]

After Woodrow Wilson signed the Federal Reserve Act in 1913, the important undertaking of choosing a board of governors for the central Washington DC branch was of utmost importance, although it was a given that the Fed would be run through the New York branch. Warburg, despite the fact that he was paramount in drafting and engineering the original bill, never thought he would be considered for the board.

When Senator Carter Glass asked him if he would accept a seat on the new board, Warburg expressed the strange and ironic situation it created: "I took the question more or less as a joke, at the most, as a compliment, and told him that I did not think the President would be at all likely to submit the name of a man associated with one of the leading Wall Street firms". After due consideration of their grand scheme to appropriately represent Wall Street interests in the system, Warburg accepted the appointment.[35]

Warburg was a partner both at Kuhn & Loeb and M. M. Warburg. He was on the boards of directors of the B&O Railroad, the US Mortgage & Trust Co., Westinghouse Electric Company and Wells Fargo Express. Not only did he have to relinquish all these positions to join the board of the Federal Reserve, but also he had to sacrifice his estimated 1914 annual salary of $500,000 (what would be $12,071,600 in 2017)[36] that he earned from all his endeavours, for the comparatively paltry sum of $12,000 per month. Warburg had never cast a vote in America. He was in Europe during the 1912 election of President Wilson (the man who appointed him to the Board) and had been a US citizen for only three years, and yet he was about to become one of the most powerful and influential financial officials in the United States.[37]

For four weeks after his nomination, Warburg was drowning in controversy and doubt. US politicians knew of Paul M. Warburg as a Wall Street banking mogul, and a European banking legacy. He was grilled at Senate hearings, and at one point he wrote to President Wilson to withdraw his name from nomination. Some Wall Street men agreed that Senate hearings might be a harsh determination of competency.

However, in an article in the *New York Evening Journal*, the necessity for the hearings was spelled out saliently: "Their friends say that they are admirable citizens. But YOU who read this DO NOT KNOW THEM. And the men in the senate, who are asking them questions, and who are supposed to represent you, ALSO DO NOT KNOW THEM ... If they do not question them, they declare themselves dummies and unworthy to hold office."[38]

The article went on to explain the intimate business relationship between

Warburg and the Secretary of the Treasury, William G. McAdoo that could well have been interpreted as a conflict of interest:

> Before he became Secretary of the Treasury, Mr. McAdoo was interested in only one great enterprise – commonly known as the McAdoo Tunnel. That enterprise was in a very bad way, unable to get money, hard pressed. It was the firm of Mr. Warburg – Kuhn, Loeb & Co. – that took hold of the McAdoo Tunnel, put it on its feet, reorganized it, financed it by inviting the stockholders to pay an assessment – and thus relieved Mr. McAdoo from worry – or, at least, from the sorrow of seeing the great practical work of his life a failure.[39]

Wilson denied Warburg's request for withdrawal and prodded him to testify. Senators hammered away at him, especially Senator Joseph Bristow of Kansas who said that instead of being a candidate for the board of the Federal Reserve, Warburg should be a "candidate for punishments for unlawful acts in violation of the Sherman Law and other criminal statutes".[40] Senator Gilbert Hitchcock of Nebraska was less direct in his accusations, but even more revealing in his line of questioning. Warburg responded "no" to each question: To the series of questions, "Have you any other interests in Europe? Nothing in the line of banking? It has also been persistently stated that you represent the Rothschilds in the United States?" Warburg replied, "No. That is not true. The Rothschilds' agents in the United States are August Belmont & Co . . . I know the Rothschilds very casually . . . We are not at all closely connected with them."[41]

Despite Warburg's cogent response, it was common knowledge that the Warburgs and the Rothschilds went back more than a century through banking and business interests. Warburg's relationship with the Rothschild family in the all-important matter of the formation of the Federal Reserve System, and their involvement together in its inception proved to be contrary to Warburg's claims to the Senate Committee. On 9 December 1913 Warburg wrote to Anthony de Rothschild of the London bank N. M. Rothschild & Sons enclosing an article he had written in the *North American Review* on the formation of the Federal Reserve. In this very cordial letter, Warburg assures Rothschild that his article ". . . will have a soothing influence on your brain". Rothschild wrote back to Warburg on behalf of his brother and family on 9 January 1914, thanking him for the information on, "American banking and currency legislation", writing that they "studied it with great interest".[42]

In his "soothing" *North American Review* article that he penned and sent to Rothschild, "The Owen-Glass Bill As Submitted To the Democratic Caucus: Some Criticisms and Suggestions", Warburg opened with a quote from President Wilson, which explained the need for US currency to be "not rigid as now, but readily, elastically, responsive to sound credit, the expanding and contracting credits of every-day transactions, and the normal ebb and flow of personal and corporate dealings".[43]

In the article, Warburg attacked any and all criticisms of the Aldrich Bill, one by one, not surprisingly since he and the other Wall Street representatives were the ones who had created most of it, on Jekyll Island. Most of the article was a demand for one, central bank and not the 12 districts Senators Glass and Owen were bidding for in their bill. He did write that he would settle on four district banks, but warned, "there will, therefor, be no natural flow of reserve money, nor any free flow of money, into these disconnected discount centers".[44] However, it was his views on the government's subservient role in central banking that would have interested the Rothschilds and their cohort the most:

> It is the world's acknowledged theory and practice to keep the obligations of the Central Banks distinct from those of the Government. History has shown that by keeping the Central Banks and the Governments separate entities, they may be mutual supports. The Government is a customer of the Central Bank; at times its largest depositor, at times its largest borrower. The Government's credit strengthens the Central Bank, the Central Bank strengthens the credit power of the Government. Where Government credit and bank credit have been mixed up, the consequence has been to weaken both . . . The friends of the present administration, and any good citizen, for that matter, cannot too earnestly warn it not to insist on any extreme measure that would antagonize wide circles of business men and the very element through the agency of which alone the benefits of the law can accrue to the people of the United States.[45]

Warburg also sent a copy of his *North American Journal* article and the Owen–Glass Bill to the head of the Swiss Bankverein (which later became UBS, a Warburg family bank) in London for his opinion. The banker sent back his impressions and praise: "I should like to present you with my compliments on your achievements".[46] It is evident that Paul Warburg's assurance to Senator Hitchcock during the hearings that he no longer had any European banking interests or relationships was far from the truth.

It seemed to many senators that appointing Warburg to the most powerful economic post in the country was like asking a wolf to look after a flock of sheep. The fact that he was ardently against a 12-district reserve concept; the fact that he was a partner at Kuhn, Loeb & Co. and would, "open the chance for the ascendancy of another group of financiers in the control of the money and credits of the country"; the fact that, "It would be just as suitable for the President to appoint Mr. Morgan [J. P. Morgan] to the Federal Reserve Board"; the fact that "Under the terms of the law, the great banking houses of the United States are not supposed to have a direct hand in the direction of the new banking system"; the fact that "Mr. Warburg also says he is actively connected with the Hamburg banking house of Max Warburg & Co. [M. M. Warburg & Co.] . . . and the appointment of Mr. Warburg would give one of the most powerful banking houses in Europe an unfair advantage"; and the fact that "Mr. Warburg has not been a citizen of the United States long enough to entitle him to such an important post",[47] apparently didn't matter, because on 10 August 1914, Paul Moritz Warburg took the oath of office and began his term of service on the Federal Reserve Board.[48]

No sooner was Warburg sworn in, than were the nations of Europe enveloped in the Great War. European markets and banks began to shut down and Warburg led the Fed into the role of global banker. His optimism for the new system's future was overflowing and he brimmed with confidence and patriotism, despite accusations of disloyalty. He was crestfallen about the horrors his countrymen were suffering back in Germany, yet exhilarated over the potential of his thriving enterprise.[49]

At a time of increasing anti-German sentiment and xenophobia, Warburg and his wife Nina distanced themselves from their German-Jewish friends, while Warburg devised reasons why the United States should not go to war with Germany. He stressed to President Wilson the need for peace above all things and the need for America to remain neutral if it were to continue to be the "balance wheel" in world banking and politics.

However, Warburg also shared with the President a plan he devised to "Keep under supervision and control the many non-naturalized Germans living in this country". His proposal was to round up Germans town by town, city by city, and state by state and make them sign a waiver saying they would not execute any covert or aggressive action against the United States. Those that did not sign the waiver would be interned.[50]

Warburg was under attack on the basis of his religion, ethnicity and economic ideology by anti-Semitic, anti-German, anti-Wall Street and anti-Federal Reserve ideologists who swarmed about his position. The British ambassador in Washington at the time, Sir Cecil Spring-Rice, tried to convince his contemporaries back in England that Jacob Schiff controlled the *New York Times* and was trying to destroy Britain. He believed that Paul Warburg's appointment to the Board of the Federal Reserve was all a part of a Jewish conspiracy, masterminded by Kuhn, Loeb & Co.: "Since [J. P.] Morgan's death, the Jewish banks are supreme and they have captured the Treasury Department by the small expedient of financing the bills of the Secretary of the Treasury . . . and forcing upon him the appointment of the German, Warburg, and the Federal Reserve Board which he dominates."[51]

Even at Temple Emanu-El synagogue, where Warburg and Jacob Schiff were members, and James Seligman and Daniel Guggenheim were trustees, the Rabbi, Revd Dr J. L. Magnes, questioned the faith and religious dedication of some of his wealthy and successful congregation:

Your Judaism is not altogether my Judaism. Your Jewish ideals are not altogether my Jewish ideals. The richer Reformed congregation have an outward appeal in the beauty of their buildings, their glorious music, and their perfect decorum. But these outward trappings have not been able to hide from me the emptiness and the shallowness of your Jewish life.[52]

In August 1916, President Wilson appointed Warburg as the vice-governor of the board of the Federal Reserve, giving him even more power and influence. It was at that point, maybe more than ever, that Spring-Rice's warnings made sense to some. Warburg drafted a statement from the offices of the Federal Reserve, warning American investors not to purchase too many securities issued by unstable, warring nations. Since Germany had never issued any Wall Street loans, this caution would directly hinder the financial stability of both Britain and France during the war and after. Edward C. Grenfell, the senior J. P. Morgan partner in London, accused Warburg of hatching a plot to undercut the Allies. He stated to the entire British Treasury that this was a scheme concocted by "Warburg and other German sympathizers . . .".[53]

Many of the German-Jewish investors and bankers on Wall Street supported the German side during the First World War. Some were quite vocal about their views on US involvement in the war. Even the staunchest Warburg supporter would be hard-pressed to deny the idea that Warburg was any different. Their collective protests to American intervention during the war led to the almost catastrophic decline of many of their careers, the tailspin of Kuhn, Loeb & Co., and in August of 1918, the failure of President Wilson to reappoint Warburg to the board of directors of the Federal Reserve System – the very institution he basically created.[54] The "Father of the Fed" got fired.

In 1919 Warburg returned from Washington to New York, and through a merger, became the chairman of the board of the Bank of Manhattan. As the 1920s roared on with spikes in the stock market, Warburg warned of over speculation and a dangerous bubble in the market. He became known as the "Cassandra of Wall Street" and those who heeded his warnings were few, and those who rejected his prognostications mocked him openly. On one occasion in 1928 upon entering the Century Club in Manhattan, one of the members shouted, "Here comes old Gloomy Gus!" and he was booed at the directors meeting later that day.

At the beginning of 1929, Warburg gave the annual report of the International Acceptance Bank. During the report he succinctly stated that, "[Climbing prices of stock were] in the majority of cases quite unrelated to respective increases in plant, property, or earning power . . . If orgies of unrestrained speculation [continued without control] the ultimate collapse is certain to not only affect the speculators themselves but also to bring about a general depression involving the entire country."[55]

Boos and hisses were the response to Warburg's apocalyptic forecast of America's economic future, but barely six months later the "ultimate collapse" was triggered, and Warburg's "I told you so" made him even less popular, as did the fact that he promised that his Federal Reserve System would shield the country from economic upheaval.[56]

Paul Warburg's meteoric rise to the top of the US economic and financial world was only as spellbinding as the Shakespearean downfall of his career as founder and board member of the Federal Reserve. However, after the war and for the rest of his life, Warburg went on to enjoy massive wealth and success as the largest acceptance banker in the world, and he died in 1932 while his prophecy of economic destruction was still unfolding.

6

The Lieutenant: Benjamin Strong, Jr

Benjamin Strong, Jr made few speeches and did not appear in public to wax theoretically on the ways of economics and high finance. He was J. P. Morgan's workhorse, and he built his reputation and his fortune on the back of the House of Morgan.

Adeline Torrey Schenck married a railroader and small-farmer named Benjamin Strong, and together they had four sons and a daughter. Her forceful personality befitted Adeline, the daughter of a prominent Presbyterian writer, theologian and minister, and her four sons continued the tradition of prominence in their respective fields. The oldest was a Princeton graduate who earned a PhD from Columbia University and became a professor of neurology at the College of Physicians and Surgeons. Her second son became the vice president of the American Radiator Company and partner in the engineering firm of Meyer, Strong and Jones. Her youngest boy went on to a highly successful career in medicine and psychiatry after earning degrees from Princeton and the College of Physicians and Surgeons.

Adeline's third son Benjamin, Jr, was left no choice but to forego college because of a lack of financial stability in the family at the time of his high school graduation. Yet, he went on to become the governor of the New York branch of the Federal Reserve and one of the most powerful and influential men in the Unites States.[1]

In 1891, at the age of 18, Benjamin Strong, Jr left the family home in Montclair, New York, to seek his fortune in finance. After being quickly fired from his first job for of all things, poor penmanship, he entered the financial firm of Jessup, Patton & Co., which became John Patton & Co., and then Cuyler, Morgan & Co. He started as a clerk, and by 1900 Strong was representing international investors in real estate and securities ventures. Basically, he was a stock and real estate speculator.

He left Cuyler, Morgan, & Co. at 26, to join the Atlantic Trust Company, which in 1903, became the Metropolitan Trust Company. He married Margaret LeBoutillier, started a family, and soon settled in the prominent New York City suburb of Englewood, New Jersey. There, he and his wife entered the social circles of their community, and Benjamin met a man who would alter the course of his life forever. Henry P. Davison was a neighbour of the Strong's and in April 1904, he offered Strong a job at the newly founded Bankers Trust Company.

The Bankers Trust was an instant success. Known as a "banker's bank", it held the reserves of banks and other trust companies as a correspondent for them, and often made loans to those banks and others, so they could repair their reserve positions or strains on their leverage. Bankers Trust wrote many of these types of loans when the Panic of 1907 hit the industry.

However, Bankers Trust was a "banker's bank" for other reasons, and Benjamin Strong quickly found himself in the middle of the Morgan vortex of mergers and acquisitions, and questionable business tactics. Bankers Trust was the first and only bank to form a voting trust, in which all power passed from the stockholders to three trustees, Daniel G. Reid, director of the First National Bank; George Perkins, partner of J. P. Morgan & Co. (who was later substituted by George B. Case of White and Case, council for the First National Bank); and Henry P. Davison, partner of J. P. Morgan & Co. and Benjamin Strong's neighbour and boss.

The striking pattern of the success of Bankers Trust was that it began its capitalization in 1903 with $1,000,000. In six months the company's deposits went to over $10 million and by 1912 had grown to a gargantuan $168 million with capital of $10 million and undivided profits of over $5 million. Why is this important? Because to do this, Bankers Trust absorbed the Manhattan Trust Co. and the Mercantile Trust Co. However, the problem for Morgan was that J. P. Morgan's Equitable Life Insurance Co. dominated the Mercantile Trust Co. So, Morgan could show no affiliation with Bankers Trust, even though he owned it; hence, the need for a voter's trust.[2]

The other problems were that Strong had already become a board member of the Equitable Trust Co., the Astor Trust Co.,[3] and vice president of Bankers Trust when the Equitable bought Madison Trust Co. He was also the orchestrator of the $9.5 million/13,000-share Mercantile Trust and Manhattan Trust buyout.[4] These practices were dangerously close to violations of the Sherman Antitrust Act. By forming interlocking directorates in the Wall Street banking industry, Morgan and his employees were playing fast and loose with the law, and Strong was at the centre of it. These activities put him on Wall Street's radar as a "creative interpreter" of the Sherman Antitrust Act and a Morgan force to be reckoned with. He fitted right in to the Morgan way of doing business.

Strong's personal pressures were more serious than the ones at his workplace. In 1905, his wife Margaret bore their fourth child. She was soon after stricken with depression and other psychological ailments, and committed suicide. His friend, neighbour, and boss Henry Davison, took the Strong children into his home, and Strong plunged himself into work. Then, in 1907, at the age of 35, he married the 20-year old Katherine Converse, daughter of Edmund C. Converse – the president of Bankers Trust. This marriage, too, ended unhappily when Katherine left Strong, took their two daughters, and divorced him in 1920.[5]

In 1909, Strong's other good friend and neighbour from Englewood, Thomas Lamont, resigned as vice president of the Bankers Trust to become vice president of the First National Bank of New York. Strong succeeded him as vice president of Bankers Trust, one year before he would leave for the trip to Jekyll Island, and worked directly under his latest father-in-law, Edmund Converse. When Converse declined re-election, Strong became the president of Bankers Trust in January 1914 – one month after the Federal Reserve Act was signed into law. By this time the company was the second largest trust company in the country with deposits of $127 million. The first was the Guarantee Trust Co., also owned by J. P. Morgan.[6]

Benjamin Strong, Jr

The position would last only ten months, as Strong resigned from his post as president of Bankers Trust, as well as from the many other business affiliations he had formed, like trustee of Seamen's Bank for Savings (which his great-grandfather helped found), board member of the Clearing House Committee, the boards of directors of two other trust companies, and more than a dozen public utility, industrial corporations, and railroads including Electric Bond & Share Co., US Motors, Utah Power and Light, and Seaboard Airline Railway. He left all this in October 1914 to accept the title of governor of the Federal Reserve Bank of New York.[7]

He was first offered the job in August 1914, but declined. His fellow Jekyll Islander, Paul M. Warburg of Kuhn, Loeb & Co., who had just been appointed to the Federal Reserve Board at that time, strongly urged him to accept the position. Strong explained that his reasons for his decision had nothing to do with the massive pay-cut he would have to take by accepting the position. Nor did it have to do with any doubts he may have had in the success of the system. He turned down the offer for reasons having to do with the pressures of his new position as president of Bankers' Trust of New York, and the status of the company: ". . . in regard to the affairs of clients, of friends and of the city and country which lead them and me to believe that it would be unfair for me to give up my present work just now. Some of these obligations are quite personal and important."

Warburg and Henry P. Davison took Strong out to the country for a week, for the sole purpose of convincing him to accept the position. They stressed his importance to the success of the Federal Reserve and the fact that no one else could understand the larger scope of what their system would accomplish. Strong finally acquiesced to his friends' influence and accepted the governorship.[8]

A few years earlier, almost a year to the day after Strong and the others returned from Jekyll Island, Strong spoke at the American Bankers' Association in New Orleans. There he gave a rundown of the projected numbers for the plan for the United States' first constitutionally codified central bank. His projected assets for the bank were $1.2 billion with earnings of $32.5 million. After explaining that the stockholders were to receive $5 million in dividends, Strong went on to say, "It is quite apparent, therefor, that the disposition of the earnings of the association may become an important question immediately upon its organization."[9] It was no wonder that during the same event, Jacob Gould Schurman, president of Cornell University, pointed out the obvious concerns, before appeasing his Wall Street benefactors: "On the dangers of Wall Street exploitation and control, the public will be sensitive and suspicious in the extreme . . . so far as it appears, it might be said that the possibility is wholly eliminated [by the Aldrich Plan]."[10]

Strong was very open and candid about the fact that he wanted a pure "central bank", run from New York, with a New York board of directors, and dominated by the Wall Street banking community. He was bitterly disappointed by the final structure of the Fed. On 2 April 1914, the locations and the number of the Federal Reserve districts were announced, and Strong was heard to exclaim, "The twelve reserve banks are eleven too many!"[11] It was Warburg who convinced Strong that he could run the Fed from New York, as its governor, and achieve the same ends of a Wall Street-run system, by means of more covert and politically diplomatic policies.[12]

It was only after the Federal Reserve was up and running did Strong realize that Warburg had been right all along about the concept of one, central bank of the United States being unsuitable for winning over the public and the political pressures against central banking. Strong was wanton and pig-headed in his ideals, and cared nothing about how his wishes played to the public. But, Warburg and Davison were reliable contributors to Strong's education on policy issues and foreign exchange, which kept his fervent opinions in check.[13] Strong soon realized the bigger picture and saw the Federal Reserve Act not as a service to the American people's economic welfare, but as, "an opportunity to expand the international operations of United States banks, particularly New York banks . . . and the development of the market for bills of exchange and acceptances was the means to accomplish this end in a manner consistent with the Act."[14]

In Strong's letter of 10 October 1914 to Warburg, he voiced his opinion about the restrictions a harsh gold reserve policy the Federal Reserve Act would have on the member banks. Strong was already showing his want for independence and autonomy from the Federal Reserve Board. But much more interestingly, the letter reflects how hierarchical the system was, and how much power rose to the top. Strong knew his place:

> . . . If the Federal Reserve Banks refuse to pay gold, they will be discredited at the outset, and gold will certainly be demanded of them if they expand their note issue when gold will be at a premium . . . Don't for a moment think that I am going to hold back in the organization of the New York institution. If you and your associates agree that it is the thing to do at once, I am here to carry out orders.[15]

Benjamin Strong, the president of Bankers Trust Company of New York, one of the most powerful and influential bankers in the country, known to all as J. P. Morgan's "lieutenant", assured Paul Warburg, whom he described as "the real head of the board at Washington"[16] that he was at his post, ". . . here to carry out orders". Not unlike a military-style chain of command, Strong's words reveal the code and the power of authority the system protected.

Warburg demonstrated his view of the balance of power in the system when he wrote to Strong regarding the authority of the "governor" position in the twelve district banks, and his obvious scheme for the New York branch, with Strong as its governor, to wield the most power: "It is important that you frame the by-laws so as to give yourself sufficient power as Governor, but bear in mind at the same time that there are many other banks where we want to be careful not to have the Governor run away from the Federal Reserve Agent and the Board, so there must be some flexibility in this respect."[17] These words would soon solidify the fact that the monetary policies of the Fed were to be run in Washington, by the board. But they were to be carried out in New York, by Strong.

When the First World War broke out in July 1914, Jacob Schiff, senior member of Kuhn, Loeb & Co., and Paul Warburg's old boss stated, "With the closing of markets around the world, with moratoriums going into effect in important European centers, agreement has practically been reached to stop the machinery of the world's financial intercourse, and to await developments, assuring safer conditions, before this machinery be once more set into motion".[18] However, this worldwide halt of all business transactions apparently excluded what amounted to hundreds of millions of dollars in gold to Europe.

Benjamin Strong, Jr was elected governor of the New York Fed at the Bank's first board meeting on 5 October 1914, six weeks prior to the opening day of organization. He was 41 years old.[19] In August, a couple of weeks after the first shots of the First World War were fired, "Benjamin Strong, Jr, President of the Bankers Trust Co., would not confirm any of the details of the private gold shipment beyond stating that the total amount would be $5,117,000. He said that it was planned to establish central stations for a relief fund of stranded Americans in various parts of Europe".[20]

The *Tennessee*, an armoured cruiser detailed as a relief ship for Americans in Europe had $8 million of gold on her. The ship left Brooklyn Harbor with $2,500,000 million in US taxpayer gold for relief, and was joined in the harbour by "revenue cutters" to transfer the additional gold amassed by Wall Street private bankers: American Express, J. P. Morgan & Co., Bankers Trust Co., First National Bank of New York, National Bank of Commerce, National City Bank, Brown Brothers & Co., Kidder Peabody & Co., Farmers Loan & Trust Co. and the Guaranty Trust Co. Another cruiser, the *North Carolina* also set sail days later with an undisclosed amount of gold. With Ben Strong heading the entire program, both ships left for Europe, and their "exact destinations were not made public".[21]

The program's aim was to send millions of dollars in gold to England to help stranded Americans in Europe as Germany had just invaded France. Both the timing and the amount of money sent red flags up the pole of many Wall Street detractors. That seemed like a lot of money, in gold, to help "stranded Americans". However, in times of war people usually think with their hearts and concern for humanity overrides distrust of institutions. To prove that Wall Street cared too, the Mayor of New York, John Purroy Mitchel announced the formation of the sweetest bunch of guys this side of the Atlantic Ocean:

> Pursuant to my wire to you, I have appointed today a Citizens' Committee to cooperate with the State Department in whatever way may be found possible in facilitating the return of Americans abroad . . . The committee will be equipped with a clerical staff, will collect funds, will undertake to compile lists of New York citizens now abroad, and will at once get in touch with the State Department to learn in what way it would be of the greatest service.[22]

Mayor Mitchel's Citizens' Relief Committee was a group of concerned New Yorkers who volunteered their services to their country by shipping millions and millions of dollars to an undisclosed part of Europe to undisclosed members of undisclosed countries' undisclosed banks. The committee was made up of Seth Low, president of the New York Chamber of Commerce; Archibald Watson, the chamber's vice president; Frank Vanderlip, president of the National City Bank; E. C. Porter, treasurer of the Merchants Association; along with other local do-gooders like Jacob Schiff, Henry P. Davison, A. Barton Hepburn, president of Chase National Bank and former Comptroller of the Currency; Irving T. Bush, and Benjamin Strong, Jr.[23]

With $8 million in gold in Europe, Jack Morgan, the late J. P. Morgan's son, made his move. In what was described by one of the Morgan men as "a very pretty transaction", the nation of France deposited $6 million into Morgan, Harjes & Co. This was the first time in history that a foreign government had established a bank account in the United States. Then, days later, the British government deposited $3 million into Morgan, Grenfell & Co. The money from both countries was collateralized by the gold that was sent out on the *Tennessee* and the *North Carolina*. Gold that was supposed to go to Europe for "stranded Americans" was used as a marker for European countries to start banking with the House of Morgan, with Benjamin Strong negotiating every transaction.

As if having full knowledge of an all-out world war on the horizon, a member of J. P. Morgan & Co. explained the process of profiting from the war, as Germany had declared war on France only two days earlier:

> It amounts to a trade to mutual advantage. The French deliver to our Paris house $6,000,000 and we hold for their order like a sum. It saves the time and expense of our getting gold across and it gives the French government funds for use in this market, which they are certain to need. The arrangement was made by them to provide for consular and other expenses . . . principally in the purchase of foodstuffs. Grain and cotton are conditional contraband of war, which means that they can be purchased here and loaded on merchant vessels . . .[24]

Strong made many trips to Europe before the war and the fact that one broke out was a huge payoff, culminating in this momentous transaction. However, he did not want to stop there. The gold and the deposits were obviously being created for war profiteering, but Strong entered a new realm of opportunistic possibility when he stated his intentions ". . . to arrange from London for the establishment of a fund in Berlin, although [Strong] did not entertain high hopes for this being accomplished now that the two countries were at war".[25] However, A. Barton Hepburn echoed Strong's longing for German business when he wrote to Senator Oscar W. Underwood, demanding that he liberalize shipping laws: "It is inevitable that all over-sea trade of Germany will be at the mercy of any nation who first seeks and can best serve the former patrons of Germany. Of all nations, the United States is in the best position to take and hold this trade . . . and when the war in Europe is over, we should hold largely the trade that is now waiting to fall into our hands".[26]

Wall Street had a foreign exchange problem. European bankers were exchanging vast amounts of dollars for their currency, as the exchange rates were high for

European currency at the time. US Bankers were in dire need of large sums of money abroad in order to meet exchange, which the Europeans had sold. These transactions with the French and British governments, along with the shipment of gold, were of great concern to the entire New York financial district. If other countries followed suit, or if France and England allowed for more large deposits in US banks for commercial use, then the US banks would be out from under their exchange crisis and would gain unbridled control over many European markets, especially with the entire continent ravaging itself through war; and "stranded Americans in Europe" were never mentioned again.

A month later Strong represented the New York Clearing House and the Federal Reserve by proposing a $200 million pool of gold to be shipped abroad, with the taxpayers accounting for $30 million of it and the Wall Street bankers making up the difference. The gold was needed to pay off any debt the United States had in Europe. But the real reason was that there existed a "certain indebtedness of the city of New York" and that debt matured in four months. The not yet organized, Federal Reserve, wasn't paying the debt, it was buying it. The $200 million was lowered to $150 million when J. P. Morgan, Jacob Schiff, and Benjamin Strong met with the Federal Reserve Board and then Secretary of the Treasury William Gibbs McAdoo and suggested the gold be collected from every reserve bank of the Federal Reserve districts, and pooled in a branch of the Bank of England in Ottawa, Canada.[27] A strangely worded letter from Benjamin Strong and Frank Vanderlip, representing the Federal Reserve (which technically didn't exist yet)[28] explained the need for the country to pull together, so that they can buy the debt that the US owed to Europe, while a month earlier they indebted Europe by profiting from the First World War:

> The banking and commercial interests of this country are suffering from the unprecedented derangement of our international trade and banking arrangements. European credits are curtailed [not true] and foreign exchange, in volume is unobtainable [not true – they just struck an historic deal with England and France for $9,000,000 in deposits] . . . The Federal Reserve Board recognizes the necessity of providing an immediate solution to the problem and asks the cooperation of the entire country. The members of the Federal Reserve Board are Government officials [not true – only two of them are, and the Fed is not a government agency] . . . [The Fed] is best able to cope with this international situation and proposes to give its indorsement [sic] and recommendation

to a request of the banks and trust companies in all the central reserve and reserve cities of this country to subscribe to this gold fund. . .The problem is a national one [even though New York owes almost all the money].[29] ·

Three weeks later, on 6 October 1914, Benjamin Strong, Jr was named governor of the New York branch of the Federal Reserve.

By 1915 America was enjoying liquidity and prosperity, thanks mostly to the war. When things are good you can count on bankers to do one thing – complain that things aren't better. William Elliott Knox, president of the Savings Bank Section of the American Bankers' Association and controller of the Bowrey Savings Bank in New York, with his friend Benjamin Strong sitting next to him, railed the US Government, stating that the country was suffering from too much activity in the field of legislation. The Federal Reserve Act was signed into law, $200 million in gold was issued to pay off New York debts, trade embargos were lifted, the country was in the best economic shape since 1836,[30] and the Westchester Banking Association joked that congress should take ten years off and go out and do some real work.[31]

This was really just a strong position trying to get stronger. Sabres rattling to keep everyone on their toes, with Benjamin Strong wielding one of the largest sabres, as the head of the most powerful branch of the Federal Reserve System. With the economy healthy, the banks would soon be clamouring for more money to loan out. Strong also wanted the loan processes to go through New York to make sure all the banks in the system had access to a money market. Strong's desire for control over the entire system began to take shape early. He formed the Open Market Investment Committee (OMIC) that comprised representatives from district member Federal Reserve banks and to ensure a continued strengthening economy and central power in New York, Strong sternly informed them not to bid against each other in the New York market for the limited supply of US Treasury paper that had become scarce since the start of the war.

With control in New York well in hand, Strong began to venture to England in the name of the United States, the Fed and J. P. Morgan & Co. Almost immediately after the formation of the Federal Reserve System, and his appointment as governor of the New York branch, Strong was single-minded in his efforts to expand the American banking system overseas. He sought to reform the currency, bring as many banks as he could into the system to acquire as much gold reserve as possible, and to develop a major international money market in New York.[32]

After a year of networking, and trade and loan negotiating, Strong set his sights on war reparations. The strange thing about his plan was that it was only 1916 when he decided to do this. The United States would not enter the war for another year, and the war wouldn't end for another two and a half years. However, in a letter to his friend, M. Percy Peixotto, president of the American Chamber of Commerce in Paris, Strong carefully alludes to his intentions regarding the "post-war commercial situation" and calls for "diplomatic and friendly treatment" of "the belligerent nations to repair the damage of war . . ." and he offered his opinions on "temptations . . . of methods that . . . may prove unsound and dangerous . . ." in regard to German war reparations. All this in a letter to a French businessman as a sidebar to accepting membership in the Parisian Chamber of Commerce.[33]

It would be irresponsible to speculate on whether Benjamin Strong had preconceived knowledge of what the outcome of the First World War would be, two years before its end. However, when the United States entered the war, it was Benjamin Strong who used his dominance as the governor of the New York Fed to double the United States money supply to finance the US war effort in Europe, and loan money to the allied forces and later to the Germans to pay for war reparations. This action was unprecedented, and some historians believe its implementation ". . . ensured an Anglo-French victory".[34]

To accomplish this Herculean task of networking all the central banks of Europe with the Federal Reserve, Strong knew he could not face the old guard of ancient European financial centres head-on. Instead he promoted cooperation with international monetary institutions. Thus, in February 1916, with the Great War raging, he sailed to Europe to negotiate with the leaders of the most powerful banks on the continent: the Bank of France and the Bank of England. He met with financial leaders from both Paris and London and interviewed the men who ran the banks.

His work with the French proved to be fruitless, as their noted conservatism mired definite agreements. However, the British were much more accepting of Strong's ideas and motives and he achieved much more material results with the Bank of England. In his dealings and meetings with bank officials, on 18 March 1916, Strong met the man he would have an association with for many years to come, Montague Norman.

Norman came from a family of bankers. Both his mother and father came from prominent British banking families. He prepped at Eton, dropped out of King's College, Cambridge after a year, and went to work at his father's banking firm, Martin's

Bank, in 1882. He journeyed to America and worked at his grandfather's firm, Brown, Shipley & Co. in New York. For reasons unknown he travelled across the United States and back, said to be learning about the American financial system, and then he returned to Brown, Shipley & Co. in 1898. Two years later he was made a partner.

The United States and Brown, Shipley & Co. have a long and storied history together. J. P. Morgan & Co. began as George Peabody & Co., which began in 1814 as Peabody and Riggs, in Georgetown, DC, dealing in dry goods and operators of the Georgetown Slave Market. In 1815 they moved to Baltimore to be closer to the supply of both dry goods and slaves. From there, Peabody's business through importing and exporting began to flourish in London, so a firm of George Peabody & Co. was established in London. Peabody was able to make this seamless entry into the London business scene with the help of his British friend in Baltimore, Alexander Brown. Alexander Brown possessed an established firm in Liverpool, Brown Brothers, and operated Alex Brown & Son out of Baltimore. Back in 1801 Alexander Brown founded Brown, Shipley & Co., which remains to this day the oldest banking house in the United States, presently operating as Brown Brothers Harriman. But, it was a young man named Junius Spencer Morgan who joined the Peabody firm in 1854 and left an indelible mark on US and London banking. In 1864 Junius took over George Peabody & Co. and changed the name to J. S. Morgan & Co. Junius's son John Pierpont then succeeded him.[35]

Never married and quite foppish, Norman did not look the part of a banking mogul, and before his experience in the Boer War he never did care for competition and was a lonely and isolated individual. In the war he was placed in charge of a unit whose duty was to hunt down Boer commandos. It was during this time where he found a sense of adventure, enthusiasm, confidence, and the killer instinct he never knew had existed in him. He found who he was in war. He wrote to his parents, "I feel a different person now . . . One looks ahead with something of dismay to the time when one will again have to settle down to civilized life".[36] So, instead of civilized life, he went back to the banking industry. He returned to England and was elected as a director of the Bank of England in 1907 becoming deputy governor, and then governor in 1920. The traditional practice at the time was that the governorship of the Bank of England was rotated after two years. Norman, unaffected, served for twenty-four years in succession.[37]

Benjamin Strong presented Norman with a letter of introduction and recommendation from James Brown, Montague Norman's former partner in Brown

Brothers & Co.[38] That evening they dined alone in Norman's house and began forging the relationship that influenced the monetary histories of both their countries.

By 30 March 1916 Strong and the representatives of the Bank of England had drafted the *Memorandum of Conversations between the Governors of the Bank of England and the Governor of the Federal Reserve Bank of New York.* Strong reported the contents of the memorandum to the Reserve board upon his return to the States in April. The memorandum began: "Confidentially and tentatively agreed upon for submission and ratification by the respective institutions, with a view to be put into operation after the conclusion of the war". It seemed unusual that the war was a non-stop conflagration at that point, and the Bank of England and the New York Federal Reserve Bank were making deals pending its conclusion. However, no one seemed to make note of this. The memorandum contained 11 points:

1. The Federal Reserve Bank of New York to act for itself and such of the other eleven Reserve Banks as might elect to join the account.
2. The Federal Reserve Bank of New York to maintain an account with the Bank of England; but because of the law permitting the Federal Reserve Bank to receive deposits from only their own members, and the United States Government, any accounts with it would have to be in the form of earmarked[39] gold.
3. The Bank of England, to purchase on request prime sterling bills[40] for the account of the Federal Reserve Bank of New York, and these bills to meet "eligibility" requirements.
4. The accounts, respectively, to be kept free of charges and commissions except for out-of-pocket expenses.
5. It is hoped that the Federal Reserve Bank of New York will eventually reach an arrangement on similar lines with the Bank of France.[41]
6. No announcement, directly or indirectly, to be made regarding the contents of this memorandum without the explicit consent of both institutions.

The other five points dealt with interest rates, earmarking gold, shipment of gold, exchange of information, and cancellation provisions.[42]

On 26 April 1916 the directors of the New York branch approved Strong's proposal. His plea for approval from the Federal Reserve Board was cut short because in early June, Strong was diagnosed with tuberculosis of the lungs, and his doctor ordered him to the thin air of Colorado for a year of rest and recuperation. Robert H. Treman was appointed deputy governor in his absence, but Strong continued his pressure on the board for approval from the healthier air of the Rocky Mountains.[43]

On 29 August the board tentatively approved the agreement with the provision that no business would commence until after the war. But the board set off a bitter controversy between itself and the directors of the New York branch by immediately violating the sixth provision of the agreement.

Officials of the New York branch, including Strong, found out about the final approval in the newspapers. The board sent the notification to chairman, Pierre Jay, in an envelope marked "Confidential", disregarding the New York board, while Jay was on vacation. The press got wind of the approval, printed it, and the board of the New York branch was left out of the loop, completely. The Federal Reserve Board had revealed its autonomy and fullness of power.

However, all was forgiven when the desperate Bank of England agreed to ratify the agreement and the Bank of France followed in February 1917, with the war still raging. This relationship with both European banks was unprecedented, and Strong's vision for "our bank" to become an international powerhouse with the cooperation of the central banks of Europe, took shape.[44]

Benjamin Strong was met by Henry P. Davison, who also travelled to England when Strong was there, meeting with Montague Norman to hammer out the *Memorandum*. Davison and Strong represented the interests of J. P. Morgan & Co. in the overseas war effort. The late J. P. Morgan's son, Jack, adroitly used these longstanding ties with the British investment banks, his father's emissary, Davison, and his "lieutenant", Strong, to get the "House of Morgan named as the sole purchasing agent in the United States, for the duration of the war, for war material for both Britain and France".[45]

Montague Norman worked with Benjamin Strong on almost every deal the New York Federal Reserve made with the Bank of England. The two men became such good friends that they would vacation together in Bar Harbor, Maine and the South of France. Steady flows of letters over years of collaboration kept their banking and personal relationships taut and up to date.

After the First World War, the League of Nations required a certain aloofness from US banking and business interests. It supported an autonomous rebuilding of nations, which would not involve foreign Dollar diplomacy, and an abandonment of postwar imperialism, in which banks would be involved. But Strong had made his intentions very clear about financing reconstruction programs for allied countries after the war. After the armistice of 11 November 1918, Strong wrote to Montagu Norman, "There is no doubt that much of the world's happiness in the future will depend upon the relations now being established between your country and ours". The Bank of England and the Federal Reserve began drawing up plans for the design of the world's new economic landscape.[46]

Since Norman was not only unbound by the restrictions of the League of Nations, many of Norman's associates were on the League's Financial Committee for relief, reconstruction, and stabilization. The League was one of his principal channels for floating loans to beleaguered countries through any central bank he wished. Since Strong and the New York Federal Reserve represented the world's greatest economic power, and the largest monetary gold stock in the world, it was the largest potential source of international loans, and the two men collaborated despite both US and global political restrictions.

To Strong and Norman, the United States and British postwar governments were dominating them and their banking interests with monetary policy intervention, and they did not believe either government had their best interests in mind. So the two men worked together through central banking, in the face of government reprisal, and succeeded by using loopholes in the charter of the League of Nations.[47] This collaboration sparked a friendship and association between Strong and Norman, that would in turn give rise to a banking coalition between the United States and England that would influence the entire economies of both countries, and even the world's. The entire time, the two men conducted their business while continuing to thumb their noses at their own political leaders.

Despite the fact that he got his start in finance as a stock and real estate speculator, Strong was extremely outspoken about what he considered irresponsibility in banking and investing. He had true disdain for shady stock speculators and viewed the average American banker as vulture-like in picking at the bones of the banks' reserves during times when he felt discretion and patience better suited the economy. He was considered by many to be a snob, and a new-money elitist.

The farm in Montclair, New York was far behind him by this point in his life and career. In a letter to Adolph C. Miller, Strong released some of his venom towards small bankers, and urged him to prepare for the worst:

Until experience has demonstrated the contrary, I fear we must calculate that the American banker, by and large, will do in future emergencies just what he has done on similar occasions in the past. He will gather up every dollar of reserve money that he can lay his hands on and lock it up so tight that the Reserve Banks will never get a hold of it until the crisis is past. I personally saw that happen in the early 90s, 1907, and 1914. Frankly, our bankers are more or less an unorganized mob.[48]

His views on his fellow reserve banks' tactics were no less harsh in their criticism. In 1922, Strong told a Harvard audience, "Practically all borrowing by member banks from the Reserve Banks is ex post facto. The condition which gives rise to the need for borrowing had already come into existence before the application to borrow from the Reserve Bank was made. The banks make their loans first, and then hunt for the money to fund them."[49]

Strong wished to head off stock speculators before they could "damage the economy". Taking absolutely no responsibility for doubling the nation's money supply and flooding the economy with so much currency, his theories only truncated the activities of the smaller investor. Large firms and individuals of considerable wealth had no use for loans at the stock speculation level. Smaller investors were obtaining credit for stock exchange investment, and Strong was intent on watching them like a hawk. In this regard he said: "The best way to control unwise extension of credit at the stock exchange was to push the discount rates at the other 11 district Feds a percentage point higher than the rate in NY. The differential would suck money out of New York to the countryside, forcing the New York banks to call their loans to stock speculators, those being the shortest loans, and the easiest to cancel."[50]

His goal, to keep an eye on these investors was important to him, but he still had to balance his disdain for speculators with his main objective of furthering American business interests. Strong wrote to the head of the Federal Reserve Bank of Philadelphia: "That orgy [of stock speculation] will always be with us and if the Federal Reserve System is to be run solely with the view of regulating stock speculation instead of being devoted to the interests of industry and commerce of the country, then its policy will degenerate simply to regulating the affairs of gamblers".[51]

He indicated how important this undertaking was to him in a letter he wrote in January 1917, to Charles S. Hamlin, a member of the Federal Reserve Board: "If I live and keep my health, you will see our bank in a close and important relationship with all the great central banks of Europe where such relationships can be of value, and it is one of the matters, which had been uppermost in my mind ever since we started our organization. When that part of the work is done maybe I will retire and grow potatoes".[52] Benjamin Strong, Jr didn't grow potatoes. Instead, years later in 1927, Strong joined a representative from J. P. Morgan & Co. and visited Benito Mussolini to convince him that to keep the Italian Lira strong, he had to make the Bank of Italy separate from the Finance Ministry. Mussolini failed to heed Strong's suggestion.[53]

7

The Emissary: Henry P. Davison

Born 13 June 1867 in Troy, Pennsylvania, Henry Pomeroy Davison was the right-hand to both J. P. Morgan and J. P. Morgan, Jr. He often spoke for the two men and represented the firm in business and political matters. The House of Morgan owned J. P. Morgan & Co., but Henry P. Davison became the bricks and mortar that held the House together.[1]

His father, George Bennett Davison sold farm equipment and invented ways to improve the products he sold. He was on the road for most of Henry's life, having little contact with his family. Henry's mother, Henrietta Bliss Pomeroy was very musically inclined as a singer and pianist. She was warm and charming and very well thought of by her family and friends. Her death, when Henry was nine years old, affected the family in many ways.

After his mother's death Henry was sent to live with his uncle Merrick Pomeroy, a Presbyterian preacher. Merrick was very strict and impressed an ideology of blind obedience of Christianity on Henry (or "Harry" as he was known as a boy). Henry's older brother and two younger sisters were sent to live with aunts and uncles as well. Inter-marriage was a part of the Davison and Pomeroy family at this time. Two of Harry's aunts on his father's side married two of his mother's half-brothers.[2] Of all the Davison-Pomeroy family members, Merrick was the toughest, yet offered sagacious advice. Harry was well liked but did not do well in school. When his grades began to suffer greatly, uncle Merrick took him to watch a team of men digging a gutter. He said to Harry, "Those men have had none of the advantages of education and, you see, their life is hard; study, my boy, so that your lot may be a different one."[3] Despite uncle Merrick's wisdom, his harsh treatment was too much for Harry. After a year with his uncle, he asked his grandmother, Lucinda if he could live with her. Lucinda was like his mother – funny and charming, and deeply religious.

Henry attended school at Greylock in Massachusetts. He applied to Harvard, but got rejected. So he continued his education at the Williams and Rodgers Business College, returned to Troy and worked in banking at the Pomeroy's local firm. His aspirations being higher than that of a local banker, he returned to New England and got a job at a bank owned by the father of one of his school friends from Greylock, Nat Bishop. Harry started his career as a bookkeeper for the Pequonnock National Bank in Bridgeport, Connecticut, earning a salary of $800 per year. Henry loved the attention to detail and routine that the job afforded his eager mind. He soon mastered his position, and one of the directors of the bank; circus-man Phineas T. Barnum took a liking to him, as did his friend Nat's father, W. D. Bishop who was not only the director of the bank, but also the president of the New York, New Haven, and Hartford Railroad.

Henry's room-mate in Bridgeport was Herbert Knapp. Herbert was a friend of a girl whose family took pride in being one of the oldest in Connecticut. This girl, Kate Trubee would become Henry's wife on 13 April 1893. Henry and Kate moved to 444 Central Park West in New York City and Henry began working as the assistant receiving teller at the Astor Place Bank, where he soon attained a fearless reputation. Not as a banker, but as the foil of a bank robber. Henry looked up from the paying teller's window one day, to find a revolver in his face. The wild-looking man with the gun demanded $50,000. Henry quickly pulled the pile of money that was on the shelf in front of him down to the floor behind the window, as he hit the deck. He then tripped the alarm, and the bank robber was captured. This act earned him praise, attention, and even a little prestige among the bankers of New York.[4]

After a few years with Astor Place Bank, Henry's wife Kate became friendly with a woman named Mary Clarke. Mary was the daughter of Dumont Clarke, president of the American Exchange National Bank and organizer and board member of the Liberty National Bank, of which the famous George F. Baker was the major stockholder. Through Mary, Henry took a job on 6 December 1894 at the Liberty National Bank as their assistant to the cashier, earning $2,500 per year. The following year he was promoted to cashier. By January 1900 he was vice president, and on 16 May 1901 Henry P. Davison was named president of the Liberty National Bank. At the age of 34, Henry became the youngest bank president in history.[5] It was at the Liberty where Henry formed relationships in the innermost circles of the New York banking fraternity, which included the most wealthy and powerful men in the world.[6]

George F. Baker had seen enough of Henry at Liberty, and knew he needed the new president working directly for him. When Baker was re-elected at the New York Clearing House Association, Henry was elected the secretary.[7] A year after Henry was appointed president of Liberty, Baker said, "Davison, I think you'd better move your desk up here with us". With that, Henry became the vice president of George F. Baker's First National Bank of New York, leaving his friend Edward C. Converse (soon to be father-in-law of Benjamin Strong, Jr) at the helm of the Liberty.[8]

Henry P. Davison

In 1903, while at the First National, Davison conceived of and helped to create, with his friend George Perkins, who worked for J. P. Morgan & Co., the Bankers Trust. Perkins' friend at J. P. Morgan, Thomas W. Lamont (author of Davison's biography) signed on to the Bankers Trust as secretary and treasurer. Davison hired his cousin, Daniel Pomeroy – the kid who caught the giggles with Henry back at the schoolhouse in Troy, as assistant treasurer. He brought in his friend E. C. Converse from Liberty to be the president of Bankers Trust, and with he and Kate now living in the posh Englewood district of New Jersey, he appointed his neighbour, Benjamin Strong, Jr, to be the vice president.

When the Bankers Trust was formed and its announcement to Wall Street was heard, it was pointed out at the time that, "Ten years ago, such a combination of banking interests . . . would have been impossible, and five years ago would have been difficult. The men who are Directors of the new trust company . . . are closely connected with out of town interests. In fact . . . there was hardly any banker in the United States who would not find a friend on the list".[9] At the time, banking laws forbade national banks from establishing interstate branches, and there were stringent capital and reserve requirements. Trust companies were a way around these laws and requirements, as Bankers Trust began interstate and international banking operations through the use of traveller's cheques. Within the first four months of business, Bankers Trust had accrued $5,750,000 in deposits, which they promptly moved into Wall Street. By 1917, Bankers Trust was a full-fledged commercial bank and became a member of the Federal Reserve System. By 1928 it had $28 million in assets, and by 1933 (before the Glass–Steagall Act, separating the commercial and investment banking sectors) its assets were over $1 billion.[10]

Davison retained outside council for the Bankers Trust with the firm of White & Case. Davison wrote of George Case to A. Piatt Andrew as, "One of the best friends I ever had, and one of the finest men on earth . . . I care more about serving him than anyone else I know".[11] In another letter Davison wrote to Andrew regarding Case, Davison referred to Case as "Fair-haired George, the man-banker" and urged Andrew to recommend him to the first Federal Reserve Board.[12] George B. Case was married to Henry's wife Kate's friend, Mary Clarke – Dumont Clarke's daughter. This incredibly tight-knit family of bankers drove the Bankers Trust like a steamroller through Wall Street, with J. P. Morgan as subscriber of the most substantial block of stock in the bank. Bankers Trust was the fulcrum on which the banking industry levered the banking failures of the Panic of 1907 (see Chapter 9). Davison and Paul Warburg worked closely together so as to minimize the damage following the Panic to their respective firms, but it was the Trust's vice president Benjamin Strong who did most to steady the nerves after the Panic. Davison picked winners at every turn.

With the Bankers Trust in full swing after the Panic, Davison's creation, and how it handled the crisis, gave him even more respect than he already had on Wall Street. This clout earned him political exposure as well, when Senator Nelson Aldrich appointed him to an advisory position on his National Monetary Commission, where he quickly learned the banking practices of England, Berlin, Paris and Vienna through trips on behalf of the NMC.[13] In October 1908, Davison, Aldrich and A. Piatt Andrew sailed from New York to Europe on one of the NMC's "fact-finding" missions.[14] Davison was recruited by Thomas Fortune Ryan to run his Morton Trust Co., and on 1 January 1909 Davison went to work for the biggest fish in the sea when he entered the offices of J. P. Morgan & Co. as a partner.[15]

In August 1909, Davison began his first sortie into global banking with a secret meeting with Paul M. Warburg and Secretary of the Treasury Philander C. Knox to discuss a possible loan to China, through the syndicate set up by J. P. Morgan, which by this time included huge financial incentive from Kuhn & Loeb, National City Bank and the First National Bank of New York. The syndicate "brought pressure to bear on the Chinese Government, through the State Department, for participation in the $27,500,000 loan about to be negotiated with English, German, and French bankers for completing the Hankow [Sze-chuen] Railway".[16]

Squabbling by the British over petty advantages ensued for months after the Americans joined the loan tangle. The fact that the Chinese Government had not even approved the railway project seemed secondary in comparison to the terms of which the money to be loaned was negotiated by the four countries involved. However, by May 1910 Davison and Warburg pushed the deal through with the US syndicate getting an equal fourth of the share of the underwriting of the loan. The total loan amount ended up being an even $30 million with the British winning the nitpicking points over engineering rights, and Davison and Warburg celebrated as a formidable banking duo.[17]

In a later quadrilateral loan to China it was Davison who received most of the credit as he pushed the loan through despite the threat of Russian banking interests taking over the entire deal: "It is understood that it was Mr. Davison who conceived the plan by which . . . the United States, Great Britain, France, and Germany – at once advanced $2,000,000 to China without guarantees and offered a further loan of $3,000,000. This at once brought China to terms and the Russian plan was thwarted."[18]

1910 was a busy year for Henry. He organized the Morgan merger of the Guarantee Trust Co. and the Morton Trust Co. He was appointed a director of Guarantee Trust, and then he orchestrated the absorption of the Fifth Avenue Trust Co. and the Standard Trust Co. Since Davison was hired by Fortune Ryan to run the Morton Trust only a year earlier, it was ironic that it was Davison who ousted most of Ryan's board members to hold one of the directorships of the new bank. Davison sat on the new board with George F. Baker, Edmund C. Converse and Thomas W. Lamont.[19]

By the Fall of 1910, Davison had acquired more banks for J. P. Morgan in six months than any other banker. All these banking take-overs took place just in time for Davison to arrange a duck-hunting trip for him and his pals on Jekyll Island. With Morgan controlling more of Wall Street than ever, it was high time for Davison to organize the meeting that would procure ultimate monopolization of banking through national monetary policy. By early 1911 Davison was lobbying Congress for the passage of the Aldrich Bill, and he helped establish the politicized union of bankers' National Currency Association by way of Congressional approval.[20]

By this time, Davison's baby (and Morgan's pet gorilla) the Bankers Trust was on a rampage. In 1910 it turned the Astor National Bank into the Astor Trust Co. Then in 1911 it absorbed the Mercantile Trust Co., then the Manhattan Trust Co. and then it absorbed the Astor Trust Co.[21] Simultaneously, J. P. Morgan & Co. absorbed the Carnegie Trust Co., the Nineteenth Ward Bank, the Twelfth Ward Bank, the Madison Trust Co. and the Equitable Life Insurance Society.[22] By 1912, after Morgan's Guarantee Trust Co. absorbed the Standard Trust Co., it surpassed the Union Trust Co. of Pittsburg to become the largest trust company in the country with a capital surplus of $35 million, deposits of $210 million and total assets of $263 million.[23]

J. P. Morgan received a lot of negative press for all these powerful moves. Davison couldn't stand the public's perception of his idol. Many economists wrote off these actions as a type of economic or capitalistic Darwinism. However, to Davison it was more like euthanasia. He saw Morgan as someone who was helping the community by buying out all these banks and trust companies. Davison saw Morgan as a saviour, thinking that no one could run a bank better than the old man, so he should run as many as possible before these inept bankers ruin it for everyone. The problem the banking world would face was the fact that every time Morgan took out the shovel to bash another bank's head in, he strengthened his grip on banking monopolization; and the banks he "euthanized" were not all as sick as he made them out to be.

After Davison's death, his son Harry, Jr recalled an anecdote to Thomas Lamont while Lamont was compiling information for Davison's biography. Harry, Jr told the story of a dream that his father had at the time of these M&As for J. P. Morgan. Harry, Jr recounted: "Father woke Mother up and said he had just had a terrible nightmare. He thought he was back in the bank at Troy and could not balance the books, and that his uncle told him he had to balance them or get a horsewhipping. Still, they would not balance, and Father was in a cold sweat. When Mother asked him how it came out, he said: 'I finally solved the problem; I bought the bank'".[24]

J. P. Morgan's corporate imperialism eventually became too much for the country's political power to idly sit and watch. The famous Money Trust hearings began in 1912, lead by attorney Samuel Untermeyer and Democratic senator from Louisiana, Arsene Pujo. Pujo was also the co-chairman of the Senate Subcommittee on Banking and Currency. Morgan's reputation was on the line. Davison's hero was finally going to have to answer for his role as banking executioner, and Davison was on the hook as his emissary. He worked tirelessly, preparing charts, graphs, and financial reports for the committee. Morgan eluded questions regarding the reach of his directorate within the banks he controlled, and the operations and deposits of their customers with retorts like, "You cannot in any bank, not in any first-class bank, at any rate – go and find out how much I have got in the bank".[25]

When Davison was on the stand on 23 January 1913, he answered questions regarding voting trusts and monopolies, among many others subjects. Davison considered voting trusts "useless now" and promised to "consider" doing away with the one that existed within the Bankers Trust and Guarantee Trust. He denounced the large directorates that had developed over the years within the two trust banks. However, on the topic of control and who should possess it, Davison was very telling with his opinions. On the question of trusts he replied, "I would not say that I am not opposed to trusts in the making, but I was certainly not opposed to them after they were made. I think they are a great blessing to the country. They are not as great a blessing as they were before they were disturbed." When Davison was asked if he believed in regulated monopolies, his answer was, "I do decidedly . . . I am not opposed to competition. I would rather have regulation and control than free competition."[26]

The inquisitors of the committee continued to grill him for answers regarding how J. P. Morgan & Co. handled the funds that interstate corporations deposited with them. Davison declined to answer every question on this topic and outlasted the committee. He finally stated, with allegiance to the firm: "I know that J. P. Morgan & Co. can do no wrong, if their endeavors and the circumstances permitted them to do as they wanted to".

The accusations of "strengthening competitors" through "interlocking directorates" wore down Davison, Morgan, and the industry. The hearings lasted from May 1912 to January 1913. They took such a toll on Morgan, that many of his loyal following, including Davison, Strong and Perkins blamed the stress of the hearings for his death on 31 March 1913.[27] The whole affair frustrated Davison and in May of the year of his mentor's death, at a meeting in Paris his tongue allegedly slipped during an interview regarding the current administration. Davison was reported to have sharply criticized the policies of President Wilson and his Secretary of State, William Jennings Bryan – especially those involving foreign policy. Some of the comments attributed to Davison included: "Now that the Government has destroyed our work over the years [the Money Trust investigation] it is inconceivable that the foreign bankers or their governments will again undertake anything with us". He continued to vent his discontent, including the American people's perception of the wealthy class:

> We gave four years of patient work to putting America, for the first time, at the head of an extremely important international financiering proposition [the Chinese loans], thus opening up a vast field for future activity; But it was all sacrificed in a moment, to make a little temporary hit with the populace . . . Personally, I'm glad the American people have at last got what they've so long been clamoring for. They really wanted it, now they've really got it. What has happened is that the long awaited establishment of a sharp class division of the country into the people with money and the people without money has come about, leaving all monied people at outs with the Government.[28]

Davison denied the entire conversation and J. P. Morgan & Co. had to send out a letter to Secretary Bryan, assuring him that Davison and the firm did not hold those views.

By January 1914 the Money Trust investigations had done an adequate job in breaking up some of the "interlocking directorates" that fuelled the consolidation of banking, business and industry. Boards were trimmed down, heads of companies were forced to relinquish their positions on many other companies' boards, and bankers were expected to keep only a few of their many corporate offices. However, only seven of the 23 bank and trust company directorships had been relinquished, and this consolidation only helped Henry Davison, as he was now one of only four men at the head of J. P. Morgan & Co., the firm still held 33 places for partners, and the Federal Reserve Act was signed into law only weeks before the restructuring.[29]

Soon the Great War began, and to the American banking industry it was seen as a literal gold mine. Davison helped to orchestrate the $500 million government-backed Anglo-French loan in 1915 to aid the Allies' war effort. Repayment of this loan (and others like it) was the key to America's monetary dominance throughout and after the war. The Europeans began to collateralize and pay-off the loan immediately, through three methods. First, through shipments of gold to the US, from the inception of the loan to 1917, $1 billion in gold was shipped overseas from England and France to the United States. Second, through the sale in US markets of European-owned American securities – of which J. P. Morgan & Co. brokered most of the sales. Third, the countries themselves took out loans directly from Wall Street banks to pay off the $500 million loan from the US government, at greater than nominal interest rates. The loan was self-perpetuating and four times larger than any American loan to date (1917).[30]

The war broke out in July 1914; the Federal Reserve was organized in November 1914; and in January 1915, Henry P. Davison and J. P. Morgan, Jr travelled to London on a "secret mission" with Herman Harjes, J. P. Morgan's long-time partner in Morgan, Harjes & Co.; Lord Walter Cunliffe, Governor of the Bank of England; Lloyd George, Chancellor of the Exchequer; Lord Reading, Lord Chief Justice of England; and British Prime Minister Asquith. The reason for the meeting was to establish a gold pool, a cotton pool (credit for financing the Southern cotton crops), arms dealings, and a reciprocal credit between the British Treasury and J. P. Morgan & Co., Kuhn & Loeb, and National City Bank. Davison's view was, "The sooner the allies got together at one table the better it would be for their interests". Davison and J. P. Morgan took control of all the US operations concerning the British and French government loans during the first three years of the war.[31] There were sections of both the British and French governments that criticized the mission, noting that British and Canadian manufacturers would be deprived from the vital business of selling war supplies to the Allies. However, Wall Street challenged this complaint with guarantees of millions of dollars in savings for the Allies by combining British and Canadian orders within the US and undercutting the commissions of middlemen.[32]

As far as the US Government was concerned, they wanted no direct part in the arrangement, even though they were notified beforehand. Martin Egan, Davison's advisor at J. P. Morgan & Co. quoted Secretary William Jennings Bryan as saying "We are not approving, we simply do not make objection. I do not think it necessary that you make public the fact that we were notified . . . You can say that the matter was not submitted to the Department for its approval, therefore it is not true that there was approval."[33]

The Anglo-French loan was too big to just ship over a boatload of cash or gold. The money was passed through the purchase of bonds. Davison and Jack Morgan, Jr, at the heart of the loan structuring, formed a syndicate of 61 banks, trust companies, and investment firms with J. P. Morgan & Co. as the exclusive agent for the syndicate. Smaller loans followed on an individual basis. In April 1915 France was given a resale loan on the Pennsylvania Railroad of $30 million through Davison. At the same time, J. P. Morgan & Co. and the Rothschilds, through the de Rothschild Fréres Loan, gave another $40 million to the French, utilizing the Chicago, Milwaukee & St Paul Railway and Pennsylvania Company franc securities, "turned in by French nationals in exchange for the new National Defense Bonds of their own country".[34]

By the late summer of 1915, the British pound was dropping heavily. The Europeans' ability to make payments on their loans was dwindling. The British froze further negotiations with the syndicate for a year, and J. P. Morgan, Jr faced other problems when he was shot twice in his home in August 1915 (he survived). However, with the massive purchases from Europe, the US economy was booming. The gold imports and the securities sales gave rise to US global economic dominance.

Davison's interest in the German and Austrian banks could be construed as a consideration of doing buisness with the enemy. The firm of Zimmerman & Forshay had started an extensive advertising campaign for the sale of German war bonds. In a letter from Martin Egan to Davison, he revealed that, "The German securities are being offered at lower rates than before. A friend has obtained for us, and I send you herewith, copies of the advertisements. We are asked to keep the information and the fact that we have copies of the advertisement as confidential".[35]

Despite the subsequent freeze, Britain had to borrow more money to keep up with payments, and in 1916, the United Kingdom Loan of 1916 was structured. Britain was running out of money, gold and securities to sell, but Davison and Morgan convinced the British government that they could continue to make the payments. But they had to also convince the American people to continue to support their interests as well, because sooner or later the US would be asked to secure government bonds with collateral and direct government obligations. Davison held a press conference upon his return from England and France in October of 1916. Regarding the success of the syndicate's foreign loans, he declared "If this prosperity is to be shared by the country at large, our investors, our bankers, and the public generally must take a broad, intelligent view of the opportunities before us and assure the peoples of these foreign governments that we desire their trade and have confidence as to their financial soundness. It's not a question of wealth or value, but purely one of exchange."[36]

A week later, Davison appeared at the home of the president of the Continental and Commercial National Bank of Chicago, George M. Reynolds, to push for a liberal overseas lending policy and "to afford an opportunity for the Western bankers to meet Mr. Davison and learn from him personally something of the credit situation in Europe and of its bearing on the financial situation in this country".[37]

That same week, Davison took a break from international finance to visit the New York tax department to protest his personal tax assessment for 1915. The assessment was for $1 million. The assessment was cancelled because Davison swore that his residence was in Locust Valley, Nassau County, NY, and not in New York City.[38]

International business soon continued for Davison and the syndicate by means of what some would call an old-fashioned shakedown. The Morgan interests tried to convince Britain to consolidate their loans with the French. When the two governments could not work out a deal, which Davison knew they would not, Britain was forced to sign the Second United Kingdom Loan of $300 million in November 1916. Not unlike a second mortgage, more than half the proceeds of the second loan went to pay off the first loan. However, this loan was to be renewed one month after the date of issuance (December 1916) at a much higher rate of interest.[39]

Another idea to stop the bleeding was a suggestion by the British and French governments to issue and sell British and French short-term treasury bills, to be sold in the US market. However, the Federal Reserve stepped in to denounce the plan: "The board deems it its duty to caution the member banks that it does not regard it in the best interest of the country at this time that they invest in foreign Treasury bills of this character".[40] Under this advisement, the plan was scrapped. With no other choice, Britain succumbed to the debt pressures and in December 1916, shipped $1.3 billion in gold from its vaults in Ottawa, Canada to the United States. Henry Davison applied more pressure and structured a Third United Kingdom Loan in January 1917 for $250 million at 5.5 per cent with a two-year term. This kept Britain buying US goods for the war, and paying for them with money the Morgan syndicate loaned them, plus interest.[41]

Historians have many theories as to why President Wilson broke his campaign promise to keep the United States out of the war. One of those theories involves the effect these loans had on England and France. If the war carried on for too long, there would be no way these countries could ever pay back these loans. Therefore, one could argue that the US joined the war so as to end it when the timing best suited it – to stop the need for the massive borrowing and spending that was breaking the European economy. Europe was the goose that laid the golden egg for American bankers. Cutting her open would have served no purpose – only eventual default on all those loans.

What followed supports this theory. In March 1917, the Federal Reserve was publicly heard from a second time in three months regarding war finance. The first time, it warned against investment in foreign bills. This time, however, the Fed changed its tune, and strongly recommended the purchase of new European treasury bills. With this announcement, $100 million in two-year, 5 per cent T-bills were offered by J. P. Morgan & Co. and they sold out. The public demanded another $16 million worth, then they sold out too, and on 6 April 1917 the United States entered the First World War with 2 million troops under the leadership of General John J. Pershing. About a year and a half later, in November 1918 the war was over, and the Morgan syndicate brokered the Fourth United Kingdom Loan of $250 million and two French Republic loans of $100 million each. $3 billion in British-owned US securities alone were sold during the war.[42]

As J. P. Morgan & Co. acted as the agent for all the war loans to Britain and some of France, Davison and Morgan were well placed to "assist the British Government in solving its problem of purchasing in the United States". Davison formed an export department of J. P. Morgan & Co., organized to handle all the purchasing of US goods by Britain, and then later, by France. The man in charge of the process in Europe was the president of the Diamond Match Company, Edward R. Stettinius, who would become the Second Assistant Secretary of War when the US joined the war, and his son became the Secretary of State under Presidents Roosevelt and Truman.[43]

One month after the US entered the war and four months after he structured the Third United Kingdom Loan Henry Pomeroy Davison was appointed the Director of the war council of the American Red Cross. Among the board members of this council were Cornelius Bliss, Jr, a member of J. P. Morgan's Jekyll Island Hunt Club, Cleveland Dodge, head of Phelps & Dodge, and President Wilson's financier, Colonel Edward M. House, President Wilson's top advisor, and Dwight W. Morrow, a partner at J. P. Morgan & Co. Davison took the job seriously, and he went to great lengths to rally support for the Red Cross: "Our Job in the American Red Cross is to bind up the wounds of a bleeding world . . . Think Red Cross! Talk Red Cross! Be Red Cross!"[44]

During his first fundraising drive for the Red Cross, Davison managed to procure $114 million in one week. When questioned at one of his speeches about his firm's involvement in the managing of the contributions, and his motivation for the appointment of the post, Davison replied: "I will tell you this: that the firm's entire connection with this fund consisted of a subscription from the partners of one million dollars, and a stipulation that not one penny of the entire one hundred million be ever deposited with the firm".[45] However, further claims of malfeasance and manipulation followed, as a portion of the donations was to be made in the form of corporate dividends from 148 companies. Although the money was registered as received, much of the dividend apportioned for donation was not received, including that of Anaconda Copper Co., which was owed by J. P. Morgan.[46]

Rumours about high salaries and selling goods, rather than donating them, to the European countries in need whirled around the Davison Red Cross camp. Davison and his fellow board members blamed these claims of dishonest dealings on German propaganda.[47] However, other countries, such as Russia, made similar claims that the Red Cross was more than just an aid to the wounded, sick and displaced of the war. Leon Trotsky arrested a Red Cross agent, claiming the organization was sending trucks to Rustov to aid the Cossacks in their fight against the revolution. Henry Davison, himself, sent 100,000 rubles to the Russian government to palliate the situation, which placed into question his and Wall Street's view of the Russian Revolution.[48]

For the purposes of both corporate convenience and to secure further aid for the Red Cross, Davison contributed to the Nicoll-Meyer Bill (later thwarted in the Senate), which prohibited the employment of women under 21 years of age, and regulated the hours that women could work.[49] The bill was given a companion rider by Davison, which included the empowerment of directors of corporations to contribute from its surplus property or assets for war relief purposes, without the authority of its stockholders. Senator Elon Brown called it, "typical of decadent citizenship" and went on to denounce the bill as, "an attempt to commit a crime in the name of liberty and law . . . It is Bolshevik in its conception, and should have a Bolshevist end".[50]

In his second pledge drive, in the Spring of 1918, Davison raised $117 million. He sent Red Cross commissions of personnel and equipment to Belgium, Britain,

Russia, Italy, Switzerland, Romania and Serbia. He reportedly spent most of the money on helping the French. By the end of the war, the Red Cross had raised over $400 million in money and material, had over 31 million members, 8.1 million workers, and produced over 370 million relief articles. The Red Cross's war council ended on 28 February 1919 and Davison retired from its chairmanship. He continued to write extensive plans for the future of the Red Cross, and even published a book, *The American Red Cross in the Great War*. [51]

At the war's end, when it came time for peace treaties and the reconstruction of the governments and economy of Europe, it was Wall Street and Henry Davison, not the US government, that took charge of proceedings. Davison stated, upon his return from postwar Europe, "The financing of rehabilitation would fall largely to bankers and not to Governments, for the Governments were rapidly getting out of banking", which he believed was "highly desirable". [52] Unfortunately, Wall Street was just as leaky as the US government, and when word of the parameters of peace in Europe began to pour out of Wall Street, bankers were compelled to appear in front of a Senate hearing. Henry Davison, J. P. Morgan, Jr, Frank Vanderlip, Paul Warburg, Thomas Lamont and Jacob Schiff were called by the Foreign Relations Committee to appear and explain their thoughts on the sources of the leaks on the text of the peace treaty. [53]

However, the leaks were the least of the US government's concern regarding Wall Street's position in the peace talks. Davison and Frank Vanderlip took the reigns and began to draft the origins of a "Super Corporation" that would put Europe to work, and fight Bolshevism from spreading. Davison urged that the labour pool in Europe would have to fend for itself while, "Debentures might be issued against the credits established in Europe . . . The debentures would really be against the whole of Europe. Then the banking interests could place these debentures with the public, distributed as widely as possible." [54] This was the first step in the banking interests of America controlling as much of the European debt that they had amassed as possible, while the super corporation could control the rebuilding process of the entire continent, and Europe's working class would be stuck with the bill. All of this was stipulated in the first drafts of the League of Nations covenant.

The United States Senate had a problem with President Wilson and his Wall Street compatriots' League of Nations agreement. It was senator William Borah of Idaho who voiced his opinion most expressively, when he adduced the fact that the Peace Treaty Petition had been written at 40 Wall Street, the Bank of Manhattan

Trust Building, owned by J. P. Morgan & Co. Borah and others accused "big business" of using propaganda and insider influence to force the Senate to accept the treaty. Borah also expressed his concern that it was Thomas Lamont and Henry Davison who had obtained a copy of the first draft of the treaty and leaked it to the rest of their banking interests. He concluded that the financial interests "were not interested in getting the copy of the treaty through any motive of its advantage to America, but from their own viewpoint". He went on to contend that Wall Street financiers were in a "combination to exploit the natural resources of Europe". And that Lamont, Davison, and J. P. Morgan, Jr were at the heart of the round-robin petition of Republican politicians, lawyers, and bankers who sought to push the League of Nations bill through the Senate.

The amount of power and control Wall Street had over the fate of postwar Europe, according to senator Borah and his supporting senators was overwhelming:

> The men who wrote the petition and most of those who signed it were either bankers in that immediate vicinity or their attorneys . . . It is significant that the first treaty, which was discovered to be in this country, was found in the possession of some big business or banking interest upon Wall Street . . . A responsible journal in England has stated that the international bankers dominated the Peace Conference, so far as the things in which they were particularly interested were concerned; that is to say, that they were influential in securing that which is of most concern to them. These things are incidents, which have led to some considerable study and investigation concerning the activities of these men, their wide-ranging efforts and influence, and as to the motives, which lie back of this action.[55]

Among the signatures of the Appeal For Peace to the US Senate were those of Jacob Schiff of Kuhn & Loeb and Henry Davison. Getting the Treaty of Versailles signed as soon as possible was of most importance to these men and others like them. The reasons they cited in their appeal were that "The world is being put in imminent peril of new wars by the lapse of each day". However, their true concern was the fact that if the treaty was not signed expeditiously, "the American people cannot, after a victorious war, permit its Government to petition Germany for its consent to changes in the treaty". In banking terms, this patriotic language was simply a plea to restrict Germany from renegotiating the terms of their loan from US bankers on reparations.[56]

As peace talks stalled and the League of Nations was losing ground in the Senate, Henry Davison went to Europe in February 1920. He visited London, Paris and Geneva on what he claimed to be further work in establishing the presence of the Red Cross in postwar Europe. However, the nature of Davison's business there seemed more concerned with the financial organization of a "money combine". The *Pall Mall Gazette* of London reported that this would be a vehicle that would control the financing enterprise in Europe through the formation of an international trading company, backed by the House of Morgan and the Guarantee Trust. Davison denied every word.[57]

In May 1920, Davison made a final request for another $500 million loan to central Europe. It was senator Borah, who again attacked Davison and his Wall Street interests, asserting "the only vitality now in the League of Nations is the interest of the international bankers . . .". Borah called this request a "money making scheme" and continued:

> I very much doubt whether we have the right to appropriate money out of our treasury and tax the near-hungry man in America to feed the really hungry man in Europe. If we can do that, Mr. Morgan and these people must understand that we have established a rule, which makes it perfectly safe for us to take the money out of Mr. Morgan's pocket and transfer it to the people of the United States who are not so well off. It is a dangerous policy to invoke.[58]

Henry Davison's name came up again in an investigation regarding political affiliation and contributions. During an inquiry into misallocation of campaign funds, a congressional committee uncovered Wall Street's affiliations with the political interests of Washington DC. Their findings revealed a two-sided affiliation, with Thomas Lamont and Henry Davison at the centre of the Morgan political machine. During the 1920 election campaign, Henry Davison spoke out in support of Republican Senator Warren G. Harding for president of the United States. What puzzled some was the fact that the New York *Evening Post* came out with its support for Democratic governor James M. Cox a week before Davison rendered his support for Cox's opponent. This was found to be quite a conflict of interest within the House of Morgan because Davison's Morgan housemate, Thomas Lamont, owned the New York *Evening Post*.[59]

By 1920 Davison started getting sick. Two operations on a brain tumour left him ill equipped to carry on the business of the Morgan firm. He would get into the office when he could, but he and his family enjoyed Locus Valley and California for most of his later years of illness. His third brain operation left him unable to recover, and Henry Pomeroy Davison died on 6 May 1922, leaving a massive imprint on the Morgan firm, the US government, the European economy, and the Federal Reserve System.

8

The Professor: A. Piatt Andrew

Every elementary school had one. The kid who tattle-taled on all the other kids; the kid who, if the teacher had forgotten, reminded her to assign homework right before the bell rang; the kid who, during recess, somehow managed to strike out in kickball; the kid who was the smartest one in class, and who knew it. That kid was A. Piatt Andrew – friendly when he wanted to be, stuck up (even when he didn't want to be), and always isolated by his penchant for knowledge. Andrew took great pains to protect his work from whom he considered the smaller minds of the economic and political world. He defended his positions on economic policy and its execution with passion, possessed a keen mind and a love for money and culture. A. Piatt Andrew was all this, and to those bankers, businessmen, and politicians who wanted to exploit his economic expertise, he was a loyal and able asset.

Born 12 February 1873 in La Porte, Indiana, Abram Piatt Andrew was bred to be an economist. His father was a successful banker and he gave his son the privileges of private schooling and a comfortable lifestyle. However, in his early days as a schoolboy, money was not something he was good at managing. As a student at the Academy of Maidenhead in Lawrenceville, New Jersey, staying as a guest in the Pershing household, he wrote home to his mother almost every day. At about 8:30 pm, after prayers, young Andrew would begin correspondence with his mother and write to her all the interesting and pressing matters of his day, and his mother always wrote back.

He enjoyed lacrosse and tennis very much. Most of his leisure time was spent collecting flowers with his best friend, Jimmy Studebaker, who Abram described to his mother as, "very handsome". He was very interested in botany, and would press flowers and send them to his mother with many of his letters. She would send him flowers from home, and the two of them seemed to have a very rich and loving relationship.But, for a kid who would grow up to be an economics professor at Harvard University and one of the leading economists in the United States of America, Abram asked for money from his mother in almost every letter, letting her know, "I'm trying to be economical", but, "My money is all gone again". He needed money for stamps, 87 cents to resole his shoes, food money, he often itemized lists of his purchases and other lists of things he needed and their cost; And then there was the tennis racquet. It cost $5 and he begged and begged in every letter for a month for the money for that racquet. He even wrote to his grandmother to "Tell Mama that a tennis racquet for one boy costs $5".[1]

It is unclear what exactly happened after he graduated fom high school. It is known that he attended Princeton University after Maidenhead (or the Lawrenceville School), but a letter to his father on 22 October 1888 reveals that he spent some time at Wabash College back home in Indiana, and was having a tough go of things. He wrote to his father on Wabash College letterhead, ". . . it seems you might better understand the situation by consulting with Dr. Tuttle and others of the faculty on the subject. I don't believe I could ever possibly complete the term at Mrs. L's . . .".[2]

At Princeton University, Abram was a nominee for the Baird Prize for English Composition in 1892.[3] He graduated in 1893, cum laude, with honours for excellence in mental philosophy. He went on to attain a PhD in economics from Harvard University, where he began teaching. He continued at Harvard until August 1909, when, at 35, he was appointed head economist for Senator Nelson Aldrich's National Monetary Commission,[4] and appointed by President Taft as director of the United States Mint on the same day.[5] From then on, A. Piatt Andrew's political career was under way.

Known as "Doc" or "Doctor" to most of his political and banking cohort, Andrew was held in the highest regard by almost all the people he worked with. His education was formidable, as was his erudition in the field of economics. Days before he was even appointed to the National Monetary Commission, Andrew wrote up a lengthy report on the economic climate of the country. He sent it out to specific members of the commission, and the overall feedback is exemplified in a letter from Charles D. Norton, personal secretary to President Taft at the time: "The solid parcel of prized Monetary Commission documents are here today and I am pleased to be included among those having these advanced sheets . . . You have certainly built a monument for yourself in this work, and I congratulate you most heartily on being able to show such ample results at so early a date".[6]

When Andrew replied to Norton, he let him know of a moving mishap: "In unpacking the numerous boxes sent down from Cambridge one of the servants, finding a box of miscellaneous papers . . . dumped it into the sea. This box . . . contained all the notes which I had prepared during the nine years of work in Cambridge." However, this disaster aside, Andrew showed no nostalgia for his days in Cambridge, MA, with strictly business interests on his mind, in the same letter, Andrew alerted Norton of the US Mint's intentions to begin coining 1 cent coins with the image of Abraham Lincoln on them. The problem Andrew had with these new pennies was that their design made them too big to fit into most of the country's gambling slot machines, and so "it will render valueless a vast amount of wealth invested in these machines".[7] It was clear from the beginning that Andrew's interests were allied to those of the wealthy in America, and he was driven to be a part of the machine that controlled it all.

By October 1909, Norton was assigning Andrew homework. As Andrew was on his way to Paris, Norton sent him a crate with "A plan of Chicago" in it. Andrew was to join Norton and Senator Aldrich on a two-week tour of the West in the hopes of convincing bankers and businessmen of their plan for a central bank. In this crate were plans for a scheme to push a different kind of monetary reform policy that did not refer to their central banking aim, but which made the idea of an eastern controlled central bank more palatable to western interests. Norton framed the scheme in his letter to Andrew by quoting a ruthless Chicago businessman: "Old N. E. Fairbanks said, apropos of his attempt to corner the lard market in Chicago, that it was easy enough to kill a man, but it was hard to get rid of the corpse. I am going to offer you a way to get rid of the corpse by a kind of clearing-house system, not in any way allied to the Central Bank idea." Andrew was to read the plan, and then nail the crate back up and send it to the wife of the head of the National City Bank of New York, Mrs J. Stillman. Norton told Andrew that the Treasury Department would pay for the shipping costs.[8]

Andrew often dined with Henry P. Davison of J. P. Morgan & Co. and his wife, senator and Mrs Aldrich, and Secretary of the US Treasury and Mrs MacVeagh. He was adjusting to his new role as economic liaison for the wealthy to the political circles of the country. He and Charles Norton became very close. Norton taught him the nature of the United States' political economy. The two men made decisions that shaped lives and careers, as well as economic policy.[9]

Norton had a run-in with an officer at the US Mint. He urged Andrew to try to get

Kingsbery Foster fired for insubordination. Abram wrote a memorandum to Senator Root to press for Foster's removal. He then redacted his request after speaking with Congressman Bennett of New York: "... he told me, to my astonishment, of his close relations with Foster, and what added demoralization involving the President, the New York county committee, and the whole state situation would result ... [in a] New York political situation." Norton suggested that they, "bide our time until the political situation in New York clears up and then renew our effort".[10] The following year, Charles D. Norton left the office of the president of the United States and became president of George F. Baker's First National Bank of New York.

A Piatt Andrew's entrée into the political realm of economics was not only to oversee US monetary policy, but also to enter a world of banking and political giants that cast shadows over all aspects of the American financial scaffold. In June 1910 he was promoted from heading the US Mint when he was nominated by President Taft to hold the position of Assistant Secretary of the Treasury, under Franklin MacVeagh.[11] From the beginning, MacVeagh was to be witness to the power and at times, insolence, Andrew brandished.

A. Piatt Andrew

During Andrew's late Spring 1910 trip through the western states with Norton and Senator Aldrich, Norton's "Chicago Plan" was put into action by the efforts of the men to form a banking "Currency Association", with the Chicago banks at the heart of the support group for banking reform. At the same time he began doing favours for his new friends like Henry P. Davison. J. P. Morgan was returning from a trip to Europe on the *Adriatic*. Although no mention of what he would be bringing back from his journey, Davison asked his new friend in the Treasury Department for a courtesy: "All that I desire (and that I desire very much) is that Mr. Morgan shall receive every possible consideration at the customs. He wants to be saved every annoyance; not money. This you quite appreciate."[12]

Secretary MacVeagh felt out of the loop almost immediately. In his correspondence with Andrew he inquired as to "what transpired in Chicago?" lacking any knowledge of their "Currency Association" intentions – having to have read the news in the *Record-Herald*. In the same letter, he referred to "the Philadelphia situation" and Andrew's assurance that Davison had "agreed to section three" of a solution. Why a partner of J. P. Morgan & Co. is involved in currency reform in Chicago and banking situations in Philadelphia was a valid inquiry on the part of MacVeagh.[13]

Andrew explained to MacVeagh that a movement towards a currency association was underway. He wrote that James B. Forgan, president of the First National Bank of Chicago was thoroughly against the plan, who, along with other western bankers feared the control of Wall Street, and who had no real problem with the existing clearing house system. Andrew explained to MacVeagh that Henry Davison castigated Forgan and the rest of the Chicago bankers, saying that they were no help during the Panic of 1907, so why should they help them now? Davison and Frank Vanderlip hoped to make the withdrawal of banks from an association conditional upon the consent of a majority of the executive board. This was a precursor of the Federal Reserve Act, wherein no bank was exempt from Fed regulation unless approved by the board. This was a bear trap for western banks, set by Wall Street, Aldrich, Norton and Andrew. With this information, Secretary MacVeagh could see very early on that his new assistant, Andrew was already burrowed deeply inside the landscape of the country's monetary affairs.[14]

Andrew wrote many reports on central banking for the National Monetary Commission. He prepared a report on the Japanese and Korean central banking systems and sent it to Senator Aldrich, for his eyes only.[15] By the summer of 1910 he was setting up meetings between him, Charles D. Norton, W. G. Brown, president of Citizens Savings Bank of Inglewood, NY, and President Taft. All this was done just months before the meeting on Jekyll Island.[16]

On 23 September 1910 Andrew informed Secretary MacVeagh that he was going to California for two weeks on National Monetary Commission business. MacVeagh was not pleased but it was obvious at this point that he knew he had no control over Andrew. By 18 November 1910, just days before he left for Jekyll Island, Andrew busily wrote letters to MacVeagh regarding changes in the divisions of loans and currency, recommendations for new positions within the department, his corrections to MacVeagh's upcoming report of the Treasury that was to go to press, and two other interesting subjects.

The first was the alert that "I am leaving on Saturday morning for a few days with Senator Aldrich preparing some general plans for the Monetary Commission to consider. I expect to be back the end of next week." This was obviously regarding his "duck hunting" trip to Jekyll Island. The second was in reference to changes he had made in the Office of the Disbursing Clerk. The letter's tone was rather frustrated, and he wanted to know why his transfers, raises, appointments, and demotions had not been carried out.

The first is interesting for the obvious reasons that he was keeping the intentions of the Jekyll Island meeting from his boss, the Secretary of the Treasury. The second is interesting because a week later, while Andrew and the gang were still in Georgia, G. K. Seet wrote to Secretary MacVeagh. In this letter Seet explained, "We have followed up the leak that appeared in last Saturday's *Times* in connection with the changes in the office of the Disbursing Clerk . . . the information was given to the *Times* by a man named Belt . . . We have Belt's address and have also learned that nearly all of the news he sends in to the *Times* comes from the Treasury." From then on the tone of the letters between Andrew and MacVeagh changed. When Andrew returned from Jekyll Island he became more demanding and arrogant, and MacVeagh became much less tolerant.[17]

When Andrew was at the meeting he telegrammed MacVeagh from Georgia in response to MacVeagh's request for his opinion on what Treasury business should be included in President Taft's upcoming speech. Secretary of State Philander Knox and MacVeagh had both been waiting for Andrew's response for two weeks. When Abram decided to grace the two of them with his opinion, his telegram said that nothing of consequence should be included in the address.

However, upon Andrew's return from Jekyll Island, he began an onslaught of demands and corrections to Secretary MacVeagh's annual report to the House and Senate. In a barrage of letters of 28 November (the day after he returned from the Hunt Club) Andrew insisted that MacVeagh include the great achievements of the National Monetary Commission and "the advisability of American banks being allowed to open branches in foreign countries" in his address. The wording of his letters was always respectful, but the passive aggressive, condescension was palpable. Regarding postal savings material, Andrew expressed his frustration with the administration:

> I fear that if an immediate decision is not made upon this matter we may find ourselves not able to deliver the postal savings material as soon as it may be desired. From my conversation with people here and there and throughout the country I am more and more impressed with the criticism directed toward the administration for not acting more promptly in this matter.[18]

It is clear that Andrew was a very diligent worker and expected as much from others as he did from himself. It is the curse of the smartest person in the room. He just didn't understand why people were not as fastidious and driven as he was; and if they weren't, they should shut up and listen to him. However, private-school boy who kept asking for money from his mother, morphed into a know-it-all who reproached his own superiors. In more letters to MacVeagh, dated 28 November, Andrew continued with his rants, asking why a new engraving and printing press has not been purchased. He inquired about appropriations for workers. He questioned MacVeagh's authority by insisting that a report Andrew wrote up should not have been edited; and he could not figure out why on earth MacVeagh did not give everyone in his offices raises – including him.[19]

Andrew did have a pure sense of justice in him. He made it clear that the new press could save the Bureau $778,000 per year. He defended his reports based on their efficiency and detailed analysis, as he defended his workers, knowing that they depended on their raises to live and remain happy and productive in their work. His memos always began with everything he had accomplished (and he accomplished a lot), before he made a request or questioned the way things were done. His intentions were good. However, the delivery of his opinions was of someone who was setting his boss up to be a fall guy, and of someone who had to cast blame on anyone else, if things didn't go his way.

After the Jekyll Island meeting, Andrew made fast friends with the men from the "First Name Club" and they all were very busy after the meeting, trying to get their Aldrich Bill off the ground and a Wall Street-controlled central bank in effect as US monetary policy. Paul Warburg began laying out the immediate plan of action:

I wrote to Mr. Nelson [Nelson Aldrich, re: the "First Names Club"] while he was in New York sending him the suggestions, of which you received a copy . . . Meanwhile, the Chamber of Commerce has made me chairman of the committee on the monetary conference in Washington on January 18th (Mr. LaLanne's fool convention) and they want me to make a speech there. I have managed to keep the Merchants' Association quiet for the time being . . . I hope very much that Mr. Nelson can come out with his plan till we meet. I should like to talk his plan now, but unless I can do that I should have to talk mine, which I dislike thoroughly since that should be relegated to the background . . . Things are moving splendidly. Not a day passes without some new evidence that the Central Bank is wanted.[20]

Hopes were very buoyant after the Jekyll Island meeting. There was a plan for a central bank in the hands of the men who wanted control over it. However, knowing how difficult it would be to pass the Aldrich Bill without nationwide support, it was imperative that Andrew get to work on convincing James Forgan that central banking was the best option for East and West. Forgan was not only the president of the First National Bank of Chicago, he was also president of the American Bankers' Association. His seal of approval would go a long way in propelling the plan forward.

Andrew wrote to Forgan and enclosed the Aldrich plan in the package. On his best behaviour, he asked Forgan if he had any suggestions on how to make the plan better. Forgan responded with a plethora of criticisms. He believed that the Reserve should be national, and not privately owned. He felt that if monetary elasticity was the aim of the Reserve, then reserve requirements should not be fixed. He not only questioned the rediscounting maturity of 28 days, but the concept of rediscounting at all. He wondered why the plan would support a rediscounting policy when collateralization of a loan would be more effective and safer. Forgan also addressed the elephant in the plan: the foreign banking branches. He suggested that national banks be able to do foreign business, which would make no need for branches in other countries.

James Forgan saw the plan for what it was. It was a way for the small union of massive Wall Street banks to put a strangle hold on national monetary policy and then monopolize foreign banking on behalf of no one but themselves. The plan had very little to do with what was best for the US economy and he knew it: "Honestly, even if my suggestions are adopted, I don't approve of the plan".[21]

The Aldrich Bill began to circulate, and received mixed reviews. Frank Vanderlip gave many speeches in support and explanation of the bill. Warburg did his part in solidifying support from the US Chamber of Commerce, and he started a Monetary Reform League in Chicago. Andrew secured support from his Harvard PhD supervisor, Professor F. W. Tausing, and continued to use his influence in the Treasury to help the plan along. However, the plan's detractors remained. H. Parker Willis, the Washington correspondent to the *New York Journal of Commerce* wrote a scathing article about the bill, which prompted Andrew to write a letter to John Dodsworth, the editor of the New York Journalists' Committee [NYJC], telling him how he thought Willis's article was misinformed and biased because Willis disliked Senator Aldrich so much. Dodsworth's reply was cordial, but clear in the fact that everyone at the NYJC didn't like Aldrich, or his plan.[22]

Aldrich was Andrew's political mentor. However, people did not like Senator Aldrich. Known as a corrupt politician from a corrupt state, his popularity dwindled as he penned the controversial Aldrich–Vreeland Emergency Currency Act and then more so, when his divisive Payne–Aldrich Tariff Act actually split the Republican Party. It was Henry Lee Huggins, a Union Army colonel and senior partner in his father's brokerage firm, who suggested to Andrew that Aldrich's name be taken off the bill:

> Let me say that I think that names injure every new scheme or institution . . . Harvard Medical School is stronger for not bearing the name of Sears, Morgan, Rockefeller, or Huntington . . . All names of individuals, all vanity, all personal feeling should be laid aside, with the conviction that every bit of credit due to any man or men will arrive in due course. It will become history, and men will know it.[23]

Instead of taking his name off the bill, Aldrich insisted that members of the National Monetary Commission who did not support his bill be thrown out, and appointments of congressmen and senators who would push the bill through be appointed.

The Jekyll Island group weighed not an ounce of dissention. They stuck together like new dollar bills, fixing the plan and supporting it and each other. By Spring 1911, Andrew wrote letters to President Taft, alerting him to the fact that he had made amendments to the bill, and thought it wise for the president to mention it during his cross-country speaking tour. Moreover, with Henry P. Davison as the new board member of the American Red Cross, on Christmas Eve 1910 Andrew thought it a good idea that he call Jacob Schiff and others of the association for a meeting regarding the Aldrich plan. Andrew would "alert Mr. McCormack and Mr. Higginson [Major Higginson]", and Davison's reply was strange, to say the least: "Dear Doc, You are a very naughty boy and should be spanked. I do not know if you should be any more spanked than you are, and I doubt if you will be. You are correct in understanding that I shall be delighted to do anything I can. Do not make any serious move without first consulting me."

Davison's interest in "the moving picture business" was also a topic of correspondence between him and Andrew. The two of them considered how the new medium could help their cause. His new friends in the banking industry harnessed Andrew's new interest in investments, as Davison and Benjamin Strong, Jr began in early 1911 to handle his financial affairs. Andrew made large investments in Goldschmidt Detinning Co. and the Inter-Ocean Steel Co. with an account he set up with Bankers Trust – the J. P. Morgan owned company of which Strong was president.[24]

The Aldrich Bill continued through the political machinations of the legislative process. By 1912 it was out of the hands of the bankers who had drawn it up on Jekyll Island, and the unpopular but hugely powerful Senator Aldrich was at the helm of its future. The National Monetary Commission and the rest of the politicians involved continued to mould the bill into something that could be passed. Andrew wrote to Paul Warburg, explaining the lack of control they had at this point, "Dear Paul, You asked the other day as to the 'baby' and all I can tell you to that it is undergoing a change of treatment in the hands of its new guardians".

The fact that this bill was the first of its kind to suggest that a private arm of the banking community run the entire monetary system of the United States of America was the reason why it took so long for the bill to be considered. The ramifications of the power this new reserve would hold was described most methodically by a friend of Andrew's, Laurence M. Jacobs, in a letter regarding the Aldrich Bill's language as to the issuance of notes, silver reserves, and subsequent lending power:

> The reason I am so much interested in the question of note issues is that I see nothing to prevent a gradual substitution in bank reserves and in the pockets of the people of National Reserve Association notes for all other existing forms of currency . . . To the extent this takes place the lending power of the association will be increased. This means that there might be an expansion of loans

through the medium of the note issue of roughly $2.5 billion, taking the total money supply as $3.4 billion and deducting all national bank notes and subsidiary silver. If there is no fallacy in this theory then in the very nature of things the National Reserve Association will in a comparatively short time dominate the exchanges of the world.[25]

Jacobs was an officer of James Stillman and Frank Vanderlip's National City Bank, in London, and in this letter, he crystalized his understanding and motives of the men who penned the Aldrich Bill on Jekyll Island. He had previously written to Andrew about the fact that Britain was in the monetary driver's seat of the world's financial sector. However, with the execution of this plan, along with the unwitting help of London bankers, America would soon outrank its European rival: "So long as we go around London with cap in hand to borrow a few dollars, London has a right to talk about our economic insolvency. When we get our reserve centralized, however, I think that London will receive a great shock to its self-esteem and pocket."[26]

While Andrew was working on the Aldrich Bill, he was still Assistant Secretary of the Treasury under Secretary Franklin MacVeagh. MacVeagh did not approve of the Aldrich Bill and disliked Senator Aldrich immensely. So the fact that his subordinate was spending so much time on a bill he openly disparaged, with a senator's name on it of whom he had nothing but contempt, not surprisingly the relationship between Andrew and MacVeagh became even more strained and uncomfortable by the spring of 1912.

Andrew was an absolute workhorse. The time he spent on the Aldrich Bill was in no way affecting his work in the Treasury. Although he did take many days off, touring the country and Europe researching and promoting central banking, he was the paragon of work ethic and efficiency in the department. Secretary MacVeagh, on the other hand proved to be ill equipped to keep pace with his underling. Andrew wrote letter after letter requesting meetings with MacVeagh to discuss everything from the cleaning of money to tinting machines, coinage operations, and employee human resources. MacVeagh dragged his feet on almost every request for meetings or decisions regarding Andrew's position on these subjects and more.

In MacVeagh's defence, he was frustrated over the amount of petty subjects upon which Andrew continued to harp. Most of the decisions were well within Andrew's capability of handling on his own. It was as if he was writing to MacVeagh to let him know all the things he was doing, so as to make himself look important. His memos were incessant, and when he didn't get an answer, or even the answer he was looking for, he became quickly frustrated: "Congress adjourned today until next Monday, July 1st, without having made any appropriations for expenditures for this coming year. I presume that on Monday some legislation will be immediately passed, but in any case there is nothing else to do but run on as we have been running, even if we go to the penitentiary."[27]

Andrew began making decisions on his own. He reported the absence of the Treasurer, Lee McClung and also attacked him for spending too much money during their trip to California the previous year. Andrew ordered expensive tinting on all the new cheques for the Treasury, he gave the Treasury employees sick leave instead of days off and he gave everyone in the department raises. He then went over or around MacVeagh when he began writing to the Solicitor of the Treasury (legal advisor to the Treasury) regarding departmental matters instead of to MacVeagh, and MacVeagh was not accepting of this: "Dear Mr. Andrew, With further respect to the obtaining of official opinions from the Solicitor of the Treasury, I wish referred to me personally, for my decision, the question of the submission of any and all questions which may affect the administrative policies or constructive work of the secretary of the Department . . . No other officials of the Department are authorized to request an official opinion directly."[28]

The last straw came in May 1912, when Andrew requested time off to accompany Senator Aldrich to the Republican national convention in Chicago the week of 17 June. Aldrich, Andrew, and the rest of the First Names Club figured the convention to be a perfect forum to push their central banking plan. MacVeagh denied Andrew's request, stating that even he could not go to the convention. But Andrew went anyway – defying the orders of the Secretary of the Treasury. MacVeagh then requested that President Taft fire him, and he did. There are many versions of what happened. The best description of the events leading up to and including Andrew's resignation is in a letter from President Taft to Congressman Gardner:

> He applied to Mr. MacVeagh for lease to go to the Chicago Convention. Mr. MacVeagh told him that the other Assistant Secretaries expected to go and had been given permission to go, and, therefore that he could not allow him to leave. Mr. Andrew went to the Convention, notwithstanding. Mr. MacVeagh reported it to me and asked that he have the right to request Mr. Andrew's resignation in view of his breech of duty. Before action, Mr. Andrew sought and had

an interview with me, at which time he criticized Mr. MacVeagh's administration of the Treasury and expressed the opinion that most of his subordinates shared his view. He said to me that if I felt it me duty to sever his relations with the Treasury Department, he would feel it necessary to vindicate himself by a full publication of the criticisms and statement that he made to me concerning Mr. MacVeagh.[29]

President Taft was in full support of MacVeagh's request for Andrew's resignation, so he requested it on 24 July 1912. But Andrew, in keeping with his usual captious behaviour, ignored the request. He was asked again on 28 July, and not only did he deny the request for resignation, he begged President Taft for his job. When it came down to the fact that if he did not resign he would be fired, Andrew wrote a letter of resignation to President Taft that was extremely accusatory of Secretary MacVeagh, not once addressing the fact that he was insubordinate and derelict of his duty by disobeying his superior:

Many able and energetic Treasury officials have had to bear the brunt of harsh criticisms from people outside who have suffered interminable delays in their business with the Treasury, for which the secretary, alone, was responsible . . . at the same time they have had to submit to criticisms even more harsh and more undeserved from Mr. MacVeagh himself . . . Mr. MacVeagh's mental attitude is difficult to realize . . . he has from time to time displayed an aversion, suspicion, and distrust . . . The conduct of business in a department under such conditions is, of course, impossible . . . There has never been a time since I have been in the Treasury when he has not labored under the delusion that some of those who have been working loyally and conscientiously for him were in a cabal conspiring against him.[30]

Then Andrew followed through with the threat he made to the president of the United States. He went public with his resignation, and the press covered it thoroughly. Again, he couched his resignation with the fact that it was impossible to work for MacVeagh, never mentioning the real reason for which his resignation was asked. The *New York Times* printed many of Andrew's accusations regarding the terrible conditions in the Treasury under Secretary MacVeagh. MacVeagh used the public forum to rebut Andrew's assertions:

If Mr. Andrew could represent himself as resigning voluntarily, when he was with unusual difficulty forced to resign, it causes no wonder that he should without warrant call as witness a group of important men of the Department, who nearly all immediately contradicted him, and whose immediate assurances to me by telegraph and telephone are among the pleasantest happenings of my official life.[31]

In A. Piatt Andrew's defence, Treasurer of the United States, Lee McClung voluntarily resigned from his office in November 1912, citing the same problems of inefficiency, lack of support, and poor administration on the part of Secretary MacVeagh.[32]

Public opinion was in full support of A. Piatt Andrew. The Taft administration was a very unpopular one, and men like Andrew and McClung were seen as justified mutineers of the sloppy regime of President Taft and his appointees. Andrew became even more popular and more widely respected for his open denigration of his boss. He received fan mail from across the country. Andrew's public resignation was the perfect marketing campaign for the bankers of Jekyll Island and the supporters of the Aldrich Bill. Andrew continued to write extensively for the National Monetary Commission. In banking and economic circles he was held in the highest esteem. His words describing Secretary MacVeagh were heard by everyone in the public and in private banking. This face-off with MacVeagh, and by default with Taft, was a fine representation of the fact that the bankers and economists were seen as the heroes, and the country's monetary policies should be in their hands, and not in those of the government agents. The conditions for a private central banking plan became even more fertile because of Andrew's public display of petulance.

A. Piatt Andrew was out of a job and the Aldrich Bill was on the brink of irrelevance. With all the political and financial contacts he had made over the years, Andrew began working full time on the passage of a central banking bill, even if it wasn't the Aldrich Bill, he knew he could get something done that would be as close as possible to the work that he and the First Names Club had drafted back in November 1910.

Andrew teamed with Democratic senator from Oklahoma, Robert Latham Owen to revise the Aldrich Bill and piece together a plan for a Wall Street operated, central bank. He continued to pave his political roads by dining with the Secretary of the Army, Franklin Delano Roosevelt, and attending Theodore Roosevelt's daughter's wedding. He procured Secretary of the US Chamber of Commerce Goodwin to disseminate copies of his and Senator Owen's new plan to the Committee on Banking and Currency. Goodwin's political ties were helpful as well. He wrote, "I know some members of both Houses with whom I can place it to advantage".[33]

Andrew did mountainous work on what would become the Owen Bill. Using the original Aldrich plan as a draft, he made amendments and clarified specifics that were needed for the success of the scheme. Senator Owen wanted to increase the surplus of the individual banks within the system, but Andrew insisted that not be done. Andrew also noted that the creation of the board of the Federal Reserve be no way contingent upon the organization of the reserve banks. He wanted a board of governors, and that was all. He suggested that the National Currency Board become the origination committee for the reserve banks.

He made it clear that the board of the Fed should have complete autonomy, and not be hampered by political influence. Therefore, he did not want the Secretary of the Treasury to become chairman of the National Currency Board – a decision undoubtedly inspired by his relationship with Secretary MacVeagh.

Regarding the country bank problem, Andrew knew that they would not want to join the Fed, as the reserve requirements were going to be too high for them to maintain. Andrew didn't care whether they joined or not because he knew they would be a liability to the Fed, as the central bank would only have to carry many of these small, moderately successful western and southern banks. "Only large city banks will make this system work", he stated. His solution was to lower the reserve requirements from 15 per cent to 10 per cent and make "reserve cities" based on cumulative populations of 100,000 people or more. This would consolidate the country banks and protect the system from smaller ones, parasitical to the Federal Reserve.

Regarding the pressing question of inflation, Andrew was adamant about the Reserve not feeding the country money, but loaning the country money. If credit is established then inflation should not be a factor as Reserve money enters the national supply: "We do not want by mere fact of establishing these Reserve Banks and the passage of this law to add either to the country's notes or to its ledger balances. The intention is only to make such additions possible temporarily when the business of the country needs them, wants them sufficiently to pay for them a rate somewhat above normal."[34] US currency as an issuance by the federal government would become extinct. It would now be a loan to the United States government from the private banks of the Federal Reserve.

In a letter Andrew wrote to President Wilson in May 1913, he spelled out the changes he and Senator Owen had made to the Aldrich Plan. Among them was the fact that there should be a limited amount of reserve banks, in keeping with the "central" banking system and enabling control to stay in New York. Paul Warburg and Benjamin Strong went kicking and screaming on this point, insisting that there be no districts and only one bank. Andrew was more versed in the matters of politics and picked his battles more wisely. However, his letter to President Wilson looked like this: "THE NUMBER OF RESERVE BANKS SHOULD NOT BE MORE THAN SIX OR EIGHT."

Andrew went on to order the president, (again, in all caps) "THE PROHIBITION OF INTEREST UPON BANKERS' BALANCES IS APT TO JEOPARDIZE THE ENTIRE PLAN". Andrew knew that interest would be charged in other ways, so its prohibition would only be a pothole in an otherwise paved street. Andrew explained to the president that the new reserve banks would make money as liquid as loans on stock collateral were. He recommended that he "prohibit subscribing banks, but not state banks, private banks, or trust banks". This ensured the dominance of his Wall Street friends and the marginalization of the smaller banks that would eventually be required to join the reserve system.

The exploitation of banks across the country was the cake. But the icing was where the profit would come from: tax and interest. The genius of the Federal Reserve was how it would work with the government for its own benefit. Andrew went on to explain to President Wilson that the US Treasury would issue gold notes to the reserve banks. The banks would then make monthly payments to the Treasury at a 5 per cent annual tax on the notes for the first year, and a 1 per cent tax for 5 years after that. However, for the term of this loan of gold notes, the banks' discount rate would be set at no less than the rate of the tax. So the banks would have to pay back the loan on the notes to the Treasury, and the loan on the currency (the discount rate) to the Federal Reserve. How do the banks pay for this? By charging the American people a higher interest rate on their personal, business and farm loans.[35]

In November 1914, the date of the organization of the Federal Reserve System, the discount rate was 5.75 per cent. So the fixed rate of 5 per cent made the Treasury and the Fed profits from the beginning. This motivated banks to loan money liberally. By July 1915, the Fed had lowered the discount rate to 3.75 per cent and it kept it there through to November 1917. The important point is the fact that from November 1914 to November 1917 the interest rate on land bank loans was

5.05 per cent, so those connected to the Fed were making profits from business and mortgage loans throughout the country due to the borrowing of the American public.[36]

Over the next few months, Andrew continued to write and speak on behalf of the central banking program. He heavily criticized Congressman Carter Glass's competing banking bill. He lied, and said that the bill allowed only 2.5 per cent of reserves to be deposited in the Fed banks. He also misinformed that Glass's bill stipulated that country banks were "permitted to keep only 1% with Federal Reserve banks" and that the provisions of the bill "represented the most dangerous and extreme forms of greenbackism". Carter Glass vehemently attacked Andrew's assertions in the *New York Times*, stating, "[A. Piatt Andrew] is obliged to know that the reserve section of the bill specifically requires that at least 5% shall be kept with the Federal Reserve bank . . ." and "[Andrew] makes a deliberate misstatement . . . [Andrew] must have known and did know that a gold reserve of 33⅓% is required behind the note issue, which is exactly 8⅓% greater than the gold reserve required behind the notes of the Aldrich scheme in which Mr. Andrew had a hand." Carter Glass had Andrew and the Aldrich Plan sized up and took a final swing at him:

> Mr. Andrew also knew, but he carefully and deliberately concealed the fact that in addition to a 33⅓% gold reserve, the entire assets, together with the double liability of the stockholders of the reserve banks, are behind the note issue provided by the new currency bill, and that these notes are made a first and paramount lien on the assets of the regional reserve bank. These and other statements made by Mr. Andrew concerning the provisions of this bill are so flagrantly untrue as to render them a little short of being shameless.[37]

Andrew licked his wounds from the attack and wrote a famous paper called, *The Benefits and Blunders of the Banking Bill* (the "blunders" being most of the Glass Bill portion of the banking bill) and published it right before the vote. Eventually, his and Senator Owen's bill merged with Congressman Carter Glass's bill to form the Glass–Owen Bill, which then became the Federal Reserve Act of 1913. With a few adjustments here and there, the men of Jekyll Island got their way, and A. Piatt Andrew was on to the next phase of his life: politics and the Great War.

In November 1913, just before the vote on the Federal Reserve Act, Andrew tested the political waters for himself and announced his candidacy for Congress in

Gloucester, Massachusetts. He ran against Congressman A. P. Gardner for the Sixth Massachusetts District, and lost. From there, he spent the next year helping to organize the Federal Reserve Board and the central banking system he fought so hard to establish. Once the Fed became fully organized in the autumn of 1914, the war had already begun. Andrew felt a calling to go to Europe and contribute to the effort, years before the United States officially entered the war. However, before he got there, he noticed that some of his powerful friends had already set up shop in war-torn Europe.[38]

When war broke out in August 1914, the American business interests in Europe got to work immediately. Many donated money, equipment, and personal services. Once the French government realized the scope of American involvement in their war effort, it offered them use of the Lycée Pasteur, a collection of brick school buildings, just blocks from the American hospital that had stood for years, for use as a depot for a newly established ambulance corps. The board of the American hospital was to run the ambulance corps with the two principal powers of the board being former American Ambassador to France, Robert Bacon and Anne Harriman Vanderbilt, the second wife of William K. Vanderbilt, who was her first of three husbands. The wives of Henry P. Davison, E. H. Harriman, Montgomery Sears, Harry Payne Whitney, and other business giants from the US, joined them on the board.

Soon after, a separate board for the Ambulance Corps was established, and J. P. Morgan took over. He established the Morgan-Harjes Ambulance Mobile de Premiers Secours. His Morgan-Harjes Co. partner's wife, Mrs Herman Harjes, joined the board, and J. P. Morgan donated four Ford ambulances and shipped them from New York. Wall Street had taken over the field ambulance service in France, and A. Piatt Andrew wanted to be part of it.[39]

Theodore Roosevelt wrote a glowing letter of recommendation to Robert Bacon on behalf of Andrew. Listing his many accomplishments, Teddy asked Bacon to take good care of Andrew while he was there. With this letter, and the fact that Andrew had hired Bacon's son as his personal secretary while at the US Treasury, Andrew's request for involvement could not be ignored.[40]

Andrew started as a driver for the corps on 30 December 1914 and he soon took over the entire operation. He made contacts with the members of the general headquarters and was quickly deployed to Dunkirk to look for wounded civilians. Proving to be very well equipped for his position, Bacon made him inspector general of the American Ambulance Field Service where he would inspect the work of the hospital squads and ambulance drivers. Andrew learned that boredom, drinking and laziness plagued the servicemen because they were relegated to driving only from train stations to hospitals. There was no real fieldwork involved in their activities so morale was very low.

Andrew reported his findings to the chief advisor on transportation in GHQ, and explained that there were no volunteers on the front lines. He suggested that the men needed to be near the action to make a difference and to feel that they were accomplishing something. Captain Aimé Doumenc allowed Andrew to send a small section of the corps to Alsace for a trial. In quintessential Andrew fashion, he instead took a large section of the corps to three different cities and was a huge success. He went on to form an elite crew of drivers called Section Z and proved to be a brave and competent leader. He then formed Section Y, and whipped his men into military shape, which is what they all were waiting for. Andrew's men responded to his exuberance with pride and wanted to perform to the best of their abilities for him.[41]

Andrew forged great relationships with the French. French officers soon gave Andrew and his men the right of way during battlefield rescues, and he made concessions to the French army in the ways of discipline, uniforms, and automobile registration. This forged strong relationships between the French army and the American volunteers throughout the war, which was to create tension between Andrew and the French/American-run Transportation Committee. He was not only circumventing the authority of the committee, but he was also directly and conspicuously serving the cause of the French army, and not remaining neutral.

Acting at par for his course, Andrew shunned authority and instead built an autonomous organization in the Field Service. He formed Section U of the elite drivers' division and wired Bacon, who was in the US by then, requesting his field station have its own treasurer and separate administration. While Bacon balked, Andrew coaxed the help of Anne Vanderbilt who gave him assistance, financial support, and access to her newly refurbished military hospital.[42]

By 1916, Andrew appointed himself to a governing committee of the Field Service. With this defiant act, the Transportation Committee kicked the Field Service out of their hospital. Once again he commissioned the help of his new friend, Mrs Vanderbilt, and rented "A delightful old 18th Century house which though in the heart of Paris, is surrounded by acres of romantic and deserted gardens . . .".[43] He called it the American Ambulance Field Service and when the US entered the war in the fall of 1917 he turned his creation, which included 34 ambulance sections,

14 truck sections and over 800 volunteers (just in the truck section) over to the US army, and was awarded the rank of lieutenant colonel.[44]

Just as many of the men under Andrew's charge undoubtedly wrote letters to their sweethearts back home, Andrew did the same, but at the time his letters had to be kept out of sight from judgemental eyes. The first letters written to and from Henry Sleeper, a Boston lawyer, were in 1906. The last were in the 1930s. Andrew carried on a friendship with Mr Sleeper for most of his life. Having never married, Andrew was known to his acquaintances as a confirmed bachelor, but to those who knew him well, he was known to prefer the company of men, especially Mr Sleeper. The letters contained requests for dates, like the one when Abram asked Henry to join him in a ride in one of those new electric cars. Henry responded, "Even if I'd had an engagement you would have caught me by the subtle flattery contained in the last line of your note". Abram sent him pictures of himself, and Henry noted "the pleasure the pictures are going to give me". Abram and Henry shared years of letters and time together. Their relationship was strong and of a sharing and devoted nature. One letter even contained a happy anniversary wish from Henry to Abram that was signed, "My Love To You, HDS".[45]

In 1921 Andrew decided to run for Congress again, but to be nominated he would need to upset a few important people in quintessential Andrew fashion. Republican Massachusetts Senator, Henry Cabot Lodge had his mind made up as to whom he was going to endorse as the Sixth District Representative for Essex County – and it wasn't A. Piatt Andrew. Despite Lodge's well-oiled political machine and family influence, the people of Massachusetts picked Colonel A. P. Andrew as their Republican nominee. A sulking Lodge was ". . . pursued by the party managers and compelled to take part in the fight, which they made no bones about telling him would be hard and close. Accordingly he suddenly appeared as the supporter of a candidate whom he disliked and had opposed, and who had won his nomination largely by the aid of Mr. Lodge's Republican enemies . . .".[46]

Andrew crushed his Democratic opponent, Charles I. Pettingell by 15,757 votes. The incumbent, Lodge's original pick, W. W. Lufkin was appointed Collector of the Port of Boston. It was a sweep for the Republicans in Massachusetts that year and Andrew issued a thoughtful victory statement: "I am infinitely grateful to the voters of the district for their magnificent tribute. I shall do my best to prove worthy of their trust."[47]

It was no surprise that Andrew became a fierce politician. He spoke out against the Germans during their negotiations for war reparations. He attacked the nation and its business interests for fraudulent actions on the part of their banks, lenders, and dry goods companies. He accused these interests of exploiting the collapse of the deutsche mark and shifting Germany's wealth into the hands of a few (how ironic). He denigrated their currency as "worthless" and told of their situation as being in "dire straights".[48]

He spoke out against Secretary of the Treasury Andrew Mellon's tax plan, and wrote his own tax bill, which he presented to President Harding, himself. Forgiving of France in regard to repaying their war debt, he believed that they should have been alleviated of their responsibility to pay. This did not go down well with his Wall Street friends who lent France a large portion of the money, through the Federal Reserve. However, he showed the appropriate allegiance to his fellow Jekyll Islanders when Democratic Congressman for Illinois, Henry T. Rainey stated the obvious as he bashed Italian Premier Benito Mussolini for "murders and outrages against property and civil rights", characterizing Mussolini as "the most cruel and murderous force even exercised in all the centuries since the days of the Invisible Ten of Venice in the Middle Ages". Rainey spouted some very interesting facts about the Italian government and their war reparation responsibilities, as to their loyalty to Wall Street and not the US Government: "Italy was willing to pay New York bankers 8% for a $100,000,000 loan, but professed incapacity to pay more than ⅛ of 1% to the United States Government". In lock step defence of Wall Street, Congressman Andrew rushed to Mussolini's side when he retorted that the United States owed Italy a debt of gratitude for "holding the line" until America got into the war, adding that without the help of Italy, "no one can estimate what our war would have cost in American lives and treasure".[49]

Over the rest of Andrew's political career he proved to be an extreme anti-Russian Republican. He praised President Hoover every chance he got, he wanted to spend $100 million per year on building up the US Navy, and he was an outspoken opponent to the Volstead Act, stating that it "hurts honest and frank living" and that the entire concept of prohibition was discrimination against the poor.[50] A. Piatt Andrew remained pro-Wall Street, pro-Republican, and pro-A. Piatt Andrew throughout his political career until his death from influenza in June 1936, at the age of 63.

9

The Farm Boy: Frank A. Vanderlip

If his employer asked Frank Arthur Vanderlip to bury a body, the only question he would ask would be, "How deep do you want the hole?". Born in 1864, when he was a boy, romps with his collie, Snap, and pigs getting out of their pens were a frequent occurrence for young Frank. He fed the calves and revelled in riding his pony, Dutchman, and enjoyed "a perfect companionship with my father and mother".[1] It's hard to believe that this happy little boy grew up to demand from the president of the United States, Franklin D. Roosevelt, "that a monetary authority should be formed to seize all [American citizens'] gold . . . and it was a good idea to get off the gold standard" so that the Federal Reserve could issue fiat paper money.[2] On the contrary, back on the farm, "There never was compulsion in the family and there never was resistance; but there were kindnesses every day".[3]

Frank's mother was from Salem, Massachusetts. Her family of distinguished pioneers settled in Cleveland, Ohio where her father owned a wagon factory. Frank's father was a farmer and a blacksmith from Ohio, who began working at the Woodworth Wagon Works. As superintendent of the factory, Charles Edmond Vanderlip met his boss's daughter, the sixteen-year-old Charlotte Louise Woodworth, and married her. When Frank was a boy his father died of consumption and his little brother died of Tuberculosis. He remembered how his mother struggled to meet the $5,000 mortgage on the farm. But, strangely, even as a young boy, he also remembered the mortgage was loaned at 10 per cent interest.[4]

Frank liked science and Shakespeare. He worked as an apprentice in a machine shop but, continued reading and indulging his studious nature through high school. He wanted to attend Cornell University for a degree in "Science and Electricity". But, upstate New York was too far a journey for college, so instead he enrolled at the University of Illinois with friends of his from high school, and pursued literature.

In 1885, at the age of 21, Frank became the city editor of the *Aurora City Post*. He later moved to Chicago and secured a job as a stenographer at an investment-counselling firm. He worked for a man named Moses Scudder who consulted for a large investment firm, W. T. Baker & Co. There, Frank took dictation, drafted letters and wrote mortgages. He later involved himself in the study of bonds and the maintenance of income accounts for a large railroad company.[5]

Frank road the train to work with a friend that he had made, Joseph French Johnson. Johnson was to get Frank a job at the *Chicago Tribune*. First as a financial reporter, before moving up to financial editor. This work was steeped in irony – Frank went after crooked businessmen, and exposed them in the articles he wrote. He was a great investigative reporter, and proved to be an excellent editor.

This job brought together all the things Frank loved and at which he was skilled. The research and digging for facts attracted his scientific mind, while the crafting of great stories was aided by his love for literature, and his experience at Scudder's consulting firm gave him the final piece of experience that he needed to uncover the "skullduggery" of businessmen like Charles T. Yerkes.

Yerkes was a Chicago railroad magnate who fell victim to the wily abilities of Frank A. Vanderlip. Suspicious of Yerkes's dealings and reputation as a crooked Chicago businessman, Frank bought one share of stock in every one of Yerkes's companies. This way, he could attend all the stockholder meetings; receive figures and earnings of all his companies, especially his railroad or "traction" company, and lists of all its passengers. Yerkes was touting the railroad as making its money purely from the volume of passengers and this was a problem to the well-versed business mind of Frank Vanderlip. Frank constructed income accounts for Yerkes' traction company. He then noticed that an officer in a trust company was signing a huge amount of railroad bonds. He later found that these bonds were being secured by an open-ended mortgage, with additional bonds being certified without the public's knowledge. Yerkes's company would buy land on which to build, through a subsidiary. Then a second, large mortgage would be recorded on the property in secret. That secret mortgage would be transferred to the railroad company. Why? Because that mortgage would have precedence over the lien of bonds which the company kept issuing, which the purchasers thought were secured by the first mortgage. Yerkes was making money off the back end of a secret mortgage that ensured his profits came sooner and were larger than every other public bond purchaser. Frank had undone Yerkes with a scathing expose. He wrote, "Afterwards when Yerkes had branched out socially, he provided himself with a family crest having a device of three wolves. He used to point to one of the most viciously fanged wolves; 'this one,' he would say, 'is Vanderlip'".[6]

Frank was fearless in his quest to root out injustice, and stand up for what he felt was right. He had a run-in with the president of the First National Bank of Chicago, Lyman J. Gage. Frank had invested $3,000 in Central Market Co. where Gage was a director. Little did Frank know, that the board members of the Central Market Co. received shares in their company as bonuses. When the company went bankrupt and Frank had lost his investment, he found out that the board members didn't have to pay for the losses in their stock. The fact that he had to pay for the loss of the stock, and the board members (who bankrupted the company) did not, incensed Frank. He made a speech at the final stockholders' meeting, railing Gage and the board members for their greed and unfairness. The board members were not impressed. However, Lyman Gage was to remember him.[7]

Soon after, the largest merchant in Chicago, Marshall Field, let his feelings known to the *Chicago Tribune*'s editor-in-chief, Joseph Medill, his frustration concerning the reporting of one, Frank Vanderlip. Frank's stories were shaking up the business world and were exposing too much of Chicago's less than scrupulous dealings. As the largest merchant in Chicago, Marshall Field was also the largest advertiser. His opinion was obviously of importance to the editor, so the three men met in Medill's office, and when Medill stood up to the goliath that was Field in support of Frank's work, Frank felt an impregnable bond of loyalty: "From that day on I think for the *Tribune* under Joseph Medill I would have hidden bodies, too, had that been necessary to make us greater".[8] Frank would later learn that the loyalties to Wall Street were much more dangerous, and the loyalties of Wall Street were much more porous.

In 1892, Frank enrolled in the University of Chicago, while working at the *Tribune*. He studied under the most reputable economists of the time, like J. Laurence Laughlin and Adolph Miller. His desire to learn more about the economic end of the businesses he was investigating was a testament to his drive, but proved to be the weak link in the chain that tethered him to reporting. Frank's long-time exposure to business and its networks in Chicago, coupled with an advanced education in economics, prompted his entrance into the fray of men who had been his media adversaries for years before.

In 1896, Lyman Gage, president of First National Bank of Chicago, was asked to be the Secretary of the Treasury under President McKinley. Frank Vanderlip went to his office to congratulate him on the appointment. Ever since the days of the Central Market Co., Gage and Vanderlip had kept in touch. This meeting was fortuitous: the following year, Gage recruited Vanderlip as his assistant and the two of them left for Washington to head the US Treasury.

Lyman J. Gage was a very interesting man. He was a Republican, but supported the Democrat Grover Cleveland in the 1884 election. Cleveland asked Gage to be Treasury Secretary when he became president, but Gage turned him down. Under McKinley, Gage proved to be the best man for the job, and when Theodore Roosevelt became president, he kept the talented Gage on as head of the Treasury. Gage secured the Gold Standard Act of 1900, re-establishing gold as the backing for US currency, which greatly helped the rise of the then stagnant US economy.[9] In 1906, Gage retired to Lomaland, California. His desire was to expand his spiritual awareness by pursuing his life-long interest in the metaphysical and astrological dimensions of the universe.[10]

Vanderlip worked under Gage for three years in the Treasury Department. His greatest accomplishment was a $200 million bond issuance during the Spanish-American War. Vanderlip worked tirelessly to oversee the issuance and strength of the bonds and the US military made Vanderlip a success when the army was victorious in a massive siege in Santiago, Cuba and won the war. The bond issue brought in over $1 billion, and brought Vanderlip respect and recognition in some of the highest circles of finance.[11]

One man whose eye was turned by the talented young Vanderlip was James Stillman. Stillman was the head of the National City Bank of New York and he asked Mr Gage about his assistant's availabilities. During a meeting in Stillman's office he told Gage, "When you're through with that young man, I want him to sit right over there". With Gage's blessing, Vanderlip scheduled a meeting with Stillman. He travelled from Washington DC to New York to dine with James Stillman, a "lady-friend" of his, and his daughter Elsie, the future Mrs William Rockefeller, Jr. Stillman's other daughter, Isabel married Percy Rockefeller. After the meal, James Stillman offered Frank Vanderlip the position of vice president of the National City Bank of New York, and he vigorously accepted.[12] A month later, Lyman Gage resigned from his post of Treasury Secretary to become the president of US Trust Co. of New York City. In this position, Gage would be able to help young Vanderlip, and especially aid James Stillman. His move marked "the culmination of plans which have been in execution for some weeks by James Stillman and Frank A. Vanderlip of the National City Bank to induce Mr. Gage to settle in New York."[13]

Frank A. Vanderlip

On the board of directors of the National City Bank of New York sat James Stillman, J. P. Morgan, Jr, Jacob Schiff, E. H. Harriman, William Rockefeller, Jr (the second largest stockholder in the bank, next to Stillman), Henry Clay Frick (ex-chairman of the Carnegie Steel Co.), John Sterling, Cyrus H. McCormick and Henry O. Havemeyer (the Sugar Trust magnate); welcome to Wall Street, Mr Vanderlip.[14] A year later on 19 May 1903 he married Mabel Narcissa Cox of Chicago, and when Stillman retired in 1908, on 12 January 1909 Frank Vanderlip became the president of the National City Bank at 45 years old, with a salary of $50,000 per year.

But, before his coronation, Vanderlip made a brilliant observation, which undoubtedly aided his rise through National City Bank. He learned that British banks had what were known as "consols" in their portfolios. He noticed that these securities were yielding huge amounts of money with little risk to speak of. When he investigated the British consols, he found that they were merely a *consolidation of* debt into an obligation, backed by the British government. After running the idea of investing in these foreign securities by Stillman, Vanderlip registered British consols in the name of the National City Bank, and began to sell these "collateralized debt obligations" to other banks.[15] This not only made National City Bank a fortune, but it also made Frank A. Vanderlip the first CDO salesman in the United States of America, exactly one hundred years before the toxic CDO market annihilated the United States economy in 2008.[16]

When Vanderlip began his work with the National City Bank in 1902, he began a tradition of writing a letter to James Stillman every Friday, to recap the week and let his boss know the status of his work within the bank, along with the business and politics that affected National City. Even after Stillman retired in 1908, Vanderlip continued the letters, asking for both permission and advice along the way. It seemed that Vanderlip didn't make a move without first checking with Stillman.

Early in Vanderlip's career at National City, he learned of the relationships throughout the Wall Street banking community. He saw how, although they were competitors, every major banking institution had vested interests in each other through business investments, the bond market, foreign affairs, and much more. Vanderlip made investments with John D. Rockefeller in telephone bonds. Together with J. P. Morgan, and Mortimer Schiff of Kuhn Loeb & Co. he floated a 30-day loan to the American Telephone & Telegraph Co., and soon after, the three banks started an underwriting syndicate.[17] He recommended British consols as a personal investment for Assistant Attorney General, James Beck. His old boss, Lyman Gage wrote a memo to him and the head of US Trust regarding the issuance of New York Central bonds, and Vanderlip helped Paul Warburg by explaining to him the nature of the existence of these bonds when they suddenly appeared in the London market. Vanderlip and Warburg's Kuhn Loeb & Co. also worked together in February 1904, on the assumption of a $5 million loan to the Pennsylvania Railroad Co.[18]

Vanderlip quickly realized the incredible network that existed between the richest and most powerful men in America. As the Vice President of Stillman's bank, Vanderlip continued National City's success by reaping the benefits of these connections, and it was impossible for him not to notice the link between access to these connections and fortune. "At the board meeting yesterday Mr. Rockefeller told me that one of his Texas friends were here and that they had a plan for a new trust company which interested him . . .". This trust company, which Vanderlip explained in his 2 March 1904 weekly letter to Stillman, was to finance the development of the railroad system of the entire southwest United States.

... There was opportunity for the organization of a strong financial institution in Texas which would, on the one hand, be representative of the best financial interests there and have the cooperation of people connected with the most important banks in several parts of the state, on the other hand, it would be desirable to have relationships with strong financial interests in St. Louis, New York, and Boston ... It is contemplated to make Mr. E. M. House [later chief advisor to President Woodrow Wilson in his signing of the Federal Reserve Act], who, I understand, has close relations to the Standard people [the Rockefellers of Standard Oil], President of the institution.[19]

Foreign policy shaped Frank's position at the bank as well. As a result of the Spanish-American War, government bonds were issued to the countries of Guam, Cuba and the Philippines. The continuance of these bond issues led him to the state of Panama. In the same letter of 2 March 1904 to Stillman, under the heading "Government Finances", Vanderlip explained how National City Bank could use its network in Washington DC to capitalize on investments in Panama:

It now seems probable that the Treasury will pay the $10,000,000 to the Government of Panama within a short time ... Mr. Shaw [Secretary of the US Treasury Leslie M. Shaw] confidentially informed Mr. Ailes [Banking lobbyist, Milton Ailes of the Riggs National Bank in Washington DC] that it is his present plan to make the payment very soon ... he will call for the entire amount from New York City banks. This will make our proportion something over $3,000,000.[20]

As Vanderlip explained to Stillman that his bank was responsible for over 30 per cent of the government bonds the US issued to Panama, he went on to reveal that Stillman's friend J. P. Morgan shared an interest in the Panamanian economy as well.

I have at once taken up the matter of the sale of $8,000,000 Governments to Panama, and unless Mr. M. [J. P. Morgan] is hostile to that, I think it can be put through. Minister Bunau-Varilla [sic][21] will do nothing without consultation with Mr. M. The payment [of $10 million in Treasury bonds] will undoubtedly be made to Morgan & Company, as they are the regularly designated fiscal agents of the Panama Government – a designation obtained through their connection with Varilla.[22]

Domestically, Vanderlip sold commercial paper to country-farm banks all over the country, and he set up endowments for the Rockefellers and Andrew Carnegie for Rio Grande College. But Vanderlip's work in other countries did not end with Panama. He captained the NCB and worked with the Russian ambassador to the United States in 1904 for the funding of a new railway project called the Trans-Siberian Railroad. However, Vanderlip, under the influence of Stillman, halted business with the Russians with the outbreak of the Russo-Japanese War in February 1904. American business interests sided with Japan, and during multiple trips to Japan and meetings with its ministers, Vanderlip and his National City Bank, in another partnership with Kuhn Loeb & Co., loaned the Japanese government $25 million, and fully funded the war on the Japanese side. Japan was convincingly victorious thanks to the financial aid of Wall Street; and President Roosevelt mediated the Treaty of Portsmouth, which ended the war.[23]

On 7 July 1905 a telegram was sent to James Stillman at the Ritz Hotel in Paris from Frank Vanderlip. What made this telegram interesting was that it was written in English, German, Italian and gibberish. This was the first time Vanderlip began to write to Stillman in code. A cipher was later sent to Stillman and the telegram was untangled to reveal a deal with a Hungarian bank. The Hungarian Credit Bank wished to organize a branch in New York. For this purpose, the National City Bank would put up a majority of the $1 million in organization fees, with Jacob Schiff of Kuhn/Loeb, Morton Trust, and August Belmont of the Rothschild family, investing the remainder.

In a follow-up letter, Vanderlip explained that the Hungarian government wished to deposit "a sufficient amount of funds with the Hungarian Creditbank", however, "the law would not permit it to make such a deposit" so for "expenses" the Credit-bank would pay up to $40,000 per year for the New York bankers' cooperation. With this, Frank Vanderlip became a board member of the bank.[24]

In 1905 an insurance scandal hit the national newspapers. The stories featured James Hazen Hyde, who had inherited the tremendous Equitable Life Assurance Society from his father, Henry Baldwin Hyde. James Hyde threw lavish, Gatsby-like parties, made capricious, ill-advised investments, kicked back money and bribed government officials, squandered profits, and grossly overpaid himself, his directors, and his executives. To some this would just be business as usual for some New York socialite offspring, but the problem was the fact that Hyde did all this by raiding the reserves of his customers' insurance policy premiums. The public was outraged, and after the court hearings, Hyde fled the country and settled in Paris to save himself the public humiliation and unyielding denigration. Many Wall Street names were mentioned as fellow pirates of the Equitable. The company was audited and the newspapers continued to cover the scandal. Wall Street and its prominent members took it on the chin as their reputations of being robber barons and elitist thieves swelled in the public's consciousness. The biggest problem to affect Vanderlip and Stillman was that Hyde's personal "business advisor" and fellow fund embezzler was E. H. Harriman – board member of the National City Bank of New York.[25]

Vanderlip wrote to Stillman of the hearings: "Every day seems to bring forth some new reason for disgust with the Equitable situation and to more besmirch, in the public's estimation, the men who were directing its affairs. It has certainly done more to lose Wall Street and Wall Street men the respect of ordinary people than anything that has happened in my knowledge of affairs." Despite all the wreckage caused by Hyde and Harriman, the powers that be still thought of a way to repair their damaged reputations. Vanderlip continued:

> Mr. McLean writes that his confidential man, Mr. McBride, met with Mr. Laffan [Publisher and Editor of the New York Sun] of the Sun, June 27th. Mr. Laffan had been in Europe for some time as a guest of Mr. [J. P.] Morgan . . . Mr. McBride found Mr. Laffan greatly interested in the Post property [Washington Post]. Mr. Laffan had stated that he thought it was a good property and that he wanted to buy it. He outlined a scheme to make a working arrangement with the Sun so that the news columns of the Post would be fed from the Sun office and of making an editorial page, which would have great influence.[26]

What would Mr Medill, Frank's old boss at the Tribune, have thought of Frank now?

Throughout 1906, Vanderlip and the National City Bank were ablaze with profit and expansion. The Rothschild families' loan contract term with the Bolivian government ran out and Frank secured the new bid with a $12.5 million loan. He added other loans to the portfolio with one for a Peruvian railroad, and a $9 million loan to the B&O Railroad. National City bought James Forgan's First National Bank of Chicago, and Vanderlip and Kuhn Loeb worked together on a Cuban banking project to benefit the sugar interests of one of National City's board members, Henry Havemeyer.[27]

When the US Chamber of Commerce Committee's 1906 banking and currency report came out Vanderlip and the rest of the Wall Street gang were not happy. The need for more "elastic currency" in the market, which the bankers had been suggesting, was not addressed the way they would have liked it. Wall Street wanted more control over the monetary system and they wanted more access to money by the government. However, the Chamber of Commerce's plan went against the easy money the banks wanted issued: "They propose further that national banks shall pay at least 2% on government deposits and they would secure elasticity from that source by making the rate of interest so high that only in times of real need for currency would banks accept Government deposits, and whenever the interest rate fell, they would retire them".[28] This plan was clearly an easier way for the government to produce currency, simply by asking for a temporarily higher interest rate on the money it deposits into the Wall Street banks. Instead of arbitrarily flooding the system with currency, elasticity could be gained through these short-term interest rate bursts.

Immediately after this report came out, Jacob and Mortimer Schiff, along with James Stillman, persuaded Secretary of the Treasury Shaw and the chamber of commerce to appoint a "Committee of Five, with the power to invite outsiders to present their views" and Vanderlip was on it. That was to be the beginning of the collective drum banging of Vanderlip and the Wall Street bankers, leading all the way up to the Panic of 1907, for a central banking system in the United States. Vanderlip's views, expressed to Stillman, on the economic landscape during the Panic would have been very interesting. But, oddly, there are no documents in his archives for the entire second half of the month of October 1907 – the exact time of the Panic.[29]

After the Panic, Vanderlip wrote many candid letters, gave many speeches, and wrote many articles, striking fear into the minds of politicians, bankers, economists, businessmen, and the general public, regarding the poor state of the country's monetary system. In a 1908 Columbia University address, Vanderlip warned the audience in Islamic metaphor:

Financial crises have occurred with such periodic regularity in the United States that many have, with Mohammedan stolidity, come to regard them as the "Will of Allah", and to look alike upon banking panics and crop failures as dispensations of inscrutable providence, just as once we regarded visitations of plagues and fevers. In no other great nation in the world are such financial catastrophes regularly enacted. Nowhere else may be found an important financial system subject to such violent turbulence as is the money market of the United States.[30]

Vanderlip educated his audience, as he did in many other speeches he made around the country, to the idea of what a "modern bank" should be. He explained that modern banking "is solely the exchange of credit – the swapping of credits" and that "the business of a bank is not in the main reception of money or its safe keeping, nor is it the loaning of money . . . almost its entire business consists of receiving from its customers their evidence of indebtedness". Vanderlip's description of his "modern bank" has banks loaning money without having the deposits to back them. To Vanderlip and the caravan of Wall Street bankers who worked for a new, updated version of US banking and currency laws, "the bank first makes a loan to the borrower and in doing so, creates a deposit".[31]

It is the creation of debt that Vanderlip and his fellow Federal Reserve architects wanted to build at the heart of their interpretation of what a bank should be. The problem of crisis does not lie within the machinations of the banking system itself. To Vanderlip, the real problem is with the banks' customers: "It should be evident that it is not possible, nor desirable that a bank should keep itself in a position to pay in money, all its deposits if demanded at once. Just as it is evident that its customers could not redeem in money its promises to pay the bank if such demand should be made by all banks at once."[32]

The ostensible problem with this point of view is the fact that a customer signs a contract with a term on a loan he or she signs with a bank. If the customer does not pay the full amount of the bank loan including interest, then penalties, lawsuits, and foreclosures by the bank are certain to follow. The bank signs no such agreement with the customer when he or she opens an account with it. The bank has an obligation to give the customer his or her money when requested, just as the customer is required to pay the loan, with interest, that he or she has taken out with the bank. Vanderlip and his "modern banking" backers fail to recognize the inherent relationship between a bank and its customers. Apparently, a new relationship must be forged between the bank and the customer for this "modern bank" to flourish. According to Vanderlip:

This cooperative quality ought to be more clearly understood by bank customers. They are clear enough in their desire to enjoy the advantages of the modern banking system . . . But even though they gain all these advantages, they frequently see with indistinctness that they themselves must play their part in the financial mechanism; that they must recognize the cooperative nature of the system and comprehend that so-called deposits are not deposits of money, but are the book entries resulting from an interchange of credits, and they are of a nature where their wholesale redemption at a particular time is impossible.[33]

This theory translates into a strange equation. If the banking industry causes a panic in their own system and customers' money starts to disappear, banks close, and peoples' life-savings are lost, then the bank is not only *not* held responsible, but it is the customers' fault for trying to get their money out of a failing institution. However, if you take out a home mortgage from a bank, and you lose your job and can't make your payments, the bank can take your house, your car, all your belongings, and any other assets you may possess. This symbiotic relationship that Vanderlip is describing, perhaps seems one-sided. Continuing with this notion, if the customers are causing the bank shutdowns by means of withdrawal runs, Vanderlip explains how to keep this from happening:

Under the development of our banking system, very little of money is ordinarily used as a store of value. Occasionally, when confidence is disturbed, distrust of banks widespread, and panic conditions prevail, that function of money assumes the utmost consequence. If the disposition to use money as a store of value increases, that is to say, if hoarding becomes general, the entire credit fabric may fall in ruins.[34]

According to Vanderlip, the solution seems to be philosophical, as people should not regard money as something that needs to be saved to store value. Customers must adopt the bankers' modern version of banking so that they view money as Vanderlip's "exchange of credit" and something they continue to owe a bank through indebtedness.

Vanderlip held the banking system responsible as well. His new system was based on the model drawn up over two years after he spoke at Columbia University in

1908. All the problems of the panics, hoarding, unscrupulous banking speculation and manipulation, the inelasticity of currency, and the public's misconception of what a bank should be, would be solved with a central bank.

> Any solution that leaves the fifteen thousand banks of this country compelled to prey upon one another in a time of panic, with reserves immobile, and with management isolated and having such secondary regard for the general welfare, will fail of its ultimate purpose . . . That the result aimed at, a currency expanding and contracting, with the larger or smaller need for currency as a medium of exchange, will be better met by a central bank having the power of issue . . . [35]

It was on 20 October 1910 that Vanderlip first mentioned to Stillman the meeting on Jekyll Island. In a space in his typed letter, Vanderlip penciled-in the shorthand sign for "A" and Vanderlip's code writing to Stillman was reintroduced. It can be deduced that "A" represents Senator Nelson W. Aldrich: "The conference with 'A' is likely to be arranged this next week. He expressed a desire to go ahead with the matter at once. It may mean taking my time completely for ten days, as the plans are now shaping up. It will be interesting and well worth doing, although I am not particularly hopeful of any early results." [36]

The meeting did not take place the following week because Senator Aldrich met with a serious carriage accident soon after Vanderlip's letter was written. The meeting took place about a month later. There is another gap in Vanderlip's correspondence to Stillman, similar to the one during the Panic of 1907, between 28 October and 28 November 1910, which were the dates leading up to and including the rescheduled Jekyll Island meeting. However, upon returning from Jekyll Island, on 28 November Vanderlip's first correspondence was to Senator Aldrich regarding a matter of great importance to Wall Street and with massive implications for their profits and power, and apparently discussed on the island:

> On my return home I find that during my absence there has been some correspondence between Assistant Secretary of State Adee and my office in regard to some matter to appear in the forthcoming message of the President, concerning foreign branches of national banks. In view of our recent conversations, it occurs to me that you may possibly object to having this subject thus handled

in the message, for the reason that you may think it inadvisable to separate this enlargement of the powers of national banks from your more comprehensive plans.[37]

The next day, Vanderlip wrote a six-page letter to Stillman in which he explained everything to him about the meeting and wondered where to go from there. However, this letter was entirely encrypted in regard to the names of the men involved. It is even evident that a different typewriter was used to type in the coded names after the original copy was written. He could hardly conceal his enthusiasm:

> I am back from Jekyll Island and I have had as keenly interesting a time as I can remember ever to have had . . . For the week we were at Jekyll Island my time was so absolutely occupied with the matter in hand that I found it really impossible to write to you. The party was made up, according to the original plans, of Zivil, Zoboj, Warburg, and the Assistant Secretary of the Treasury, Dr. Andrew.

He continued,

> The Zivil has been making good use of his time in studying the subject . . . but he had made no progress at all of crystalizing his ideas further than that he was certain that some sort of central organization, which should hold reserves for the whole country, was the necessary foundation . . . I will enclose herewith an absolutely confidential copy of our conclusions.

From the context of the letter, it can be concluded that "Zivil" is Aldrich. It is revealed later in the letter that "Zoboj" worked for J. P. Morgan, so he could either be Henry P. Davison or Benjamin Strong, Jr. However in this and other letters to follow, encrypted names were the norm. Vanderlip wrote to Stillman of Zewel, Zotob, Zuneb, Zogon, Zomes, Zomit, Zoyed, Zuvij, Zipef, Zovac, Ziwel and Zidux-Ziemy.[38]

From then on, Vanderlip went on to interlock as many directorates as he could. He joined the boards of dozens of companies. He took a month-long trip to the southwest in order to investigate the expansion and merger of the Southern Pacific and Union Pacific railroads. He and Henry Davison of J. P. Morgan & Co., yielded huge profits on that deal and Davison joined the board of the National City Bank, giving J. P. Morgan two seats on that board.

Vanderlip joined the boards of the Short Line and Navigation Line railroads as well as the Timber Land Company. Railroad man W. C. Brown insisted that a Wall Street man like Vanderlip be on the board of a timber company because timber meant railroad ties. The more ties, the more railroads can be built, and the more railroads there were, the more railroad bonds Wall Street could issue. This meant millions of dollars for the railroad companies and for National City Bank of New York and its affiliated Wall Street banks.[39]

The connections were limitless, and it was the bond markets that NCB was keenly interested in. When a bank can inject massive amounts of money into a bond, it only earns a small percentage on each bond investment. But, if it does this with many companies, the overall yield can be significant, with the risk being the success or failure of the company. If Wall Street agents like Frank Vanderlip and the other Jekyll Islanders obtain seats on the boards of these companies, they can control the company and make decisions to better the bond prices, which are not necessarily decisions that are better for the company or its employees.

But, what was this obsession Vanderlip and the other Wall Street behemoths had with what Vanderlip referred to as, "this enlargement of the powers of national banks?". The National Banking Act of 1864 stated that US banks could not set up foreign branches, and foreign banks could not be established in the US. European banks did not have these restrictions, so US overseas manufacturers, importers and exporters had to deal with foreign banks for their foreign business. One of the lesser known, but incredibly advantageous, things that the Federal Reserve Act accomplished for Wall Street was that it allowed US banks to establish overseas branches, and compete with European banks. This new law, along with Vanderlip's work to exploit it, made the National City Bank of New York the most powerful bank in the United States within four years of the Act's passage.

Vanderlip was the first to recognize the need for this expansion, as he believed it would be better for trade, manufacturing, and the National City Bank. In 1909 he instructed his banking lobbyist, Milton Ailes to push for legislative regulations to be lifted so as to allow US banks in foreign lands. To Vanderlip's surprise, they were denied. The illegality, foreign competition, and the lack of trained personnel were the reasons given. However, Ailes believed it was more likely because of feuding senators and Washington bureaucracy.

In 1910, they made a second effort to amend the law. This time a fierce lobby gained the support of the Secretary of State, the Attorney General, and President

Taft. Vanderlip sought to get a looser interpretation of the law approved. But, again he was denied. While Vanderlip was dealing with politicians to change the law, he was also looking for the best area in which to expand, knowing that at some point he and the bank would get their way. When they did, Vanderlip had South America in his sights.

1913 and 1914 proved to be miraculous years for banking. Woodrow Wilson's presidential platform was a vow to expand US business interests. With his 1913 election and his signature of the Federal Reserve Act that same year, which completely overrode the National Banking Act of 1864, the first opportunity occurred and Vanderlip and his bank were on their way overseas. However, England and Germany both had a strong presence in South America, and the original worries of serious foreign competition and the lack of qualified US personnel loomed as daunting realities. Another opportunity was needed.

On 28 June 1914 a man from Bosnia named Gavrilo Princip, assassinated another man named Franz Ferdinand and his wife, Sophie. A world war began, and the entire continent of Europe was shut down. Not only could the US banks begin to finance the war in Europe, they also took advantage of the fact that European banks could no longer service the needs of underdeveloped nations throughout the world: opportunity number two.

Frank Vanderlip swooped down on South America with predatory precision. He immediately struck a deal in Argentina, with James Farrel, the president of US Steel, worth $100 million per year. Vanderlip was granted a charter by the US government on 22 September 1914 and opened the first foreign branch of the National City Bank of New York in Buenos Aires. Before 1914 ended, National City Bank had a branch in Chile, and branch in Italy, two in Uruguay, two in Cuba, and four in Brazil.

In 1915, Vanderlip purchased the International Banking Corp., or the American International Corp. [AIC]. It was originally set up during the Spanish-American War for the US government to facilitate trade with China.[40] Vanderlip attracted a powerhouse of names to sit on the board of National City's newly acquired AIC, and he and James Stillman picked their team. To head the company as its president Stillman chose Charles Stone, president of the Boston engineering and construction firm of Stone & Webster. The secretary-treasurer was Richard A. Tinsley, former treasurer of John D. Rockefeller's Standard Oil Company of New York. William S. Kies, a corporate lawyer and vice-president of National City Bank accepted a vice-presidency with AIC with particular responsibility for Latin American investment, and the other vice-president was Willard Straight, former Far-Eastern diplomat and financier for J. P. Morgan & Co.

According to AIC's charter, its initial stock subscription was $50 million and the company's articles of incorporation allowed it to perform anywhere in the world and to engage in almost any type of business. Banking, corporate takeovers, exploitation of natural resources, and heavy construction – no business practice was off-limits. There were massive opportunities for foreign development. Although it began in South America, AIC and the National City Bank quickly went global.[41]

Over the years it opened branch banks all over the world. With this single purchase of AIC, Vanderlip turned the National City Bank into the largest international bank in the world. By 1917 banks sprouted up in Russia and Venezuela; in 1918, Puerto Rico; by 1919 there were 33 branches in Cuba alone; and by 1920 the National City Bank along with it's subsidiary, AIC owned 56 Latin American banks, along with 12 in Europe, and 17 in Asia.[42]

Vanderlip served the National City Bank of New York and the Stillman family for ten years as president with all the loyalty he had learned decades earlier from Mr Medill at the *Chicago Tribune*. In 1919, however, a plot to get his resignation was instigated by the late James Stillman's son, Jimmy. Jimmy wanted the presidency and he conspired with the board members to force Vanderlip out. When Vanderlip heard that William Rockefeller was backing Jimmy Stillman, he knew the end was near.

Vanderlip couldn't stand William Rockefeller. Although the bile was bottled in the pages of his memoirs, the undercurrent of distain was evident in the stories he unfolded about his neighbour in Scarborough, New York. The first of which concerned stock in National City Bank. Vanderlip had optioned, and then purchased, 10,000 shares from the Morgans, and William Rockefeller demanded that he split them with him. Vanderlip refused the ridiculously entitled order, and in so doing made an enemy of a Rockefeller.

Vanderlip recalled a scandalous appropriation of railroad bonds, by Mr Rockefeller. William Rockefeller was a director of the New York Central Railroad. When bonds were issued for the railroad, Rockefeller agreed to sell them as the director of the railroad. However, as a director of National City Bank of New York, he agreed to buy them as well. This was a blatant conflict of interests and was totally illegal. But as Vanderlip put it, "this sort of thing was the means of some of the worst abuses that occurred in Wall Street".[43]

However, Vanderlip and the National City Bank had their own sins to atone for as well. Accusations were made, via an anonymous tip-off to the Treasury Department that a woman named Lotta M. Taylor, employed by National City Bank's "man in Washington", Milton Ailes compiled confidential information regarding the condition of all national banks, and handed that information over to the National City Bank. The Riggs National Bank was the authorized agent to the office of the Comptroller, and would have access to these documents. The charges stated that Miss Taylor was given unauthorized access to these documents by the officers at Riggs, copied the confidential information and illegally transferred them to, and for the benefit of, the National City Bank of New York.[44]

In 1905, another National City bank vice-president, Archibald Loomis, was forced to resign following disclosures that, as an agent of NCB, he was responsible for the Montreal and Boston stock-washing deal, particularly for the brokerage firm of Munroe & Munroe, managers of the stock syndicate. National City Bank made loans of $60,000, in eight consecutive days, of unendorsed Munroe & Munroe notes. Stillman knew all this was going on, and referring to his vice-president's transgressions, was later quoted as saying, "we all make mistakes from time to time".[45]

Vanderlip created a shell company for the purposes of acquisitions called the National City Company. In 1913, when the "Money Trust" investigations by Senator Lindbergh, Samuel Untermeyer and Senator Pujo were underway, the creation and existence of the National City Company, and many others like it, were shown to be a threat to the entire free market system. According to the government, the game was fixed, and all the major players ran almost all of it together. Vanderlip wrote to Stillman on the seriousness of the government's claims:

> There is a force in the premise which the Attorney General lays down; that in large measure, or at least in some measure, we have passed from a competitive to a monopolistic condition in industry, and that the prices of some commodities at least are fixed under monopolistic conditions, and in the market for these commodities there is no free and unfettered play of supply and demand.

Vanderlip explained to Stillman how he covered their tracks as well as he could, knowing full well how badly the situation looked:

We have proceeded with great caution in the whole matter . . . We have transferred all the securities owned by the US Investment Co, and have paid off the
US IC bonds. We have also transferred to the NCIC the Morgan participation
in the south side RR in Chicago, and two or three things in which we had
stock interests. There was also a fund which had accumulated in the hands of
the Cashier and was not on the books of the [National City] Company, that
embraced some miscellaneous stocks we had long held, and some miscellaneous profits that had been extraordinary in character, and had been segregated
in that fund as sort of a rainy day provision . . . It was held in the Cashiers vault
and not on our books at all. I believe we are going to work this whole thing out
without embarrassment, except the admission that . . . we may still have been
going against what is, in the present temper, good public policy.[46]

Knowing that a "Money Trust" investigation was inevitable, and that the Wall Street
banks were going to have their day of reckoning, Vanderlip quoted Jacob Schiff
in one of his weekly letters to Stillman, where Schiff outlined an idea to protect
National City Bank and skirt responsibility for any wrong-doing:

There is every reason to believe that there will be some Money Trust investigation this winter. Now, as a matter of fact, the City Bank has a dummy board
and if any of us were put on the witness stand and asked questions we would
have to admit we know nothing about a great many things that the bank does
and it will make us look very foolish and will be bad for you . . . I still think there
should be an executive committee . . . of such men as Taylor, Steve Palmer or
Post, men who are not in any way directly connected with the banks.[47]

Vanderlip finally lost his cool in another letter he wrote to Stillman regarding Samuel
Untermeyer's involvement in the Money Trust investigations. Vanderlip's close connection with the Jewish men of Kuhn, Loeb & Co. did not seem to influence his
anti-Semitic tendentiousness:

Untermeyer has mixed into the situation very effectively. He wrote a letter to
the Committee on Rules declaring that the Money Trust was the mother of all
other trusts and that all the evils of the trust question could best be reached
through control of the fundamental trust evil, the money power . . . Just what

his game is, I don't know . . . the principal thing he is advocating, is a law prohibiting banks dealing in securities; it is also suggested that some of the Hebrew private bankers are inspiring him, with the emphasis on the "spire".[48]

Vanderlip justified the bank's actions with swift rationalizations. He truly believed that some wrong-doing should be overlooked if most of what he did was legal or of significant success. Vanderlip and the rest of the Wall Street bankers seemed to think that a little cheating wasn't really cheating, and the fact that the bank handled its dealings without breaking the law, most of the time, should give them a pass when it acts illegally: "One of the troubles of the situation is that the city bank, for instance, might handle, $200,000,000 of its business in an absolutely correct way and go wrong on $100,000 and the one thing that it did wrong would in no way be counterbalance by the $200,000,000 it did right – in the public's mind".[49]

In terms of retirement, Vanderlip would have gladly stepped down. But he did not want to be thrown out. However, Jimmy Stillman handed Vanderlip a cheque for his stock in the bank on 4 June 1919, even though he had been the president of the bank for five years and was "not down as one of the principal shareholders [of NCB]".[50] He attended a meeting of the board of directors, with his nemesis William Rockefeller in the room, and he announced that Jimmy wanted to be president and that he would not put up a fight. The decision was settled. After 17 years of service to the National City Bank of New York, he was handed his hat by the boss's son; packed up his things; and Frank Vanderlip left the bank for good.[51]

It is hard to feel sorry for Frank Vanderlip, but this was not the only inauspicious ending in his career. Although he went on to even more financial success after his departure from the bank, it would transpire that he and his wife would be attacked on all sides by the very systems to which they were so loyal. After the infamous "Teapot Dome Scandal" in which President Warren G. Harding's Secretary of the Interior, Albert Bacon Fall was jailed for taking bribes from an oil company in 1924, Vanderlip testified about his beliefs regarding the scandal and the Harding administration. Because he spoke out so vehemently, and paradoxically, in defence of the public's right to know about this and other important issues, Vanderlip was forced to resign from the boards of directors of almost 40 companies.

Frank's wife, Narcissa was accused by many to be a communist and, in 1924, the same year Frank was being released from his seats on so many boards, she was named in the *New York Times* with her friends and fellow suffragettes, Esther Lape and

Eleanor Roosevelt, when they were called to appear before Congress as "dangerous internationalists eager to get America into that un-American body of the World Court".[52] It seemed that the minute the Vanderlips began to finally exorcize their consciences and their beliefs in those things that are greater than banks or money – things that hold the greater good in mind – they were denounced and preyed upon because of it.

10

The Panic, the Pirate and Pujo

The Panic of 1907 was the economic shock that sent waves of banking reform throughout the country. It was responsible for American politicians and Wall Street bankers beginning to work together to find solutions to the rigid American monetary system. The 1910 meeting on Jekyll Island, the Aldrich Bill of 1911, and the Aldrich–Vreeland Emergency Currency Act of 1908, and the Federal Reserve Act were all responses to the Panic and its fallout. "Central" and "Banking" were two dirty words before 1907. But, the Panic changed that forever.

The commonly known story of the Panic is that in October 1907 an attempt by an overzealous Wall Street banker to corner the copper market led to a run on many major banks. The effects of the run caused a panic that reverberated throughout Wall Street and the rest of the US banking and manufacturing industries. At the height of the Panic, J. P. Morgan stepped in to aid the banking community and quell the massive drop in bank reserves and avert market collapse. He was touted as a true patriot and selfless beacon of financial hope for the country.

Compared to the panics of 1837, 1857, 1873 and 1893, the Panic of 1907 was by far the most volatile. The major companies that were affected included Amalgamated Copper, US Steel, and the railroads of New York Central, Pennsylvania, Reading, Southern Pacific and Union Pacific. The market began to drop ten months before the actual panic, with tremendous stock disposals throughout the span of January to October 1907. From 18 February to 14 March, the market dropped 29 points. In March, Secretary of the Treasury George B. Cortelyou provided a stimulus of $71 million after the first large drop in the market. The New York bankers were expecting much more, so they were unable to hold off the second hit that occurred in August because of the mass buying of low-priced securities in March and the subsequent short sales over the summer. The fall of 17 points that followed from 29 July to 15 August hurt even more because the securities that were purchased low in March were now even more undervalued. Once the Panic started, between 8–24 October another bottoming out of 18⅜ points occurred.[1] The US government and the major bankers of New York began to pour money into the market for bank bailouts and for financial positioning.

In 1906, harbingers of the encroaching crisis were unseen to the untrained eye. The US economy was fantastic, and threat of a panic was the last thing on the minds of Americans. It could even be said that the reason for the crash was the fact that the market was too good the previous year. US credit was so strong in 1906 that an estimated sum of $500 million was borrowed by Wall Street banks from European markets in order for corporations to seize opportunities of leveraged buyouts and mass consolidation throughout the year.

For example, the Union Pacific Railway, having received its shares of Northern Pacific and Great Northern in the Northern Securities liquidation, sold off a large tranche of them in June 1906. This meant that Union Pacific had $55,968,000 in cash and money on call against $7,345,000 a year earlier. It then began a period of mass acquisition, borrowing $75 million on its notes and buying $131,970,000 in railway stocks. Union Pacific's activity, along with many others like it, put the country's corporate structure into a dangerous position of debt-held capital, along with massive market consolidation.[2]

Agriculture was doing well in previous years. Crop yields were strong and the whole country was enjoying prosperity, especially in the South and the West. Unemployment was very low, as manufacturers were riding an industrial torrent, enabling them to pay very high wages. Everyone was happy. It is in these times when greed usually overtakes better judgement and disrupts what would undoubtedly be a time of peace and financial security. The forming of syndicates to underwrite the huge amount of new bond issues and the attempt to control the stock market under what became adverse conditions, led to the mass sale of securities to pay off these Himalayan European and Wall Street loans, as well as the margin calls of the market.[3] The commissions earned by these syndicates ranged from 2.5–10 per cent, and J. P. Morgan and his sea of investment banks, trust companies, and railway and steel company interests were at the core of the bond, underwriting, and loan scramble.[4] As Henry Clews, contemporary Wall Street observer, wrote:

This over-extension of Wall Street capitalists, with their efforts to unduly inflate prices, had its counterpart elsewhere, for such trading was by no means confined to them, but extended to, and was conspicuously shown by, railway and industrial corporations in their efforts to keep up with the increasing demands upon them consequent on the country's great prosperity and natural growth.[5]

The country was on high alert against the greed of the American financier and industrialist. 1907 was a year that not only saw these seemingly involuntary reflexes of cupidity of the wealthy sect, but also the cannibalistic monopolies of the industrial capitalists. In January 1907 John D. Rockefeller's Standard Oil was indicted in the Ohio court on 539 counts of rebate practicing and price fixing. Two weeks later, the Interstate Commerce Commission had charged Standard Oil with "a practical monopoly over the petroleum industry". J. D. Rockefeller wrote an autobiography, hoping to clear his name in the court of public opinion. However, by this time, the people and the muck-rakers had had their last straw of big business and industry getting free passes. The Indiana branch of Standard Oil was hit with a $29,240,000 fine for criminal acceptance of rebates. Judge Kenesaw Landis ruled that the parent Standard Oil Co. had to pay the fine. However, Rockefeller did not pay the fine, and a "higher court" ordered that the government pay Standard's legal fees. Months later, Standard Oil, the American Tobacco Co., and E. H. Harriman's railroads were all brought up on charges in violation of the Sherman Antitrust Act.[6]

With increasing shares in decreasing markets, industrial monopolization, over-leveraged capital, debt, and other dark conditions, the Panic of 1907 began long before the October run on copper, and J. P. Morgan was at the centre of it all. According to J. P. Morgan's company records, the Panic of 1907, which drew out over the last three weeks in October proceeded as follows.

On 17 October 1907 there was a violent break in the United Copper and Consolidated Steamship Co.'s stock. F. Augustus Heinze, president of the Mercantile National Bank attempted to corner the copper market with Gross & Kleeberg as his brokers. C. W. Morse, head of Consolidated Steamship, was also the head of the National Bank of North America, and a director of the Mercantile National Bank. That night, the Clearing House Committee decided that if Mercantile needed a bail-out, it would aid the bank under the condition that the entire board resigns.

On 21 October the Clearing House Association denied aid to the failing

Knickerbocker Trust Co., and the resignation of its president, Charles T. Barney was then announced.

On 22 October the Knickerbocker Trust Co. closed its doors.

On 23 October a run began on the Lincoln Trust Co. dropping their deposits from $21 million to $6 million.

On 24 October the *New York Times* published an article linking Barney to the Trust Company of America, which began a run on that bank until 7 November, during which time their deposits drained from $56 million to $18,500,000. The following banks closed on the same day: Hamilton Bank of New York, International Trust Co., Williamsburg Trust Co., Borough Bank, and Jenkins Trust Co. On this date, J. P. Morgan invited 14 banks to loan $23,550,000 at interest rates varying from 10 per cent to a gargantuan 60 per cent and renewed the next morning at 20 per cent.[7]

On 25 October $1 million was jointly loaned to the Lincoln Trust Co. by the First National Bank of New York, National City Bank of New York, and J. P. Morgan & Co., and the same was done for the Trust Company of America, including another $9,700,000 at 25–50 per cent interest.

On 26 October the Clearing House Committee decided to issue $100,925,000 in certificates.

On 29 October a syndicate composed of J. P. Morgan, First National Bank, and National City Bank took for cash at par of $30 million.

On 14 November Charles T. Barney of the Knickerbocker Trust Co. committed suicide.

On 21 November the following members of Borough Bank and International Trust Co. were arrested: Howard Maxwell, William Gow and Arthur D. Campbell.

On 22 November Secretary of the Treasury Cortelyou announced the issue of $100 million in Treasury Loan Certificates.

On 26 November Arthur D. Campbell committed suicide.

On 21 January 1908 the Hamilton Bank resumed business.[8]

A total of $6 million representing nineteen banks was loaned directly to Lincoln Trust and the Trust Co. of America. After that, another $10 million was raised for more bailouts.

When the panic started, J. P. Morgan was in Richmond, Virginia. He was attending the annual Episcopal conference and getting over a cold when he got the call from New York that something terrible had happened. He and his entourage of Bishop William Lawrence, Bishop Greer and others drove to Washington, and then took a train to Jersey City, and then it was off to Morgan's offices in New York. The entire time, Morgan was seen with "no suggestion of care or anxiety on his part, indeed rather the contrary. He was in the best of spirits." Later, upon arrival in Jersey City, he was heard, "singing lustily, some tune which nobody could recognize . . .".[9]

While Morgan was singing, other bankers were apparently either closing their banks, getting arrested, committing suicide, or dancing to his tune of financial rehabilitation. Benjamin Strong, Jr, president of Morgan's Bankers Trust Co. was familiar with banks in trouble, as the trust company was known as a "banker's bank". It held the reserves of banks and other trust companies as a correspondent for them, and often made loans to those banks and others, so they could repair their reserve positions or strains on their leverage. Bankers Trust wrote a lot of these types of loans when the Panic of 1907 hit the industry.

Strong was appointed to a committee to determine which institutions could be saved after the panic, and which would be sacrificed. The committee answered to three men: J. P. Morgan, George F. Baker and James Stillman. According to Strong, Morgan mercilessly locked prominent bankers in his library and pocketed the key until they found a way to aid the institutions he saw fit to rescue or buy out. Strong summarized these trying times later in life as, "the endless incidents, some tragic, some humorous, many of them exciting or depressing, which characterized those weeks of strain and anxiety".[10] When the dust settled, three banks were left off the list to save; the Hamilton Bank (which J. P. Morgan ended up taking over), the Twelfth Ward bank, and the Empire City Savings Bank – all three banks were in Harlem.[11]

In the popular mind, the origins of the Panic started with the greed of a banker, in his attempts to corner the copper market. But, as stated, the Panic was brewing for well over a year before the crash and bank runs actually took place. However, copper mining did have a part to play with the introduction of the major players in the Panic itself. Henry H. Rogers, backed by money from John D. Rockefeller, set up a mining trust called the Amalgamated Copper Co. When he decided to add a smelting trust he approached Meyer Guggenheim, who had many active silver mines and a smelting company, to sell his company and buy into his newly formed American Smelting and Refining Co. After a harsh negotiation, the Guggenheim brothers finally sold their shares for $42,500,000 to acquire a controlling interest in American Smelting. Guggenheim also partnered with J. P. Morgan to form another mining and smelting company called Kennecott Copper Corp.

American and Kennecott had competition in the form of Frederick A. Heinze.

Heinze challenged the big guys in court and in the field by undercutting their mining operation by tapping into veins of ore owned by Amalgamated. He cited the "apex" theory in which a mining company has the right to mine under the land owned by another party, if the vein he was mining came to an apex upon another vein, even into an adjacent property. With this defence and a Judge William Clancy in his pocket, Heinze was not only able to reap the ore from Morgan and the Guggenheims and other properties; he was also able to persuade the judge to render Amalgamated an illegal combine and restricted its subsidiaries from paying their dividends to their parent company. Eventually, all of Amalgamated was shut down, Heinze sold his company for $10,500,000, moved to New York to become president and controlling head of Mercantile Bank, and in the process made some very powerful enemies.[12]

From his bank, Heinze began promoting another company, the United Copper Co., with another banker, former ice merchant, and head of the Consolidated Steamship Co., Charles W. Morse. Both Heinze and Morse were reputed for their unscrupulous nature in their former professions and in the banking business. After the two big dips in the market in March and August 1907, Heinze and Morse saw an opportunity to buy as much copper stock as they could, in an attempt to corner the market. Their United Copper Co. stood firmly as the other copper stocks fell. Heinze then began to call all short sales. Unfortunately for Heinze, stockholders began to dump stock in droves and a corner was impossible. Heinze began to sell stock to regain liquidity, but it was too late. Even his brother's investment firm of Otto Heinze & Co. failed.

A run on Mercantile National ensued along with the collapse of many of Morse's other banks. A bailout was pending, but only under the condition that Heinze and Morse resign. They did. Heinze was sacrificed because in both the mining industry and the banking industry, he refused to play by the rules that the giants had set. What he did was nothing new. The problem was that when he did it, it was illegal; when the industrial and banking trusts of America did it, they were advancing the economy and protecting it from men like Heinze.[13]

It was at then that J. P. Morgan swooped in and absorbed the Mercantile Trust, and six more trust companies and banks, including the two largest banks that were hit the hardest: the Trust Company of America and Lincoln Trust. Morgan's Guarantee Trust and Manhattan Trust companies would control them with the Rothschild US emissary, August Belmont, at the helm of the merger.[14] He promised Charles Barney that he would help to save the Knickerbocker Trust (one of the largest trust companies in the country, and competitor of his Bankers Trust Co.), but decided to pull the plug at the last minute. He did not stop there.[15]

Banks in other states began to fail. Banks in the cities of Providence, Philadelphia, and Pittsburgh sought aid. Secretary Cortelyou released $25 million of government money for the bailout and J. P. Morgan's approximated private pool of about $30 million, included a $10 million loan from John D. Rockefeller. Publicly, Morgan railed the working people of America for trying to rescue their own money from the teeth of Wall Street greed:

> As I have already said, I cannot too strongly emphasize the importance of the people realizing that the greatest injury can be done to the present situation in thoughtless withdrawal of funds from banks and trust companies and to hoarding their cash in safe deposit vaults or elsewhere, thus withdrawing the supply of capital always needed in such emergencies as that which we have been confronted with during the past week.[16]

While J. P. Morgan was ordering the public to "keep cool heads" and he and his Wall Street cohort were charging massive interest rates on their bailout loans, it was payback time. Morgan called the collateral on the loans he gave to Morse's banks. He used the collateralized bonds to acquire Morse's Consolidated Steamship Co., which was his competitor, as he owned the International Mercantile Marine Co. – the parent company of the famous *Titanic* White Star Line.

Morse scrambled to raise enough money through the liquidation of Consolidated Steamship to pay off Morgan and keep his company. However, Morgan saw to it that the stock plummeted to $17 per share, and Morgan obtained control of the company, which was originally capitalized at $60 million for a paltry $3 million. Morgan kept the acquisition a secret for two weeks, until word got out that he was able to buy his competitor at the lowest rate possible, and ruin one of his financial foes in the process.[17]

Along with many steel and railroad stocks, Morgan began to gobble up interest in hundreds of companies. One in particular set off more monopoly alarm bells in the public eye, and even in Washington DC. The Panic struck the Tennessee Coal & Iron Co. as hard as it did many other major US companies. Like the trust companies, banks, and Consolidated Steamship, J. P. Morgan's radar for easy prey located another victim.

Tennessee Coal and Iron's stock was melting away. It was a direct competitor of Morgan's US Steel Corporation. So Morgan used a sinking fund of $30 million of 5 per cent bonds in US Steel to be given in exchange for TC&I stock on the basis of 84 for the bonds in exchange for 100 in the stock. This way, whoever owned TC&I stock, now owned a smaller part of US Steel, and Morgan then owned both companies with US Steel stock even higher than it was before the buyout.

The only problem was that this was not exactly legal. This transaction came dangerously close to violating the Sherman Antitrust Law. E. H. Gary, H. C. Frick, and J. P. Morgan visited President Theodore Roosevelt to talk him into overlooking the monopolistic implications of the takeover. Their argument was one of proximity. The iron and steel plants of the companies had their own, separate district territories. Therefore, they were not technically competitors, as they did not cater to a common market, and a union of these two corporations would then not be a monopolistic combination of capital ownership. President Roosevelt blessed the deal, and Morgan owned another one of his competitors (with estimated mineral reserves of 700 million tons of iron ore and 2 billion tons of coal), while expanding the reach of US Steel and usurping valuable southern real estate at the same time.[18]

When the Panic began to subside in November, J. P. Morgan and J. P. Morgan, Jr attempted to broker a deal with the Banque de France for a loan of gold to the US. This loan would circulate 3 per cent notes "being simply a method of attracting the hoarders' money". The problem was that the French wanted US government assurance on the loan. To do this they would have to take money out of circulation against treasury bills, and there was no way they were going to do that during a panic.

Morgan also passed on an offer of $100 million by the Rothschilds to endorse commercial bills. This too was an unsavoury deal for the Morgans and the US government. However, with knowledge that the Panic had adversely affected British currency, the Morgans, with J. P., Jr in London at the time of the Panic, seized an opportunity to profit from Britain's hardship. They raised the rate on 60-day sterling loans to the Bank of England. They knew the bank needed the money, so they knew it would pay the increase. When the sovereign bank took the deal, J. P. Morgan swapped the demand on the 60 days and discounted them at 6 per cent.[19] Morgan Harjes, J. P. Morgan's London securities company, made millions on the deal.[20]

John Pierpont Morgan was exalted as the nation's saviour after the Panic. Countless newspaper articles lauded him as a genius that had saved the national economy from imminent collapse, a selfless patriot who had come out of retirement to transition Wall Street back to stability. He received hundreds of letters of thanks from businessmen, politicians, bankers and world dignitaries. The country fell in love with J. P. Morgan, and for the most part fell in love with capitalism, industry and Wall Street all over again. Big money had saved the nation, so the propaganda push to support it and uphold it was relentless. It was like the trust busting of Standard Oil had never happened, and the country was once again captured by the lure and security of wealth.

Still, there were many who viewed Morgan's role in the Panic in a different light. His opportunism and consolidative business practices were too ostensible for much of the public to overlook, as the *Washington Mirror* was to point out:

> J. Pierpont Morgan is today receiving encomiums from the subscribed press as the savior of the financial interests of the country. Mr. Morgan may have called a halt on the desperate runs on the banking institutions of New York, but far from being a Samaritan he has proven himself a hold-up operator of the highest order. Instead of a Captain of industry, he has again proven himself a buccaneer on the Financial Main . . . The usurer who lends his money at rates that are legally prohibitory never drove a more damnable bargain than financial blackmail . . .[21]

The Panic of 1907 was the catalyst for banking reform on the grandest scale in US history. The desire for reform swept the nation and President Wilson was determined to put his administration in a favourable light, as the man who would save the nation from its economic ills. By January 1913, Democratic Congressman Carter Glass, then Chairman of the House Banking and Currency Sub-Committee, and soon to be Secretary of the Treasury under President Wilson, submitted the first draft of the Glass Bill (soon to be the Federal Reserve Act) on Banking Reform to the president for review and polish before it was seen by the public or Congress. While the Carter Glass bill remained under great consideration and scrutiny, the other half of the House Banking and Currency Sub-Committee, chaired by Democratic representative from Louisiana, Arsène Pujo began an investigation into the big bankers and Wall Street men who would benefit the most from the passing of the Glass Bill, or other reform bills like it. At the heart of the investigation was the concept of a "money trust". Attorney Samuel Untermeyer, who headed the Committee to investigate the major Wall Street oligarchs, defined a "money trust" as,

... An established identity and community of interest between a few leaders of finance, which has been created and is held together through stock-holding, interlocking directorates, and other forms of domination over banks, trust companies, railroads, public service and industrial corporations, and which has resulted in vast and growing concentration and control of money and credits in the hands of a few men.[22]

The Pujo Committee findings were astounding. They unanimously determined that a small cartel of financiers, namely J. P. Morgan and other of New York's most powerful bankers, had created a money trust by gaining consolidated control of numerous industries and monopolized them through the abuse of public trust, mostly during and after the Panic of 1907.

The Pujo Committee (Pujo seated fifth from left) (courtesy of FAY 2018/Alamy Stock Photo).

The committee issued a scathing report on the banking trade, and found that 341 officers of J. P. Morgan & Co. also sat on the boards of directors of 112 corporations with a market capitalization of $22.5 billion (the total capitalization of the

New York Stock Exchange was then estimated at $26.5 billion). In other words, Morgan had influence or outright control over so many corporations' boards of directors, that they represented over four-fifths of the value of every corporation on the entire New York Stock Exchange.[23]

The Pujo Committee Report also concluded that Morgan, and a handful of similar titans of American and international banking and industry, had gained control of major manufacturing, transportation, mining, telecommunications and financial markets throughout the United States. The report revealed that no less than 18 different major financial corporations were under the complete control of a consortium led by J. P. Morgan, George F. Baker and James J. Stillman. Just these three men, personally, represented the control of over $2.1 billion through the resources of seven banks and trust companies: Bankers Trust Co., Guaranty Trust Co., Astor Trust Co., the National Bank of Commerce, Liberty National Bank, Chase National Bank and Farmer's Loan & Trust Co.

The Pujo Report also named individual bankers, including Paul M. Warburg, his brother, Felix M. Warburg, Jacob H. Schiff, Frank E. Peabody, William Rockefeller and Benjamin Strong, Jr. The report revealed that this handful of men held the New York Stock Exchange hostage, and attempted to evade interstate trade laws.[24]

The Pujo Committee investigations sent alarm through Wall Street. Frank Vanderlip of National City Bank of New York expressed his unease to his superior, James Stillman in a fear-stricken letter of April 1912:

Dear Mr. Stillman, I wrote to you on Saturday that there was nothing new in the Money Trust Investigation. I appear to have been as innocent of impending danger as were the Titanic passengers. All our plans have certainly been ripped from stem to stern now, and everything we have done is apparently of little value . . . Pujo has asked for new powers from the House in a set of whereases [sic] and resolutions, which read like a stump speech. I will send you a copy. These resolutions go to the Rules Committee and will undoubtedly be favorably reported. Then, I should say we are in for it.[25]

Vanderlip even had 200 bankers to his home in Scarborough, New York to convince them not to testify in the Money Trust hearings if called to do so.[26] Despite Vanderlip's fears, and those of many other Wall Streeters and industrialists named in the report, there is no evidence that any of the men named were ever arrested, prosecuted, or fined for any crime; and yet no group or investigative committee had proven the Pujo Committee inaccurate. Instead, financial reform continued to sweep through the country with the Federal Income Tax Act of 1913, which taxed the income of every American worker, and the Federal Reserve Act of 1913, which favoured the large Wall Street banks rather than punishing or regulating them.

There were many who even believed that the Panic of 1907 may have been pre-meditated and manufactured by the Wall Street elites to gain ultimate control over banking and industry in America. When testifying before the Committee on Rules, when Senator Aldrich's 1911 banking reform bill was on the table for consideration, Congressman Charles Lindbergh, Sr. made this telling protest:

> In 1907 nature responded most beautifully and gave this country the most bountiful crops it ever had. Other industries were busy too, and from a natural standpoint all the conditions were right for a most prosperous year. Instead, a panic entailed enormous losses upon us. Wall Street knew the American people were demanding a remedy against the recurrence of such a ridiculous, unnatural condition. Most senators and representatives fell into the Wall Street trap and passed the Aldrich-Vreeland Emergency Currency Bill. But the real purpose was to get a monetary commission, which would frame a proposition for amendments to our currency and banking laws, which would suit the Money Trust. The interests are now busy everywhere, educating the people in favor of the Aldrich plan. It is reported that a large sum of money has been raised for this purpose. Wall Street speculation brought on the Panic of 1907. The depositors' funds were loaned to gamblers and anybody the Money Trust wanted to favor. Then when the depositors wanted their money, the banks did not have it. That made the panic.[27]

11

The War

On 14 June 1917 President Wilson explained America's need to defend itself as it was ushered into a war it did not want to fight: "It is plain enough how we were forced into the war. The extraordinary insults and aggressions of the Imperial German Government left us no self-respecting choice but to take up arms in defense of our rights as free people and of our honor as a sovereign Government." So said Secretary of the Treasury, William Gibbs McAdoo, in an address to the American Bankers' Association while encouraging the issuance of war bonds. He also defined the necessity of war on the part of the United States as an imperative: "We entered the war primarily because of the persistent insults and aggressions of Germany, the wanton disregard for American rights within our own boarders as well as on the high seas, the contemptuous violation of international law, and the ruthless destruction of American life and property".[1]

Despite these arguments, the United States was to form a more altruistic version of its role in the war. The postwar landscape found an ailing Europe and a thriving America at economic odds. The United States painted itself as a saviour of a ravaged European continent through its military aid during the war and its economic aid after it. As Richard Edmunds wrote: "Newspapers, ministers of the Gospel and public men, overlooking entirely the reasons which caused us to go to war for our own preservation, began in 1919 a campaign of praising ourselves with pious unction . . ."[2] This hypocrisy was evident in the fact that the United States faced arduous economic trials before the war and the outbreak of the war became a chance for economic redemption for the US as, Edmunds again, "the Allies were buying from us foodstuffs and ammunition by the billions of dollars, and at exorbitantly high prices . . . there came a rush of activity in practically all industrial interests . . . During the next two or three years our prosperity was fertilized by the blood of millions of soldiers dying on the battlefields of Europe."[3]

Did America go to war to defend itself? The sinking of the *Lusitania* was the catastrophic event that hurled the United States into the war, strangely, two years after 1,200 people were killed when German U Boats slammed torpedoes into her side. This was a British ocean liner serving the transatlantic route. However, it was a surprise to many that the *Lusitania*, on a course for Britain, was carrying millions of dollars in munitions as well. The larger surprise was the fact that the *New York Times* printed an article in their 8 May 1915 edition that described the warnings the German embassy had put out to American travellers, the shocking advertisement the German government had taken out in the *New York Times* itself, and the fact that no American agency had warned the passengers of the *Lusitania* of this threat. The article stated: "Just before the Lusitania sailed there was a report that some of the passengers had received warnings in the form of unsigned telegrams that it would be best for them to sail by some other vessel than the Lusitania, and that the Lusitania would be torpedoed when she neared or got into European waters."[4] The article the German embassy took out in the *New York Times* read as follows:

> NOTICE. Travelers intending to embark on the Atlantic voyage are reminded that a state of war exists between Germany and her allies and Great Britain and her allies; that the zone of war includes the waters adjacent to the British Isles; that in accordance with formal notice given by the Imperial German Government, vessels flying the flag of Great Britain or any of her allies are liable to destruction in those waters and that travelers sailing in the war zone on ships of Great Britain or of her allies do so at their own risk. IMPERIAL GERMAN EMBASSY, Washington D.C. April 22, 1915.[5]

These words are very threatening, and would be a cause for war in any country at any time. However, the fact that so little was done by the US government to defend and even inform the passengers of the *Lusitania*, make the argument for defence against the German aggressors as the sole reason for America's entrance into the war much less cogent.

As for altruism, the First World War cost well over 100,000 American lives, and approximately 20 million European lives. Countries mobilized men and weaponry on mass scales to fight, kill, and die for a cause. However, economically, the spoils of war are glaringly evident. According to two-time United States Congressional Medal of Honor recipient, US Marine, Major General Smedley Darlington Butler, "War is a racket. It always has been. It is possibly the oldest, easily the most profitable, surely the most vicious. It is the only one international in scope. It is the only one in which the profits are reckoned in dollars and the losses in lives."[6]

For centuries before, the New World had been fought over, exploited, and bought and sold by European interests. The First World War changed all that history within a few years. It marked the coming of age for the United States as the most economically powerful nation in the world. The war had a tremendous effect on the United States economy before, during, and after US military involvement. And the outbreak of war proved to be quite serendipitous for America's new central banking system. America went from being a debtor nation before the war, to becoming the wealthiest creditor nation in the world by the time the war was over, thanks, in great part, to the Federal Reserve and the men who controlled it.

The Federal Reserve was fully organized and began its reign as the nation's central banking system on 16 November 1914 – less than four months after war broke out on 28 July 1914. The war was considered a time of economic crisis in America, and the Federal Reserve came through it with flying colours. It was given public accolade as a major contributor to winning the war, as an efficient fiscal agent to the office of the Treasury, as a reliable source of reserve currency, and was upheld as an indispensable part of the US banking system.[7]

The Federal Reserve had to act immediately, as the war in Europe curtailed ocean transportation and immediately affected trade. The cotton crop in America in 1914 had been the largest to date, and the cotton export market was on the verge of collapse because of restricted trade in the war zones of the eastern Atlantic and Mediterranean sea. In January 1915, the Federal Reserve Board approved the Cotton Loan Fund, in which member banks would give loans to farmers.[8] Although these loans contributed to the wealth of the Federal Reserve, it was not until the United States declared war on Germany on 6 April 1917 when the Fed gained its immense control over the US economy, and later the Fed would prove to be much less concerned with the financial interests of the American farmer.

As the 1916 presidential election neared, Edward Mandell House, about whom President Wilson wrote, "Mr. House is my second personality. He is my independent self. His thoughts and mine are one . . ."[9] began meeting with Sir William Wiseman, an official in the British embassy in Washington DC. House also sailed to England to meet with many British military officials on more than one occasion that year. These salient yet secretive meetings were thought by many to be the beginnings of a scheme to bring the United States into the war.[10] Because of this, President Wilson's Secretary of State from 1913 to 1916, William Jennings Bryan, resigned. He would not accept the president to go back on his word of US neutrality in the war, especially by such surreptitious means.[11] Bryan's wife, Mary Baird Bryan wrote: "While Secretary Bryan was bearing the heavy responsibility of the Department of State, there arose the curious conditions surrounding Mr. E. M. House's unofficial connection with the President and his voyages abroad on affairs of State, which were not communicated to Secretary Bryan . . . The President was unofficially dealing with foreign governments."[12]

It is important to remember that both Benjamin Strong and Henry P. Davison were in England in 1916 as well. They were there to finalize the draft of the "Memorandum of Conversations between the Governors of the Bank of England and the Governor of the Federal Reserve Bank of New York", and to get J. P. Morgan & Co. named as the sole purchasing agent in the United States, for the duration of the war, for war material for both Britain and France. Mr. House was secretly visiting England at the same time.

As early as November of 1914, rumours of Wall Street involvement in war loans had reached across the globe. In a letter from the Japanese ambassador to the US to Martin Egan – an affiliate of J. P. Morgan & Co., close friend of Henry P. Davison, former member of the Associated Press, and later advisor on censorship to General Pershing[13] – the ambassador asked Egan "a great many questions as to what had been done here by Germany and France and told me that he had heard through confidential channels that one or two of the New York Houses with German affiliations had discussed the plan of establishing German credits here without appealing to the public or taking the public into their confidence".[14]

President Woodrow Wilson, who in 1912, had run on a platform totally against central banking, signed the Federal Reserve Act into law two years later, in 1914. In 1916, he was elected again, this time on the promise that he would keep America out of the war in Europe. A year later, in 1917, he declared war on Germany. 4,355,000 US troops were mobilized; 116,516 were killed; 204,002 were wounded; and 4,500 were POW or MIA.[15] The United States spent a total of $30 billion on the war, with just over $20 billion spent on its own expenditures, and almost $10 billion on aid to other countries; and the Federal Reserve oversaw every penny.[16]

After the war, Secretary of the Treasury McAdoo, who although on the board of the Federal Reserve, battled endlessly with the bankers on the board with whom he served, and pleaded for the issuance of short-term treasury certificates to float the $2 billion Liberty Loan of 1917. The board of the Fed, under the prodding influence of Paul Warburg balked; claiming that the 2 per cent interest rate for the first $50 million McAdoo was suggesting was much too low. The money was finally lent to the US government and by October 1918, $17 billion in bonds had been floated expanding the federal government's debt to Federal Reserve banks from $1 billion in June 1916 to $21 billion in December 1918.[17] As a result of these debts the Federal Reserve, which had only been in operation one year, already had a stranglehold on the United States government and its economy.

The bloodletting was not contained to the government. The spectre of the postwar Federal Reserve System soon reached the individual investor as well. By 1920 the Reserve banks, which were originally seen as the lifeguards of the agricultural industry with their Cotton Loan Fund, saw liquidation of discount credits.[18] Instead of aiding the farmers, the Fed called for the restriction of the circulation of currency. This, along with the postwar collapse in prices, contributed to the epidemic of farmers who could no longer afford their loans and mortgages to Federal Reserve member banks, and by 1921 more than 500 small farm banks closed. Like a modern-day "big-box store" the Federal Reserve was eliminating its smaller more vulnerable competition, and honing in on full market domination.[19]

The purchasers of the volatile Liberty Bonds (war bonds) suffered as well. The low interest rates at which the bond buyers purchased their Liberty Bonds, proved to be a Trojan horse when they discovered that when market rates rise, bond prices fall. To compound the problem, the Fed imposed capital losses on the bond purchasers immediately after they bought them and the public was incensed. Paul Warburg knew the bonds would suffer long before the public did. However, the Fed issued them in mass to the unsuspecting American citizens anyway:

> After the issue of the first Liberty Loan it became clear to me that inasmuch as we were making a strong appeal to the whole country to devote every penny that could be saved to subscriptions to the war loan, conditions might arise soon where the industries of the country, including the railroads, might find great difficulties in securing funds required to carry on their business, or necessary to take care of maturing obligations. The danger that this might happen

was increased by the fact that propaganda for the war loans stimulated a great many people to sell other securities they owned, even at a loss, in order to be able to subscribe heavily to the new war loans.[20]

The Federal Reserve System, the Federal Reserve Board, and governor of the board, Harding, personally, were brought up on charges by Congress on the grounds that the system was acting for its own benefit, discriminated against certain sectors of the US economy (especially agriculture), misused funds, and even Comptroller of Currency Williams, who sat on the board, accused his own board members of driving up interest rates to create deflation for the profit of Reserve bankers. A Joint Congressional Commission of Agricultural Inquiry began hearings in August 1921. By January of 1922 they submitted a report to Congress finding that the Federal Reserve was responsible for merely not acting quickly enough to raise interest rates after the war. All other charges were dropped and deemed to have no basis.[21]

The First World War changed the status of the United States from debtor nation to creditor nation. Before the war the United States owed most of its money to Britain. As the war continued, however, many financial centres in Europe disintegrated, stock exchanges closed, London gave way to New York as the major world credit market, and the US overtook Britain as the richest nation in the world. The headquarters of the world's acceptance market (the trading of short-term credit instruments) moved from London to New York as well, and Kuhn & Loeb's Paul Warburg became the most powerful trade acceptance banker in the world.[22]

After the war the Federal Reserve truly operated as the "fiscal agent" for the United States federal government. In 1914, 17 state banks joined the Federal Reserve System; by June of 1919 the total number of state and national banks was 8,822.[23] The Fed became responsible for managing the country's bank account. It took in the tax receipts, made payments, and managed and borrowed money if needed for the government – and yet, the country went deeper and deeper into debt. The Federal Reserve became the private accountant for the country, and did so with little to no government regulation or control.

The question of European indebtedness to the United States became a looming topic in American politics and culture after the war. If America entered the war to defend itself, or to be the light in the darkness of European upheaval, did it also have a responsibility to alleviate the debt in which Europe drowned, due to its advantageous position and their time of need? General Pershing; the man who ran the war and who dined with Vanderlip, Andrew and Davison revealed his perspective during a speech he gave in Denver, in 1926:

While I am on the subject I want to say something I have never said in a public address before. It seems to me that there is some middle ground where we should bear a certain part of the expense in maintaining the Allied armies on the front, while we were preparing, instead of calling all this money a loan and insisting on its payment. We were responsible. We gave the money, knowing that it would be used to hold the Boche until we could prepare. Fifteen months! Think of it! We sent our first men in June, and they were not ready to go into the front line until the following year.[24]

The amount of money the US made from the war was significant. From 1910 to 1914 the United States made $6,751,408,000 in export sales to Europe. From 1915 to 1919 it collected $19,494,779,000 in European imports. After the war, from 1920 to 1924 exports slowed, but remained double the level before the war, totalling $13,451,252,000.[25]

The benefits did not stop at banking and industry; they spilled into the US job market as well. Every farmer, wage-worker, manufacturer, and banker demanded and received higher prices for their goods and services due to Europe's insatiable need for survival during the war. With almost everyone gainfully employed and hard at work, US tax revenues hit an all-time high. In 1910 the federal government received income just under $20 million. By 1915 tax revenues had jumped to over $80 million, and by 1920 they were just under $4 billion.[26]

In a speech Henry P. Davison gave to the American Bankers' Association in September 1919, he discussed what the war had done for the US economy and the banking industry: "The United States was left in an exceedingly strong position. It had unimpaired and vastly expanded credit, it had surplus food and raw material, it had machinery in large organized units that had not been broken up, and there had been no serious decrease in its available manpower." As a banker, and a fundamental player in getting the firm of J. P. Morgan & Co. named as the sole purchasing agent for the British government during the war, Davison was not as quick to forgive Europe's indebtedness, which amounted to numbers that were unheard of at the time: ". . . Europe, during the course of the war has become our debtor to the extent of nearly ten billion dollars, a debt that has an annual interest charge of half a billion, and that for a good many considerations besides principal and interest we want a Europe that can meet its obligations".[27]

Davison went on to explain that through exchange stabilization and the continued extension of credit to the European nations, in time, Europe would be in a position to make its required payments to the United States' banks, which had loaned them the money. He then addressed the elephant in the room:

> It has been said lightly that European credit and exchange was a banking problem and that these bankers, including myself, who were concerning themselves about it were interested primarily in the profit that woud acrue to themselves and to their institutions. Some of the critics went so far as to say that legislative and executive aid was sought for the purposes of creating a money trust that was to be solidified and made monopolistic by legislation and governmental support. All this is on parity with the charmingly consistant criticism, whch once accused bankers of growing rich on the profits of war and now charges them with conspiring for an experiment in permanent peace. We are by some damned if we do and damned if we don't.[28]

The British were uncooperative in their responsibilities of paying off their debts. They referred to the United States as "Uncle Shylock" in many of their daily newspapers. Members of Parliament accused the United States of entering the war with "commercial importance as their God, and the ledger as their Bible". France also regarded the American debt settlement as a major cause for their own ills. Other than for the millions of men who died on the battlefields of Verdun, Somme, and the rest of Europe, perhaps a few less tears should be shed for those who borrowed money and were unwilling to pay it back.

The United States' banking industry controlled European war debt. Obviously, they wanted to ensure the progress and stability of certain European nations who were indebted to them. Entering the war at the time the United States did, guaranteed an Allied victory, allowed the United States to set the tone for war reparations, and put countries like Britain and France in positions of postwar economic growth, so as to ensure those nations' ability to pay their debt to the Wall Street banks and the Federal Reserve. J. Paul Getty explained it best when he quipped, "If you owe the bank $100 that's your problem. If you owe the bank $100 million, that's the bank's problem". Wall Street went to great lengths to ensure that the countries that owed them money had the ability to repay it – with interest. For an idea as to how much money was owed, in an August 1925 report of the National City Bank of New York, disbursements for the fiscal year of 1924 for receipts on foreign government indebtedness were $23,088,687 for principal and $159,215,670 for interest.[29]

After the war, Italy received the port city of Trieste from Austria. France received the Saar Valley coal mines and Alsace-Lorraine, which was rich in coal mines, had established steel mills, and a population of over two million people. The British (who owed US banks the most money) received massive territorial appropriations from the postwar treaties. They acquired territory in North Africa of 930,000 square miles with an approximate population of 11 million. This gave the British a continuous stretch of territory from Egypt to Cape Town. They also received 143,000 square miles of land in Asia Minor and the oil-rich kingdom of Iraq. In addition, they appropriated from the German government the Bismark Archipelago, Samoa, the Nauru Islands, and the Kaiser Wilhelm Islands, totalling another 1,500,000 square miles.[30]

For the continued insurance of European stability, Benjamin Strong and Paul Warburg worked side-by-side to make sure that Wall Street controlled the outcome of the economic viability of the nations of Europe. Fred I. Kent, president of the Bankers Trust Co., and leading British and Dutch financiers, joined them and together they were instrumental in drafting the Amsterdam Memorial. This was an international petition that mainly called for the extension of large-scale American credits and loans to European businesses and governments. The petition also warranted pre-arranged intergovernmental debt settlements, and a lenient postwar reparations assessment, generous to Germany.

The leading European and American statesmen, bankers, and industrialists signed the Amsterdam Memorial, including Warburg and J. P. Morgan, Jr. However it was Benjamin Strong who, typically, went against the grain, and although he firmly approved of the Memorial's prescriptions, declined to sign it. His grounds were, "My relations to our treasury department are of such an intimate character that I feared the possibility of its being misunderstood and causing embarrassment which would, of course, have done harm rather than help the effort."[31]

12

The Journalist: Bob Ivry

B ob Ivry is a senior editor of enterprise news for Bloomberg News, in New York
City. Bob and I met through a mutual friend at Bloomberg when she found
out about my interest in writing a book about the Federal Reserve. Bob and I cor-
responded and found that our interests were more aligned than we thought a
journalist's and a historian's would be. After a couple of meetings and great conversation, Bob agreed to an interview for this book. The reason I was so interested
in his story was the fact that Bob's partner at the time, Mark Pittman was the only
person to ever sue the Federal Reserve Board, and after his death in 2009, Bob took
his place.[1]

After a series of "crappy" jobs, which Bob believes gave him more insight into the
real world than some journalists who get more traditional work right out of journalism school, Bob started out reading the news at KPFA radio in San Francisco. He was
the sports guy for the San Francisco Bay *Guardian*, worked at the San Francisco *Examiner*, and made his way to the east coast as the movie reviewer for the New Jersey
Record. After his first year there, 9/11 happened. Bob asked to do a story on the security of a nearby nuclear power plant, and the editor gave him the go ahead to work on
it with a lead investigative reporter. The running joke in their offices was that this
reporter was less than thrilled to share such an impactful story "with the fucking
movie reviewer". Bob's foray into the field of investigative reporting brought him,
in 2006, to the real estate team of Bloomberg News – when the banking collapse of
Wall Street started to reveal itself, and Bob, furthering his education at Bloomberg,
became a part of history.

The interview began with Bob refuting the most common misconception about
the Fed; that it is part of the government. It is, as Ivry put it, "of the banks". This is a

particularly important distinction for journalists and members of the public who are trying to obtain information regarding currency, monetary and banking matters. The Freedom of Information Act of 1966 (FOIA) provides that the executive branch of the government must give information that is not a matter of national security to any and all who petition for it. The Federal Reserve is not a part of the federal government, so it is technically exempt from FOIA petitions. However, the Fed realizes that since it is so big, "it can't and shouldn't get away with everything", so they do respond to some FOIA requests.

By 2006 the writing was on the wall: there was a real estate bubble and things could get very bad. However, as far as the Federal Reserve was concerned, they didn't flinch until 2007, when Bob and his partner at Bloomberg, Mark Pittman noticed the Fed announcement that it would be issuing swap agreements[2] with US banks and other central banks overseas. These agreements could only be interpreted as a widespread emergency program, although they were not framed that way. The Fed's public persona at the time was as if it just had a lot of money lying around, and would offer some loans at great rates to its overseas friends. To Pittman and Ivry, this was greater proof of a bubble and a possible meltdown.

In May 2008, six months before the Troubled Asset Relief Program (TARP) was established, Pittman and Ivry sent a FOIA request to the Federal Reserve on the basis that the Fed, the Fed Treasury, the Federal Deposit Insurance Corporation (FDIC), and other financial regulators were providing "extraordinary support to the financial system at the time" but they were doing it in complete privacy. Pittman and Ivry requested the names of the banks the Fed was providing assistance to, they wanted to know how much money was being lent out, and what the Fed was accepting for collateral.

The Federal Reserve Board denied their FOIA request. With backing from Bloomberg's lawyers, Pittman and Ivry appealed. The Fed then denied the appeal, knowing that the FOIA states that if a request is denied and information is not provided, the requestee may sue for that information. So after meetings with attorneys and Bloomberg management, a lawsuit was given a green light. Bloomberg News, led by Bob Ivry and Mark Pittman, sued the Federal Reserve System.

Judge Loretta A. Preska of the US District Court for the Southern District of New York heard the case. The Fed argued that if the names of the banks were to be made public, it would "stigmatize" them within their banking circles, their customers and their shareholders. Judge Preska ruled in favour of Bloomberg, stating that "embarrassment is not a reason to withhold information" and that "the public interest is more important". The Fed appealed the case.

In the appeals court, the Clearing House Association joined the suit on the side of the Fed. It made no difference as they lost the suit again. The Fed then appealed the case to the United States Supreme Court, and three interesting things happened. Firstly, the Federal Reserve dropped out of the case. Second, the Obama administration voiced its support for Bloomberg and urged the Supreme Court to rule in their favour. They only did this belatedly, for the notoriety, when they knew they would be on the winning side of a case between Bloomberg News v. the Clearing House Association. Third, the Supreme Court refused to hear the appeal, and the Fed had to turn over the information requested by Pittman and Ivry, about a year and a half after the original request.

Just weeks later, as the paper work came pouring in, Mark Pittman died on Thanksgiving Day 2009. Immediately, rumours began to circulate that the Federal Reserve had something to do with his death. Mark's widow wondered if there was any way to really know if the Federal Reserve had her husband killed. So Bob called the medical examiner. Bob explained the circumstances and the strange timing of Mark's death to the ME, who replied, "I'm Russian, believe me, I get it". The ME conducted a special examination of Pittman's body and concluded with certainty that there was no foul play and that Mark had died from a heart attack brought about by an unhealthy lifestyle.

Since the original request to the Fed for information the government bailout for ailing firms had mushroomed from two or three cases of relief to ten cases and counting. With Pittman deceased, Ivry was left with Bloomberg's team of data guys and other reporters to sift through all the information the Fed had relinquished. In hindsight, Ivry thought that they should have been more specific in their request for information, as the Federal Reserve handed over 29,000 data entries in PDF form, rather than Excel. It was "hellish". Bob had his computer screen magnified and went through every line with a ruler, marking and noting every entry.

The work was gruelling and sometimes raised more questions than answers, such as, if a bank takes out a billion dollar loan on Monday, and rolls it over for five days, is that a $1 billion loan or a $5 billion loan, according to the Fed? How to present all this information accurately, fairly, and to make it understandable was another challenge they faced. This information had to cater for the scrutiny of bankers, politicians, regulatory agencies, and the general public. It had to be as in-depth yet as accessible as possible. Bob decided to use a "peak lending" formula. For example, to determine how much money Morgan Stanley, for example, had out in discount window loans, mortgage-backed securities (MBS),[3] money market guarantees, etc., Bob's team would figure out the "peak day" that Morgan would have the most money borrowed from the Federal Reserve. On one day in December of 2008, the Fed had $1.2 trillion in assistance out to banks in one form or another – in one day.

As the team went over the charts, they noticed an acronym, "ST OMO". No one had any idea what it was, so they nicknamed it, "Saint Omo". The charts had bank's names and colour-coded bar graphs denoting money borrowed by the banks from the Fed. For example, Citibank borrowed X amount of money from the discount window, and that would be in blue; and X amount from this source would be in yellow, etc. In all the entries, in bright pink, it kept reading ST OMO and they couldn't figure out what it was. Finally, Bloomberg sources directed Bob to a totally obscure memo from 2008, which explained that the Fed had this ST OMO program since the late 1940s. It stood for "Single-Tranche Open Market Operations" and through this system, the Federal Reserve would buy or sell MBS to help regulate the amount of currency it has in the system. However, in the case of the 2008 crash, the Fed used the ST OMO as a quasi-bailout. It started lending money to cover all the toxic debt the banks had incurred, using MBS as collateral. The borrowing rates were determined by a bidding process, so at one point a Goldman Sachs interest rate on a loan for their bad debt was 0.01 per cent, and this and all the other loans through Saint Omo were collateralized with toxic MBS and collateralized debt obligations (CDO). Bob actually called up Congressman Barney Frank, then head of the House Financial Services Committee and later, co-author of the Dodd–Frank Act, to see if he knew what ST OMO was. Frank did not, and Bob made him aware of it.

Since the 1940s, the Fed had lent or purchased a couple of billion dollars a month, every so often, throughout the life of the ST OMO program. In 2008 the Fed did 100 times that volume in one year. The Fed insisted that it was not an emergency bailout because it had been using the program for so long. However, this was obviously not the case, and Bob and his team added STOMO to their widening list of money lent.

It was time to tally all the money lent out from the Fed to the banks. Back in 2008, Bob called the former governor of the St Louis Federal Reserve Bank, Bill Poole, and asked him about all this money he saw going out the back door of the Fed, with seemingly no one keeping track of it. Poole used a term that Bob had never heard before – "quantitative easing": when the Federal Reserve buys securities in order to inject money into the financial system. The Fed had begun doing this in early 2007, but had never called it that. So with a white board and dry-erase markers, Bob added up all the information he had received from the Fed along with the 6–8 week press releases of the Fed records over the course of the crash, and the Fed's balance sheets, which it releases every Thursday at 4 pm, and the final peak lending figure, in March 2009, was $7.77 trillion, all lent by the Federal Reserve to, mostly, Wall Street banks. Once Bob had factored in the other agencies that had helped the banks after the crash like the US Treasury's TARP bailout, the FDIC, and since it was a real estate collapse, the Department of Housing and Urban Development (HUD), as well as the Fannie Mae and Freddie Mac bailout, the total figure lent to the banks reached $14 trillion, which at the time was about equivalent to US GDP. The federal government and the Federal Reserve had supported the banking system to the tune of everything that had been produced in the United States in a single year.

The team at Bloomberg now knew how much money was going out. What they did not know was for what, and to whom. After more digging, Bloomberg found that the Fed was lending to everyone they could. A Japanese fishing collective got a US Federal Reserve loan, along with an insolvent Belgian bank called Dexia, which is a gross violation of Fed lending protocol. Moreover, all this secrecy completely masked how dire the situation really was in 2008. There were international companies and banks that were bailed out, which had no business being allowed to survive. The worst part of it, according to Ivry, was the fact that Congress had no idea what was going on. If they had known the extent of the Fed's lending practices, would they have provided TARP? Would they have voted down attempts to make the big banks smaller? The banks had been getting money for years before TARP. There were banks that publicly stated that they didn't need the TARP bailout money because they were in such good shape. It was a lie. They were merely surviving because they had been receiving ultra-low interest rates on massive loans from the Federal Reserve. Even more reprehensible was what the banks did with the TARP bailout money – they purchased US government Treasury bills at 2.5 per cent and made $14 billion in one month.

Bob and I discussed what was known on Wall Street as the "Lehman weekend". The crash happened on a Friday and Lehman Brothers filed for bankruptcy on Monday morning. That weekend, Henry Paulson, Treasury Secretary, Ben Bernanki, chairman of the Federal Reserve Board, and Tim Geithner, the governor of the New

York Fed all gathered for a meeting in New York to figure out a way to save the US financial system. Who did they call for help? The heads of the ten largest banks in America. No business representatives, no labour representatives, no diversity of opinion.: just ten or twelve bankers were asked how to save the financial system. "Of course they're going to say 'We have to save the banking system!'" Bob shouted. ". . . And they're the one's who got themselves into the trouble in the first place", I continued.

After the peak borrowing was calculated, Bob found that J. P. Morgan was the least in hock, receiving only $50 billion in assistance from the Fed. Bloomberg hunted around for statements from all the executives of the Wall Street banks and every one said that their bank was in perfect shape. Their balance sheets were awesome and their investors should be very content. They all lied. But not enough for them to have been stopped, arrested or to get in trouble with the Securities Exchange Commission (SEC). No one was punished. Bob thinks that the election of Donald Trump and the UK's referendum vote for Brexit are a direct repudiation by average citizens of the lawlessness of 2008.

When I asked Bob what he thought the relationship was between the Federal Reserve and Wall Street, he paused for a while. He had never heard that question before. His answer was, "You know what? Until 2009, the Fed *was* Wall Street". When the Fed chairman is out to save the country from financial collapse and all he does is take advice from the big banks, "there's your answer". The Dodd–Frank Wall Street Reform and Consumer Protection Act, signed in July 2010, has shackled the banks enough so that they will not be the cause of the next crisis. The big banks and the Fed remain very politically powerful, but the new shadow banking system has taken over. Hedge funds and private equity firms are replacing banks as the investment arm of the economy. They are now rolling the dice in the casino, not the big banks. Since the Fed cannot oversee these entities, they, along with the big banks, are not in the game the way they once were and had been for over a century. The banks can't make money the way they used to and it is dividing the industry with some banks lobbying for greater regulation of these hedge funds and the like, while others are investing in them as a sign of the future of the banking industry.

The Fed has become more of a breeding ground for Wall Street executives, and no one personified that more than Tim Geithner. After 2009, picking Geithner as the US Treasury Secretary was "the original sin of the Obama administration", according to Ivry. Obama had stated that he was going to take a more sceptical view of the people and their world that gave us the 2008 crisis, but it never happened. If overhaul was required, Geithner was the wrong person for the job. As Treasury Secretary, he was basically a sycophant. In early 2009, Larry Summers, head of the Council of Economic Advisors to the President, and Tim Geithner got together and decided that they were going to break up Citigroup. Geithner was assigned to start the process. Bob noted that Ron Suskind's book, *Confidence Men* showed how Geithner slow-walked the assignment, stalled the process, was never checked, and it never happened. After his term as US Treasury Secretary, Tim Geithner was named CEO of the private equity firm, Warburg Pincus.

We went on to discuss the relationship the Fed has to the US Treasury. Bob recognized that there was a strong bond between Bernanke and Paulson. Geithner going to the Treasury from the New York Fed kept that bond going. However, Bob was not sure if that bond remained as strong between Janet Yellen and then Treasury Secretary Jack Lew (or current Treasury Secretary, Steven Mnuchin). Bob's hope is that they remember the events of 2008 and act accordingly. As time passes, people forget things. Bob pointed out that there is now an entire generation that was in elementary school when the crash of 2008 occurred. "They know nothing", he said, "2008 is like ancient history to them", and "when we forget we are doomed to repeat".

I asked Bob if there were any unofficial capacities of the Federal Reserve. He replied, "Its unofficial job is central bank to the other central banks. It proved itself in 2007 to 2009 that it is the central bank of the world". Its other unofficial role is to sustain the power and growth of Wall Street. It takes employees from Wall Street and spits them back out into Wall Street. Its advisors are Wall Street veterans and its main focus is "Wall Street's reaction or opinions to its moves". Its goal is to keep Wall Street strong. This has much to do with the global opinion of America. The stock market is the face of capitalism, as it embodies the essence of free market enterprise with the ability for the public to share in the risk and reward of each company. As the Fed dithers over interest rates, it is "paying too much attention to what Wall Street is telling it", said Ivry. I then explained a little of the history of the founders of the Federal Reserve to Bob, and it all began to make sense to him. The Fed was founded as a symbiotic partner to Wall Street, as the remora is to the shark. As Bob put it, "On Capitol Hill the banks are more powerful than the Fed. Wall Street is gaming the Fed. The Fed is there to serve Wall Street."

When I ask Bob about the role of the government in oversight of the Federal

Reserve, he was, ironically, forgiving: "I have sympathy for Congress because they are limited in intelligence and logic. Cut them a break. [Most of them] are stupid, not necessarily corrupt". He continued to explain how the Fed is more transparent now than ever before in its history. He gives credit to Bernanke, in comparison to Greenspan (who was a friend of Ayn Rand). "Lawmakers can't force the Fed to make sense. A lot of it makes no sense . . . You can be transparent without being enlightened."

Bob and I then spoke about the power the Federal Reserve System has on the average American citizen. Bob brought up a salient point about the Fed dropping interest rates after the crash. With that monetary policy the Fed was one of the key contributors to income and wealth inequality in the country. The Fed bailed out the banks and did nothing to help the American homeowner. In fact, cutting interest rates to close to zero severely damaged all Americans who were on a fixed income – relying on their banks' savings account interest rates and money market accounts for growth and income. The rich could borrow at miniscule interest rates and consolidate more capital, while the middle class earned nothing on their savings, and were given no ability to borrow money for their homes or businesses, as the banks took all that bailout money and enforced massive lending restrictions for years after the crash. "Our central bank has made things harder for ordinary people and better for those who are already well off."

I asked Bob if he failed to uncover anything that he really wanted to know regarding the Fed's bailout of the big banks. He said one word, "Collateral". If Citigroup requests a $10 billion loan from the Fed, and they ask what the collateral is, Citigroup could say, "We got some swampland in Florida and some beat up, old Chevys. And the Fed would OK the loan." Besides the toxic MBS, Bob and his team never found out what collateralized many of the Fed loans to the banks. We discussed how this lending practice goes against every basic economic principle, including the most cited "Bagehot Principle", which states that an entity must lend money at above market rates only to solvent companies during a crisis. The Fed did the exact opposite. However, it is not the Fed's function to be fair. The Fed was not designed to put a chicken in every pot. The Fed makes its own rules and can lend to anyone it wants, at any rate it wants.

As far as Wall Street is concerned, the thing that took down the whole real estate market – consolidated debt obligations – is back. These toxic, synthetic investment instruments, which were bundled, illegally rated by credit rating businesses, and sold to anyone Wall Street could trick into buying them, proved to be the poison for the financial system of the nation, and in 2015 Goldman Sachs introduced the "Bespoke Tranche Opportunity", which is a CDO, and as you read this, they are earning more that Treasury Bills.

Conclusion

In researching the founders of the Federal Reserve I found no lizard alien races or satanic cults. I found men – men who conspired to form a central bank large enough and powerful enough to rule the world's financial markets, and at the same time, control the entire monetary system of the United States from their Wall Street offices. I found collusion with other countries to do so, and I found ultimate economic power in the hands of a few, who with empty promises and political support became the original "masters of the universe", free to do as they pleased with the knowledge that the largest monetary safety net in the world would save them from their recklessness and inimical greed.

A conspiracy is merely a hidden or secret plan, usually to do harm, so why does the term "conspiracy theory" have a connotation that those who believe it must be dim-witted, gullible, or crazy? Perhaps it is because some conspiracy theorists are those things and more. Or maybe it's because it is easier for those who conspire to brand those who see them for who they are, as crazy or moronic. Perhaps those in authority accuse their accusers because they can. They sit in high offices, behind thick walls, and laugh at those who question their motives, their practices, and their authority. In the end, the people must choose for themselves who to believe, and it is much easier, more convenient, and much more comforting to believe that those in charge are doing the right thing, and those who question them are crazy, stupid, or most popular these days – un-American.

In 1961 a Yale University psychologist named Stanley Milgram began an experiment. Basically, the experiment consisted of regular people in a room with people who they thought were being "tested" in an adjoining room. Very important men in lab coats asked questions of the people being tested, and if they got a question wrong it was up to the unwitting participant to send an electric shock to the person who answered the question wrong. With each wrong answer, the voltage was raised and the pain increased. In truth, those who were "tested" were not being shocked at all – instead voice recordings of different levels of screams were played in the adjoining room so that those administering the painful shocks could hear.

Milgram's findings were frightening. A hugely disproportionate amount of people blindly obeyed the instructions of the "professionals" who ordered them to deliver shock after shock to their fellow man. Despite the screams of pain for merely answering questions incorrectly, ordinary people would do what they were instructed to do by others in authoritative positions. Milgram wrote an article on the experiment called, "The Perils of Obedience" and later he wrote a book entitled, *Obedience to Authority: An Experimental View*.

But what Milgram's findings also showed was that it is sometimes safer to question authority. Sometimes those who know more than us do not have our best interests in mind and use this to take advantage of any given situation. Questioning authority is never easy as authority is predicated on the fact that most people will believe those in positions of authority. Accusers do not hold those elevated positions, typically, and their findings can be debunked with strategies of distraction or reward. Authority always knows best, or so we are told.

The founders of the Federal Reserve claimed that they organized the Fed to protect the United States economy from itself, and that with its formation, panics, depressions, even inflation and unemployment, would be things of the past. The pre-Federal Reserve American monetary structure was attacked by Wall Street bankers as antediluvian and impractical. The Panic of 1907 was the spark that ignited the bonfire of change, from which arose the Federal Reserve System. The authors of the Federal Reserve Act contended that a central banking system would have shielded the economy from that infamous and controversial panic, and that is how they obtained the momentum from the public need for change, to implement their "new and improved" monetary system.

After the Panic of 1907, how has the Federal Reserve fared in keeping its promise to the American people, by protecting them from further troubling economic times over the past century, since its inception? The Federal Reserve, to quote again from William Greider ". . . has presided over the crashes of 1921 and 1929; the Great Depression of 1929 to 1939; recessions in 1953, 1957, 1969, 1975, and 1981; the nightmarish interest rates of the late 1970s; a stock market 'Black Monday' in 1987;

a 1000% inflation which has destroyed 90% of the dollar's purchasing power;"[1] And the recession of 1991–93; and the investment banking and real estate crash of 2008, in which the Federal Reserve secretly loaned many Wall Street banks $7.7 trillion.

The seeds of change had been planted in the first few years of the twentieth century, and the relationships between the founders of the Federal Reserve System began to take shape and strengthen. These relationships were as binding and as strange as any, but they were the beginnings of what would become the group of men who would run America's monetary system and control its currency. The interweaving of the founders' lives and careers is what makes what they created so impactful. Like the Italian mafia used to call it, "cosa nostra" or "our thing", the Fed was their thing. This core group of men, families, and banks kept things private and strictly between each other, and the US government and the citizens of America were viewed as interlopers.

Their "thing" began with Paul Warburg and his connections with Kuhn, Loeb & Co., M. M. Warburg and N. M. Rothschild. But, it was not until 1907, only a month after the Panic, when Paul Warburg and Nelson Aldrich began the first realistic discussions about forming a US central bank in the Kuhn, Loeb offices. Warburg and the Secretary of the Treasury, William Gibbs McAdoo (President Wilson's son-in-law) began their relationship during the McAdoo Tunnel project. And lest we forget, the intermarriage between the Kuhn, Loeb & Co. officers made Paul Warburg his own brother's uncle; Benjamin Strong's second wife was his Bankers Trust boss's daughter – Katherine Converse, and he then went on to be president of Bankers Trust – succeeding his father-in-law. Strong's next-door neighbour was Thomas Lamont of J. P. Morgan & Co.; the wife of Strong's other neighbour, Henry P. Davison of J. P. Morgan & Co. befriended the daughter of Dumont Clarke. This relationship enabled Davison to work for George F. Baker, and found the Bankers Trust Co. of which he appointed positions to E. C. Converse, Thomas Lamont (who authored Davison's biography), Benjamin Strong, Jr, and George Case who was Dumont Clarke's son-in-law; the daughters of Senator Nelson Aldrich and James Stillman, head of the National City Bank of New York both married Rockefellers; A. Piatt Andrew had a very close relationship with Anne Vanderbilt while in France, and it was his allegiance to Senator Aldrich that got him fired from his job with the US Treasury; and Frank Vanderlip, A. Piatt Andrew, Henry Davison, and Paul Warburg were all appointed by Nelson Aldrich to his National Monetary Commission.

The relationships of individual bankers and politicians were merely the beginning of a teleological process of widespread control of national and global dimensions. Banking syndicates were formed throughout this burgeoning Wall Street era, usually with J. P. Morgan spurring their creation. Morgan created a banking syndicate to fund banks after the Panic of 1907; Kuhn, Loeb & Co., the First National Bank of New York, National City Bank, and J. P. Morgan & Co. formed a syndicate for participation in the $27,500,000 loan negotiated with English, German and French bankers for completing the Chinese Railway; J. P. Morgan & Co., along with their European affiliate, Morgan, Harjes & Co., formed another syndicate with the British government and Kuhn & Loeb, and National City Bank for the purposes of establishing a gold pool, a cotton pool, arms deals, and reciprocal credit between them and the British Treasury; even the First World War peace treaty was penned at 40 Wall Street with a banking syndicate funding the war and its reparation process.

Before any of this could be possible, the Federal Reserve System had to be established. Wall Street needed to become more powerful than its European counterparts and the Federal Reserve Act enabled that usurpation. As Lawrence Jacobs of National City Bank put it, ". . . then in the very nature of things the National Reserve Association will in a comparatively short time dominate the exchanges of the world". The Foreign Branch banking provision of the Federal Reserve Act allowed for Wall Street to dominate global banking while European nations warred. This along with the loans that Wall Street issued to Europe to fund the war made the collective of Wall Street banks the wealthiest and most powerful banking centre in the world.

Wall Street feigns competition while it monopolizes credit and currency to keep the power among itself. National City Bank, Kuhn & Loeb, and J. P. Morgan formed an underwriting syndicate to float loans to the American Telephone and Telegraph Co. of which John D. Rockefeller became a primary investor; Frank Vanderlip introduced CDOs to Paul Warburg and Kuhn & Loeb while working together on a loan to the Pennsylvania Railroad Co. and Warburg and Henry Davison worked on the China Railway loan together. When the US Chamber of Commerce Committee's 1906 banking and currency report came out and clearly did not address Wall Street's want for more elastic currency, it was James Stillman and Jacob and Mortimer Schiff who together petitioned Secretary of the Treasury Shaw to form the "Committee of Five".

Just as every other syndicate, loan, interlocking directorate, or collusive banking deal these top Wall Street bankers created together, the Federal Reserve was one more entity which reflects the union and solidarity of these select few in economic and monetary power. They promised the US government and its people a way out of economic instability and delivered a system that was designed to aid them and only them. The Federal Reserve creates debt. Banks are indebted to it and citizens are indebted to banks, and those who created the Fed sit atop the financial forum with unchecked, oligarchical autonomy, and now entire nations are indebted to them.

Not unlike the aforementioned mafia, Wall Street promised protection while extorting money from the nation. Their central banking solution was a Trojan horse that ravaged the country's economy from the inside out. Central banking proved to be even less sound than the system its proponents denigrated. According to Frank Vanderlip, a central bank would save the banking system from its cannibalistic nature by making money more elastic. Paul Warburg predicted that central banking would stop panics, altogether, and Benjamin Strong promised it would weed out unscrupulous stock speculators. These theories, that continue to be the cornerstone of our entire monetary system can be challenged by three words: the Great Depression. Much more than a panic, when the Great Depression began in 1929, only 15 years after the organization of the central banking system of the Federal Reserve, there were 25,000 banks in America. By the end, in 1933, there were only 12,000 with only 3,000 eventually reopening. The effect on money supply was so dramatic that from 1929 to 1933, it plummeted by 27 per cent. For every $3 in circulation in 1929, only $2 was left in 1933. This was exactly what Wall Street said the Fed could prevent by having the power to create or destroy money ("a currency expanding or contracting"). Even the GNP crashed, as it reached $100 billion in 1928 and bled down to $56 billion by 1933.[2]

Wall Street bankers and their foreign counterparts staged a revolution in America. Not a shot was fired nor a blade drawn. It was done with paper and gold, and its effects are as binding today as they were when the nation got its first taste of bankers controlling the currency. About a year before the Federal Reserve Act was signed, J. H. Tregoe, the Secretary-Treasurer of the National Association of Credit Men wrote a letter to Paul Warburg informing him of a speech he heard that described the basis of what would soon be the Federal Reserve System:

> I had in Cincinnati on Tuesday evening a rather disagreeable experience. The meeting of the Credit Men on that evening was addressed by Mr. C. O. Crozier, who advanced himself as a very thorough student of finance, and a strident

opponent to the monetary bill. During the course of his address he claimed that the bill was virtually a conspiracy upon the part of "Wall Street" to control the finances of the Nation, and through the finances, the nation itself. In addition, he claimed it was also an international conspiracy whereby our country would become a part of an international money trust.[3]

I did everything I could to find out who Mr. C. O. Crozier was. Alas, the conspiracy theorist was lost in history, never to be known. Yet, the framers of the Federal Reserve have gone down in history as some of the richest and most powerful men in American finance. Authority is truth, again.

Is that it? Do Wall Street and the immense corporations who sway her mood affect the rest of our lives based upon their level of greed that day? Capriciously deciding who's rich and who's poor, who starves and who eats, who lives and who dies, just as long as their financial appetites are sated. As Bespoke Tranche Opportunities prove that Wall Street continues to operate without remorse or without learning lessons from the crash of 2008, and the fact that new securities that bundle car loans and student loans, just as CDOs operate, are being sold off it is proving difficult to keep up with the level of indifference to those who struggle to meet the financial demands of a system that favours the wealthy and exploits those with less.

Sometimes the ball game is fixed. Sometimes the bad guy gets away. Sometimes we all get the rug pulled out from under us and we sit there and think, "How did this happen?" But, how badly do we really want to know? Are we too afraid of the answer to that question? Is that why so many people know so little? Is that why the average American can't tell you who Janet Yellen is, but Kim Kardashian's ass is plastered across everyone's iPhone?

The powers that be count on that ignorance. They rely on the fact that it breeds the two things they want most in us – confidence and fear. The confidence of people who want to walk in between the raindrops, who put on their rose-coloured glasses and just know that everything will work out just great because this is America, damn it, and we're the best country in the world! Or the fear of the people who do what they're told, and watch what they're told, and wear what they're told, and say what they're told, and think what they're told. That confidence and that fear ensures the dark and wistful fact that the only thing more dangerous than a fool who thinks he's right, is a wise man who is too scared to speak the truth.

The founders of the Federal Reserve were the pioneers of a system that remains in place to this day, and has stayed true to its design as the most powerful financial entity in the United States. But was it a quest for change they sought, or a quest for control? Were they really the architects of this system, or were they servants to men like J. P. Morgan, John D. Rockefeller, James J. Stillman, Jacob Schiff, and the Warburg and Rothschild dynasties?

From the Federal Reserve System's deceptive name, to the clandestine First World War dealings of the founders of the Fed, to the consolidation of power and the ignition of fear from the serendipitous Panic of 1907, to the secret meeting on Jekyll Island where the early stages of the Federal Reserve Act were conceived by Wall Street bankers and a politician known for malfeasance, to the Pujo Committee Report and its unmitigated findings of greed, control and illegalities – the Federal Reserve System was born in darkness, created by dark men, and has remained a dark instrument of control and power ever since.

When an artist paints a picture or creates a sculpture, it is said that the artwork is a reflection of the artist. Similarly, the creation of the Federal Reserve is a reflection of the men who created it – who these men were and what they were made of. The Federal Reserve is a banking entity, and yet it was the opus of Warburg, Strong, Vanderlip, Andrew, Davison and Aldrich, who sunk their very beings into their creation. The Fed was their work of art, and art remains subjective.

Nothing born of weakness could last as long as the Federal Reserve System has. As the system exceeds its centennial birthday, the study of the questionable inception of this gargantuan economic machine and its Frankensteinian creators, may give much needed insight and courage to ask questions about today's Federal Reserve System and the type of hold it has on the American economy. If the future is to change, the past must be known.

In an address to Congress in June 1932, Representative Louis T. McFadden, former president of the Pennsylvania Bankers' Association, former president of the First National Bank of Canton, and, at the time of his speech, chairman of the House Banking and Currency Committee, filed a petition for impeachment of the entire Federal Reserve Board. In his speech to his fellow congressmen, his passionate words echoed:

Mr. Chairman, we have in this country one of the most corrupt institutions the world has ever known. I refer to the Federal Reserve Board and the Federal Reserve Banks. The Federal Reserve Board, a government board, has cheated the Government of the United States and the people of the United States out of enough money to pay the national debt. The depredations and iniquities of the Federal Reserve Board has cost this country enough money to pay the national debt several times over. This evil institution has impoverished and ruined the people of the United States, has bankrupted itself, and has practically bankrupted our Government. It has done this through the defects of the law under which it operates, through the maladministration of that law by the Federal Reserve Board, and through the corrupt practices of the moneyed vultures who control it.[4]

Notes

1. The Genesis

1. Smith, *The Freedoms We Lost*, 134.
2. Ibid., 141–2.
3. Ibid., 151.
4. Ibid., 179.
5. Ibid., 184–8.
6. Ibid., 189.
7. Howard Zinn in *The Corporation* (Zeitgeist Films, 2004).
8. "*Pembina Consolidated Silver Mining Co. v. Pennsylvania*, 125 US 394 (1888)".
9. Mary Zepernick in *The Corporation*.
10. Mullins, *The Secrets of the Federal Reserve*, 4–5.
11. Lane, *A Nation Wholly Free*, 87–91.
12. Ibid., 92.
13. Dearinger, *The Filth of Progress*, 9.
14. Ibid., 201.
15. Ibid., 188–91.
16. Ibid., 200.
17. Ginger, *Age of Excess*, 111–2.
18. Ibid., 108–10.
19. Ibid., 34.
20. Josephson, *The Robber Barons*, 92–3.
21. Ibid, 93.
22. "Greenbacks" were paper currency printed by the US government during the Civil War. Hitherto, the only money issued had been gold and silver coins.
23. Edwards, *New Spirits: Americans In the "Gilded Age", 1865–1905*, 81.
24. Ibid.
25. Ibid., 80–1.
26. Strouse, *Morgan: American Financier*, 170.

27. Ibid., 171.

28. Gold and silver are both permitted as legal tender and both are coined by government mints in unlimited quantities.

29. Quoted in Strouse, *Morgan*, 319.

30. Postel, *The Populist Vision*, 269.

31. Strouse, *Morgan*, 348–9.

32. Quoted in ibid., 356.

33. Livingston, *Origins of the Federal Reserve System*, 47.

34. Ibid., 63–4.

35. Fraser, *Every Man a Speculator*, 27.

2. The System

1. Dykes & Whitehouse, "The Establishment and Evolution of the Federal Reserve Board: 1913–1923", 227.

2. Quoted in Greider, *Secrets of the Temple*, 276.

3. Laughlin, *The Federal Reserve Act*, 6.

4. Ibid., 6.

5. Ibid., 7.

6. Rothbard, *The Case Against the Fed*, 58–9.

7. Ibid., 60.

8. Laughlin, *The Federal Reserve Act*, 8–9.

9. Homer, "The Aldrich-Vreeland Emergency Currency Act", 49–50.

10. Laughlin, *The Federal Reserve Act*, 14.

11. Ibid., 14.

12. Ibid., 16.

13. Quoted in ibid., 18.

14. Quoted in ibid., 18.

15. Quoted in ibid., 35.

16. Ibid., 59–61.

17. Ibid., 133.

18. Ibid., 138–40.

19. Ibid., 157–8.

20. Quoted in ibid., 156.

21. Quoted in Livingston, *Origins of the Federal Reserve System*, 216.

22. Laughlin, *The Federal Reserve Act*, 160.

23. Ibid., 161–70.

24. Quoted in Mayer, *The Fed: The Inside Story of How the World's Most Powerful Financial Institution Drives the Markets*, 68.

25. Discounting a short-term debt security for a second time, typically less than its par value. In times of low liquidity in the market, it enables banks to generate cash.

26. Livingston, *Origins of the Federal Reserve System*, 180.

27. Warburg, *The Federal Reserve System*, 141.

28. Livingston, *Origins of the Federal Reserve System*, 180–1.

29. Vanderlip, *From Farm Boy To Financier*, 219.

30. Kemmerer, *The ABC of the Federal Reserve System*, 28.

31. Thomas Jefferson to John Taylor Monticello, letter 28 May 1816, Available at: http://www.let. rug.nl/usa/presidents/thomas-jefferson/letters-of-thomas-jefferson/jefl245.php (accessed 1 March 2018).

32. Livingston, *Origins of the Federal Reserve System*, 179.

33. Kemmerer, *The ABC of the Federal Reserve System*, 28–9.

34. Leffingwell, "The Cavalcade of Greed", 9.

35. Friedman, *Money Mischief*, 143.

36. Law Librarians Society of Washington DC, "Public – No. 43 – 63D Congress {H.R. 7837}".

37. Kemmerer, *The ABC of the Federal Reserve System*, 29.

38. Law Librarians Society of Washington DC, "Public – No. 43 – 63D Congress {H.R. 7837}".

39. Mullins, *The Secrets of the Federal Reserve*, 34–5.

40. "Institution History", National Information Center. Available at: https://www.ffiec.gov.

41. Law Librarians Society of Washington DC, "Public – No. 43 – 63D Congress {H.R. 7837}".

42. *Ibid.*

43. *Ibid.*

44. Dykes & Whitehouse, "The Establishment and Evolution of the Federal Reserve Board: 1913–1923", 228–9.

45. US Bureau of Labor Statistics, "US Bureau of Labor Statistics CPI inflationary Calculator 1914–2017". Available at: http://www.bls.gov (accessed 24 July 2017).

46. Dykes & Whitehouse, "The Establishment and Evolution of the Federal Reserve Board", 232.

47. Kemmerer, *The ABC of the Federal Reserve System*, 41.

48. Law Librarians Society of Washington DC, "Public – No. 43 – 63D Congress {H.R. 7837}".

49. Dykes & Whitehouse, "The Establishment and Evolution of the Federal Reserve Board", 235.

50. *Ibid.*, 232–3.

51. Mullins, *The Secrets of the Federal Reserve*, 123.

52. Rothbard, *The Case Against the Fed*.

53. Greider, *Secrets of the Temple*, 226.

3. The Island

1. Jekyll Island Club Resort, http://www.jekyllclub.com/jekyll-island-history/ (accessed 1 February 2018).

2. Mullins, *Secrets of the Federal Reserve*, 3.

3. Nelson W. Aldrich Papers, reel 43.

4. *Ibid.*

5. Wicker, *The Great Debate on Banking Reform*, 52–3.

6. Ahmed, *Lords of Finance*, 55.

7.   Laughlin, *The Federal Reserve Act*, 16.

8.   Wicker, *The Great Debate on Banking Reform*, 54.

9.   Quoted in Mullins, *The Secrets of the Federal Reserve*, 1–2.

10.   Irwin, *The Alchemists: Three Central Bankers and a World on Fire*, 35.

11.   Lowenstein, *America's Bank: The Epic Struggle to Create the Federal Reserve*, 109–12.

12.   Laughlin, *The Federal Reserve Act*, 18.

13.   Dodge, "The Aldrich-Vreeland Emergency Currency Act", 61–2.

14.   Irwin, *The Alchemists*, 36.

4. The Politician: Nelson W. Aldrich

1.   Sternstein, "King Leopold II, Senator Nelson W. Aldrich and the Strange Beginnings of American Economic Penetration of the Congo", 189.

2.   Philips, "The Treason of the Senate".

3.   Chernow, *The Warburgs*, 131.

4.   Stephenson, *Nelson W. Aldrich: A Leader In American Politics*, 6. Stephenson collected these notes from a collection of letters Aldrich wrote to his wife. He is the only credible secondary source for information on Aldrich's youth and early career.

5.   *Ibid.*, 11.

6.   Biographical Directory of the US Congress. Available at: http://bioguide.congress.gov/biosearch/biosearch.asp (accessed 1 February 2018).

7.   Stephenson, *Nelson W. Aldrich*, 5.

8.   Steffens, "Rhode Island: A State For Sale", 5.

9.   *Ibid.*, 6.

10.   Lucious Garvin in his speech to the General Assembly of Rhode Island, "Special Message Concerning Bribery in Elections . . .", 1903.

11.   Sternstein, "Corruption in the Gilded Age: Senator Nelson W. Aldrich and the Sugar Trust", 16–21.

12.   *Ibid.*, 24–7.

13.   Theodore Roosevelt Papers, "A letter from Stephens to Roosevelt, June 9, 1909".

14.   "The Sugar Trust in Politics", *New York Times*, 14 June 1894.

15.   "Concerning Two of Mr. Aldrich's Assertions", *New York Times*, 4 June 1894

16.   "Stupid Falsehoods", *New York Times*, 5 June 1894.

17.   "Senator Aldrich and Sugar: The Republican Tariff Leader Owned by the Trust, Indebted to it for Financial Aid", *New York Times*, 20 June 1894.

18.   "Providence Railways and the Sugar Trust", *New York Times*, 20 June 1894.

19.   Sealander, *Private Wealth and Public Life*, 219.

20.   *Ibid.*, 221.

21.   Finlay, *Growing American Rubber*.

22.   *The Times*, 11 December 1906.

23.   Sternstein, "King Leopold II, Senator Nelson W. Aldrich, and the Strange Beginnings of American Economic Penetration of the Congo", 189–204.

24. Wuliger, "America's Early Role in the Congo Tragedy".

25. Theodore Roosevelt Papers, "Letter from Bellamy Storer to Theodore Roosevelt, 22 October 1903".

26. *New York Times*, 19 March 1905.

27. Sternstein, "King Leopold II . . .", 196. In a letter he cited from the Library of Congress' Nelson W. Aldrich Papers.

28. Ellis, *The Life of Cardinal James Gibbons*.

29. *New York American*, 14 December 1906.

30. *Wall Street Journal*, 15 November 1909.

31. *New York American*, 10–14 December 1906.

32. *Wall Street Journal*, 24 June 1910.

33. *Wall Street Journal*, 12 August 1910.

34. Rockefeller Archives, "The Papers of Nelson Aldrich", General Correspondence: microfilm reel 44.

35. Nelson W. Aldrich Papers, reel 24.

36. *Ibid.*

37. *Ibid.*

38. *Ibid.*, reel 43.

39. *Ibid.*, reel 44.

40. *Ibid.*

41. "Personal", *Wall Street Journal*, 11 August 1910.

42. "Visit to Ex-Senator Aldrich", *Wall Street Journal*, 20 August 1914.

43. Nelson W. Aldrich Papers, reel 44.

44. *Ibid.*

45. "Estate of Ex-Senator Aldrich Estimated at $30,000,000", *Wall Street Journal*, 4 June 1915.

46. http://www.govtrack.us/staffreports (accessed 1 February 2018).

47. Phillips, "The Treason of the Senate: Aldrich, the Head of it All".

5. The Architect: Paul M. Warburg

1. Farrer, *The Warburgs: The Story of a Family*, 11–17.

2. *Ibid.*, 22.

3. *Ibid.*, 22–3.

4. Griffin, *The Creature from Jekyll Island*, 218.

5. Farrer, *The Warburgs*, 24–5.

6. *Ibid.*, 25.

7. *Ibid.*, 30–3.

8. Birmingham, *"Our Crowd": The Great Jewish Families of New York*, 158.

9. Farrer, *The Warburgs*, 34–41.

10. Birmingham, *"Our Crowd"*, 9.

11. Farrer, *The Warburgs*, 383–4.

12. "Kuhn, Loeb & Co. Leave All Railroad Boards", New York Times, 27 February 1906.

13. "Kuhn Loeb in Shaw's Bank", New York Times, 2 June 1907.

14. "Leather Trust's Good Year", New York Times, 1 March 1906.

15. Farrer, The Warburgs, 353.

16. Kellock, "Warburg the Revolutionist", 16.

17. Farrer, The Warburgs, 354.

18. Paul M. Warburg Archives, Sterling Library, Yale University; Box 1, Folders 1–15.

19. Griffin, The Creature from Jekyll Island, 18–19.

20. Chernow, The Warburgs: The Twentieth-Century Odyssey of a Remarkable Jewish Family, 130.

21. Ibid., 130–1.

22. Livingston, Origins of the Federal Reserve System, 169–71.

23. Paul Warburg, "Defects and Needs of Our Banking System", New York Times, 6 January 1907.

24. "Mr. Warburg Urges Government Bank", New York Times, 14 November 1907.

25. Chernow, The Warburgs, 132–3.

26. Paul M. Warburg Archives; Box 1, Folder 1–15, "Letter from Warburg to Aldrich".

27. Chernow, The Warburgs, 137.

28. Warburg, "Defects and Needs of Our Banking System", New York Times, 6 January 1907.

29. Paul Warburg, "A Plan for a Modified Central Bank", 4.

30. Ibid.

31. Paul Warburg, "Principles That Must Underlie Monetary Reform in the United States".

32. Among Warburg's more important speeches were: A Plan for a Modified Central Bank (1907), American and European Methods and Bank Legislation Compared (1908), A Central Banking System and the United States of America (1908), A United Reserve Bank of the United States (1910), Principles That Must Underlie Monetary Reform in the United States (1910), The Discount System in Europe (1910), Circulating Credits and Bank Acceptances (1911), The Glass-Owen Bill as Submitted to the Democratic Caucus: Some Criticisms and Suggestions (1913), The Glass-Owen Bill: Should There be Four or Eight Federal Reserve Banks, and The Glass-Owen Bill: Gold or Lawful Money, Note Issue, and Government Bonds (1913).

33. Quoted in Griffin, The Creature from Jekyll Island, 19.

34. The Papers of Nelson Aldrich, reel 43; "Letter From Warburg to Aldrich".

35. Chernow, The Warburgs, 137–8.

36. US Bureau of Labor Statistics, "US Bureau of Labor Statistics CPI Inflationary Calculator 1914–2013".

37. Chernow, The Warburgs, 138.

38. Paul M. Warburg Archives; Box 14, Folder 142.

39. Ibid.

40. Chernow, The Warburgs, 138. The Sherman Antitrust Act of 1890 prohibited certain business activities that federal government regulators deemed to be anti-competitive.

41. Paul M. Warburg Archives; Box 7, Folders 83–4.

42. Paul M. Warburg Archives; Box 9, Folder 120.

43. Warburg, "The Owen-Glass Bill As Submitted To the Democratic Caucus: Some Criticisms and Suggestions", 527.

44. Ibid., 539.

45. Ibid., 553–4.

46. Paul M. Warburg Archives; Box 1, Folders 1–15.

47. "Faction In Senate Opposing Warburg", *New York Times*, 14 May 1914.

48. Chernow, *The Warburgs*, 139–40.

49. Ibid., 158–60.

50. Paul M. Warburg Archives; Box 3, Folder 42.

51. Chernow, *The Warburgs*, 160–2.

52. "Rabbi Attacked Reformed Judaism", *New York Times*, 12 May 1910.

53. Chernow, *The Warburgs*, 162.

54. Rothbard, *The Case Against the Fed*, 70.

55. Quoted in Birmingham, *"Our Crowd"*, 354.

56. Ibid.

6. The Lieutenant: Benjamin Strong, Jr

1. Chandler, *Benjamin Strong, Central Banker*, 21–2.

2. "Five Men Control $368,000,000 Here", *New York Times*, 11 December 1912.

3. "Carnegie Blamed in Bank Report", *New York Times*, 13 May 1911.

4. "Equitable Life Sold Mercantile Stock", *New York Times*, 17 June 1911.

5. Chandler, *Benjamin Strong, Central Banker*, 30.

6. "E.C. Converse Drawing Out", *New York Times*, 9 January 1914.

7. Chandler, *Benjamin Strong*, 31.

8. Ibid., 38–9.

9. "Aldrich Answers Critic of His Plan", *New York Times*, 23 November 1911.

10. Ibid.

11. Meltzer, *A History of the Federal Reserve: Volume I, 1913–1951*, 76.

12. Rothbard, *The Case Against the Fed*, 69.

13. Chandler, *Benjamin Strong*, 51.

14. Meltzer, *A History of the Federal Reserve Vol 1*, 75

15. Chandler, *Benjamin Strong*, 61.

16. Spencer & Huston, *The Federal Reserve and the Bull Markets*, 12.

17. Chandler, *Benjamin Strong*, 67–8.

18. "To Send Gold To Tourists", *New York Times*, 4 August 1914.

19. Federal Reserve Bank of New York, "About the New York Fed". Available at: https://www.newyorkfed.org/aboutthefed (accessed 16 March 2018).

20. "Gold Cruiser to Sail Today", *New York Times*, 6 August 1914.

21. Ibid.

22. "Congress Votes $2,500,000", *New York Times*, 6 August 1914.

23. Ibid.

24. "Foreign Credits Here $9,000,000", *New York Times*, 7 August 1914.

25. Ibid.

26. Ibid.

27. "Bankers Approve Forgan Proposal", *New York Times*, 11 September 1914.

28. The Federal Reserve Act was passed in December 1913, but the Fed was not fully organized until October 1914.

29. "Call For Gold To Export", *New York Times*, 23 September 1914.

30. The year Andrew Jackson lifted the country out of debt and disbanded the second Central Bank of the United States.

31. "Wants Congress To Rest Ten Years", *New York Times*, 7 February 1915.

32. A "money market" is the use of a system or institution for the borrowing and lending of liquid money in the short term. Examples would be T Bills (or Treasury Bonds), municipal bonds and banker's acceptances (or loans).

33. Benjamin Strong, Jr Archives, Mudd Library, Princeton University; Box 6, Folder 2, "Letter from Benjamin Strong to M. Percy Piexotto, 25 April 1916".

34. Rothbard, *The Case Against the Fed*, 71.

35. Mullins, *Secrets of the Federal Reserve*, 48–9.

36. Ahmed, *Lords of Finance*, 26–7.

37. Chandler, *Benjamin Strong*, 258–62.

38. Ibid., 258.

39. "Earmarking" is setting aside funds (or in this case, gold) to pay for something specific.

40. "Sterling bills" is a reference to the pound sterling, the British national currency.

41. The Federal Reserve Bank of New York, led by Benjamin Strong, did reach arrangements with the Bank of France.

42. Chandler, *Benjamin Strong*, 93–4.

43. Ibid., 94.

44. Ibid., 94–8.

45. Rothbard, *The Case Against the Fed*, 70.

46. Ahmed, *Lords of Finance*, 132.

47. Chandler, *Benjamin Strong*, 262–3.

48. Quoted in Mayer, *The Fed*, 120.

49. Ibid., 96.

50. Ibid., 72.

51. Spencer & Huston, *The Federal Reserve and the Bull Markets*, 7.

52. Chandler, *Benjamin Strong*, 93.

53. Mayer, *The Fed*, 81.

7. The Emissary: Henry P. Davison

1. Henry P. Davison is the only one of the men who met on Jekyll Island to have no personal papers compiled. This chapter will cite other personal papers of men who worked with Davison, as well as his biography (*The Record of a Useful Life*), written by his friend and fellow partner of J. P. Morgan & Co., Thomas W. Lamont, and articles from the *New York Times*.

2. Lamont, *The Record of a Useful Life*, 15–20.

3. *Ibid.*, 24.

4. *Ibid.*, 26–45.

5. "Liberty Bank's New President", *New York Times*, 17 May 1901.

6. Lamont, *Record of a Useful Life*, 46–7.

7. *New York Times* "Clearing House Report" 2 October 1901.

8. Lamont, *Record of a Useful Life*, 47.

9. "Bankers Trust Company", *New York Times*, 31 January 1903.

10. Macey, *The Death of Corporate Reputation*, 55–7.

11. Abram Piatt Andrew Papers, Hoover Institute, Stanford University; Box 9, Folder 4, "Letter from Davison to Andrew, 17 June 1910".

12. Abram Piatt Andrew Papers, 23 August 1913.

13. Lamont, *Record of a Useful Life*, 92.

14. "On the Way Home", *New York Times*, 15 October 1908.

15. Lamont, *Record of a Useful Life*, 51–62.

16. *New York Times*, 4 August 1909.

17. "We Get a Fourth of Chinese Loan", *New York Times*, 25 May 1910.

18. "American Settled Chinese Loan", *New York Times*, 23 June 1912.

19. "New Guarantee Trust Board", *New York Times*, 10 January 1910.

20. Lamont, *Record of a Useful Life*, 94–118.

21. *Ibid.*, 62.

22. *Ibid.*, 126.

23. "Guarantee Soon To Be Biggest Trust Co.", *New York Times*, 12 September 1912.

24. Lamont, *Record of a Useful Life*, 121.

25. *Ibid.*, 140.

26. "Holds Voting Trusts Unnecessary Now: Davison May Advise . . .", *New York Times*, 24 January 1912.

27. Lamont, *Record of a Useful Life*, 138–45.

28. "Davison Disavows Attack On Wilson", *New York Times*, 25 May 1913.

29. "Morgan Partners Retain 33 Places", *New York Times*, 4 January 1914.

30. Lamont, *Record of a Useful Life*, 186–7, 195.

31. *Ibid.*, 188–91.

32. "Davison To London On Secret Mission", *New York Times*, 22 June 1915.

33. Martin Egan Papers, Morgan Library, New York; Henry Pomeroy Davison folder, "Letter from Egan to Davison, 30 March 1915".

34. Lamont, *Record of a Useful Life*, 192.

35. Martin Egan Papers; Henry Pomeroy Davison folder, "Letter from Egan to Davison, 29 December 1915".

36. "Davison Sees Prosperity Long After War", *New York Times*, 31 October 1916.

37. "Davison Meets Bankers", *New York Times*, 4 November 1916.

38. "Many Have Taxes Reduced", *New York Times*, 5 November 1916.

39. Lamont, *Record of a Useful Life*, 201–5.

40. "Bankers Withdraw Offers Of War Notes", *New York Times*, 2 December 1916.

41. Lamont, *Record of a Useful Life*, 209–11.

42. Ibid., 206–19.

43. Ibid., 221.

44. Ibid., 274.

45. Ibid., 297.

46. "Explain The Delay In Red Cross Gifts", *New York Times*, 19 July 1917.

47. "Teuton Propaganda Attacks Red Cross", *New York Times*, 4 November 1917.

48. "Trotzky Misled, Denounces America", *New York Times*, 23 December 1917.

49. "Meager Work of New York Legislation", *The Survey* 40 (April 1918), 73.

50. "Sees Harm In Relief Bill", *New York Times*, 27 February 1918.

51. Lamont, *Record of a Useful Life*, 288, 310–20.

52. "Davison Hopeful For World Finance", *New York Times*, 24 May 1919.

53. "Bankers Testify Today On Leak", *New York Times*, 11 June 1919.

54. "Vast Corporation To Rebuild World", *New York Times*, 16 June 1919.

55. "Borah Assails 'Round Robin'", *New York Times*, 1 July 1919.

56. "Ratify The Treaty, Say 250 Leaders In America", *New York Times*, 15 September 1919.

57. "Money Combinetale Denied By Davison", *New York Times*, 20 February 1920.

58. "Borah Against Help Until Europe Works", *New York Times*, 20 May 1920.

59. "Democrats Press Charge On Funds", *New York Times*, 2 September 1920.

8. The Professor: A. Piatt Andrew

1. Abram Piatt Andrew Papers; Box 5, folder 1, "Letters from A. Piatt Andrew to his mother, grandmother, and father".

2. Ibid.

3. "Princeton University", *New York Times*, 30 October 1892.

4. *New York Times*, 6 August 1909.

5. "Andrew To Head Mint", *New York Times*.

6. Abram Piatt Andrew Papers; Box 13, folder 3.

7. Ibid.

8. Ibid.

9. It was curious that as the secretary to the president of the United States, all of Charles Norton's letters to Andrew were on US Treasury letterhead. The seal on them read "Assistant Secretary – Treasury Department", but Milton Ailes (of the infamous Riggs Bank fiasco) was the Assistant Secretary of the Treasury at the time of these 1910 letters.

10. Abram Piatt Andrew Papers; Box 13, folder 3.

11. "Three Taft Nominations", *New York Times*, 7 June 1910.

12. Abram Piatt Andrew Papers; Box 9, folder 4.

13. Abram Piatt Andrew Papers; Box 21, folder 1.

14. Ibid.

15. Abram Piatt Andrew Papers; Box 20, folder 18.

16. Abram Piatt Andrew Papers; Box 20, folder 21.

17. Abram Piatt Andrew Papers; Box 21, folder 1.

18. *Ibid.*

19. *Ibid.*

20. Abram Piatt Andrew Papers; Box 22, folder 7.

21. *Ibid.*

22. *Ibid.*

23. *Ibid.*

24. Abram Piatt Andrew Papers; Box 9, folder 4.

25. Abram Piatt Andrew Papers; Box 22, folder 7.

26. *Ibid.*

27. Abram Piatt Andrew Papers; Box 22, folder 1.

28. *Ibid.*

29. Abram Piatt Andrew Papers; Box 22, folder 4.

30. *Ibid.*

31. "Andrew Inefficient, Retorts MacVeagh", *New York Times*, 5 July 1912.

32. "Treasury Row Finds Victim in McClung", *New York Times*, 15 November 1912.

33. Abram Piatt Andrew Papers; Box 9, folder 1.

34. Abram Piatt Andrew Papers; Box 13, folder 10.

35. Abram Piatt Andrew Papers; Box 16, folder 20.

36. National Bureau of Economic Research. Available at: https://alfred.stlouisfed.org/ (accessed 1 February 2018).

37. "Federal Bond Drop Arouses Mr. Glass", *New York Times*, 4 July 1913.

38. "Piatt Andrew After Gardner's Place", *New York Times*, 8 November 1913.

39. Hansen, *Gentlemen Volunteers: The Story of American Ambulance Drivers in the Great War August 1914– September 1918*, 3–4.

40. Abram Piatt Andrew Papers; Box 14, folder 23.

41. Hansen, *Gentlemen Volunteers*, 39–44.

42. *Ibid.*, 45–50.

43. *Ibid.*, 51; "Letter to Parents, 18 August 1916", American Field Service Archives.

44. *Ibid.*, 54.

45. Abram Piatt Andrew Papers; Box 15, folder 1.

46. "Senator Lodge Worried", *New York Times*, 21 September 1921.

47. "Bay State Election Republican Sweep", *New York Times*, 28 September 1921.

48. "Figures Big Fraud On German People", *New York Times*, 11 October 1923.

49. "Scores Mussolini In House Debate", *New York Times*, 14 January 1926.

50. "A. Piatt Andrew Urges Dry Repeal", *New York Times*, 18 July 1930.

9. *The Farm Boy: Frank A. Vanderlip*

1. Vanderlip, *From Farm Boy To Financier*, 1–5.

2. King, "Should a Federal Monetary Authority Be Established To Exercise Complete Control Over the Currency?", 99.

3. Vanderlip, *From Farm Boy To Financier*, 9.

4. Ibid., 14–16.

5. Ibid., 23–35.

6. Ibid., 54–6.

7. Ibid., 53–4.

8. Ibid., 58–9.

9. "Gage, Lyman Judson", *Encyclopedia Britannica*, eleventh edition, 1911.

10. *Washington Times*, 15 July 1906.

11. Vanderlip, *From Farm Boy To Financier*, 79–83.

12. Ibid., 94–100.

13. "Mr. Gage's New Position", *New York Times*, 19 February 1902.

14. Vanderlip, *From Farm Boy To Financier*, 141–55.

15. Ibid., 188. This is also cited in a paper I co-authored with Liam McDermott, "Quantifying Derivative Market Distortion and Monetary Policy Expansion: Welfare for Wall Street".

16. Vanderlip, *From Farm Boy To Financier*, 188.

17. Frank Arthur Vanderlip Papers, Columbia University Rare Books and Manuscripts Archives Library; Box B-1-2 (all folders in this collection are unmarked).

18. Vanderlip Papers; Box B-1-1.

19. Ibid.

20. Ibid.

21. Philippe Jean Bunaua-Varilla in 1903 led a US-backed revolt to separate the area now known as Panama from the country of Columbia, in order to make it an independent state. The following year, in 1904, US construction began on the Panama Canal.

22. Vanderlip Papers; Box B-1-1.

23. Ibid.

24. Ibid.

25. David Nasaw, "A Real Nice Clambecque", *New York Times*, 21 September 2003.

26. Vanderlip Papers; Box B-1-2.

27. Ibid.

28. Ibid.

29. Ibid.

30. Vanderlip, "The Modern Bank", 3.

31. Ibid., 4–5.

32. Ibid., 6.

33. Ibid., 6–7.

34. Ibid., 10.

35. Ibid., 17–18.

36. Vanderlip Papers; Box B-1-3.

37. *Ibid.*

38. *Ibid.*

39. Vanderlip Papers; Box B-1-4.

40. Mayer, "The Origins of the American Banking Empire in Latin America", 60–8.

41. Mazuzan, "Our New Gold Goes Adventuring: The American International Corporation in China", 212–16.

42. Mayer, "The Origins of the American Banking Empire", 69–70.

43. Vanderlip, *From Farm Boy To Financier*, 272–3.

44. Kane, *The Romance and Tragedy of Banking*.

45. "Loomis's Resignation Follows Munroe Case", *New York Times*, 14 January 1905.

46. Vanderlip Papers; Box B-1-4.

47. *Ibid.*

48. Vanderlip Papers; Box B-1-5.

49. *Ibid.*

50. "Banks' Stock List Full Of Surprises", *New York Times*, 23 September 1914.

51. Vanderlip, *From Farm Boy To Financier*, 302–3.

52. Wiesen Cook, "The Impact of Anti-Communism in American Life", 475. The World Court is also known as the International Court of Justice and was touted by conservative American politicians as an arm of liberal and communist conspiracy.

10. The Panic, the Pirate and Pujo

1. Balgue, "The Big Panics Since 1837", 479–81.

2. Noyes, *Forty Years of American Finance*, 355–6.

3. These observations on the causes of the Panic of 1907 were written by William M. Kingsley in a July 1909 financial periodical of the time called, *The Ticker and Investment Digest*. Ironically, he was the vice-president of the United States Trust Co. of New York City at the time of the panic.

4. Gertenberg, "The Underwriting of Securities by Syndicates", 328–32.

5. Clews, *Fifty Years in Wall Street*, 121.

6. Filler, *Crusaders for American Liberalism*, 308–13.

7. Note that interest rates this high were completely illegal at the time. They were only accepted because of the much-needed influx of currency into the market during the Panic. Morgan and his Wall Street friends took full advantage of the vulnerability of the industry.

8. Vincent Carosso Papers, The Morgan Library, New York; [ARC 1214] Box 37: Morgan & Co. – Panic of 1907, file 2. Syndicate Book #5.

9. Vincent Carosso Papers [ARC 1214] Box 37: Morgan & Co. – Panic of 1907, file 1: Lawrence, Bishop William, *Memoir of John Pierpont Morgan (1837-1913)*, 32–3.

10. Vincent Carosso Papers [ARC 1214] Box 37: Morgan & Co. – Panic of 1907, file 2: Notes from Benjamin Strong on the Panic of 1907.

11. J. P. Morgan Papers, The Morgan Library, New York [ARC 1196] Box 18, folders 1–4 (Clippings): *Daily Herald*, Rutland, Vermont, 25 October 1907.

12. Groner, *The American Heritage History of American Business and Industry*, 210–12.

13. Ibid., 213–14.

14. J. P. Morgan Papers [ARC 1196] Box 18, folders 1–4 (Clippings): *New York Press*, 6 November 1907, 1–2.

15. Groner, *The American Heritage History*, 215.

16. J. P. Morgan Papers [ARC 1196], Box 18, folders 1–4 (Clippings): *The Sunday States*, New Orleans, Louisiana, 27 October 1907.

17. J. P. Morgan Papers [ARC 1196], Box 18, folders 1–4 (Clippings): *The Ledger Dispatch*, Norfolk, Virginia, 12 November 1907.

18. *The Commercial and Financial Chronicle*, 9 November 1907, 1177–80.

19. In other words, Morgan traded the existing 60-day loan for another 60-day loan with a higher interest rate. The Bank of England needed the money, so the Morgans took full advantage of the opportunity by swapping one loan for another.

20. J. P. Morgan, Jr Papers, Morgan Library, New York [ARC 1216], Box 4, Letterpress Book 3.

21. J. P. Morgan Papers [ARC 1196], Box 18, folders 1–4 (Clippings): *The Washington Mirror*, 13 November 1907.

22. "Money Trust Is Now Disclosed", *New York Times*, 12 January 1913.

23. Bruner & Carr, *The Panic of 1907: Lessons Learned from the Market's Perfect Storm*, 31–2.

24. Pujo Committee Report, 28 February 1913, "Report of the Committee Appointed Pursuant to House Resolutions 429 and 504 To Investigate the Concentration of Control of Money and Credit". Available at: https://fraser.stlouisfed.org/scribd/?title_id=1329&filepath=/files/docs/historical/house/money_trust/montru_report.pdf (accessed 16 March 2018).

25. Frank Arthur Vanderlip Papers, Box B-1-5, Letter from Vanderlip to Stillman, 23 April 1912.

26. Ibid.

27. Congressman Charles Lindbergh testifying before the Committee on Rules, 15 December 1911. Available at: http://modernhistoryproject.org/mhp?Article=FedReserve&C=2#Lindbergh (accessed 16 March 2018).

11. The War

1. Edmunds, "One of the Greatest Economic Problems the World Has Ever Faced", 1.

2. Ibid., 3.

3. Ibid.

4. "Disaster Bears Out Embassy's Warning", *New York Times*, 8 May 1915.

5. Ibid.

6. Butler, *War is a Racket*, 2.

7. Chandler, *Benjamin Strong*, 102.

8. Dykes & Whitehouse, "The Establishment and Evolution of the Federal Reserve Board", 237.

9. Griffin, *The Creature from Jekyll Island*, 240.

10. Ibid., 241.

11. Friedman, *Money Mischief*, 108.

12. Bryan & Bryan, *The Memoirs of William Jennings Bryan Vol. II*, 404–5.

13. "Military Office For Martin Egan", *The Bankers Magazine* 96 (1918), 752.

14. Martin Egan Papers, Morgan Library, New York; Henry Pomeroy Davison Folder: "Letter from Egan to Davison, 1 November 1914".

15. "WWI Casualty and Death Tables". Available at: http://www.uwosh.edu/faculty_staff/henson/188/WWI_Casualties%20and%20Deaths%20%20PBS.html (accessed 16 March 2018).

16. Dykes & Whitehouse, "The Establishment and Evolution of the Federal Reserve Board", 238.

17. Ibid.

18. A discounted credit is a lower closing cost option for a borrower. With less money and higher closing costs, farmers and farm banks were heavily restricted in their ability to work together.

19. Ibid., 239.

20. Paul M. Warburg Archives; Box 10, folders 124–7: Warburg's writings on the "War Finance Corporation".

21. Dykes & Whitehouse, "The Establishment and Evolution of the Federal Reserve Board", 240.

22. Mullins, The Secrets of the Federal Reserve, 122. A banker's acceptance is a loan with a time draft, drawn on and accepted by a bank. The investment market handles the method of financing short-term debts in international trade, usually including import-export transactions.

23. Dykes & Whitehouse, "The Establishment and Evolution of the Federal Reserve Board", 238–9.

24. Abram Piatt Andrew Papers; Box 36, folder 10, a prospectus entitled, "Why The War Debts of the Allies Should Be Cancelled", 3.

25. Ibid., 6.

26. Ibid., 15.

27. Martin Egan Papers; Folder: "Henry Pomeroy Davison (1914–1924)", Speech given by Davison to the American Bankers' Association, 16 September 1919.

28. Ibid.

29. Abram Piatt Andrew Papers; Box 36, folder 6, National City Bank of New York, August 1925 Report.

30. Abram Piatt Andrew Papers; Box 36, folder 9, Ralph Beaver Strassburger, "Is America A Shylock?", written for the Committee of American Businessmen in 1927.

31. Roberts, "Benjamin Strong, the Federal Reserve, and the Limits to Interwar American Nationalism", 75.

12. The Journalist: Bob Ivry

1. Some of what was covered in this interview can be found in the chapter called "Wrath" in Bob Ivry's book, The Seven Sins of Wall Street. Also, Columbia University Journalism School's Case Consortium holds the copyright in a paper by Lisa Armstrong entitled, "Cumulative or Discrete Numbers: How Should Bloomberg Measure the Bailout?", which is a chronicle of the non-disclosure lawsuit that Bloomberg, Pittman and Ivry brought against the Federal Reserve. According to Alan Meltzer, there was also a lawsuit brought against the Fed in the 1950s, but it never went to trial.

2. "Swaps" are when two parties exchange financial instruments, which can be almost anything, but are usually the exchange of one stream of future interest payments, typically fixed rate, for another, typically floating, or vice versa.

3. A "Mortgage-Backed Security" (MBS) is a bundle of mortgages, consolidated together for use as an investment vehicle.

Conclusion

1. Greider, *Secrets of the Temple*, 20.
2. Moore (ed.), *Business Cycle Indicators*, vol. II, 135.
3. Paul M. Warburg Archives; Box 1, folder 1–15, "Letter from J. H. Tregoe to Paul Warburg, 16 January 1913".
4. Congressional Record, June 1932, 12595–603, "Louis McFadden on the Federal Reserve". Available at: http://www.modernhistoryproject.org (accessed 25 April 2013).

Bibliography

PRIMARY SOURCES

Abram Piatt Andrew Papers, The Hoover Institute, Stanford University.

ALFRED: Archival Economic Data, St Louis Fed: https://alfred.stlouisfed.org/

American History: From Revolution to Reconstruction and Beyond: http://www.let.rug.nl/usa/

Benjamin Strong, Jr Archives, Mudd Library, Princeton University.

Biographical Directory of the United States Congress: http://bioguide.congress.gov/biosearch/biosearch.asp

Commercial and Financial Chronicle.

Federal Reserve Bank of New York: https://www.newyorkfed.org/

Frank Arthur Vanderlip Papers, Columbia University Rare Books and Manuscripts Archives Library.

Jekyll Island Club Resort: http://www.jekyllclub.com/jekyll-island-history/

J. P. Morgan Papers, The Morgan Library & Museum, New York.

J. P. Morgan, Jr Papers, The Morgan Library & Museum, New York.

Law Librarians Society of Washington DC: http://www.llsdc.org/

London Times, NYPL Database.

Martin Egan Papers, The Morgan Library & Museum, New York.

Nelson W. Aldrich Papers, Rockefeller Archive Center, Sleepy Hollow, New York.

New York American, New York Public Library, microfilm division.

New York Federal Reserve Archives.

New York Historical Society.

New York Times, New York Public Library, ProQuest database.

Paul M. Warburg Archives, Sterling Library, Yale University.

Theodore Roosevelt Papers, Library of Congress, manuscript division.

United States Department of Labor, Bureau of Labor Statistics: https://www.bls.gov/

Vincent Carosso Papers, The Morgan Library & Museum, New York.

Wall Street Journal, NYPL Database.

Washington Times, New York Public Library (NYPL) Database.

SECONDARY SOURCES

Balgue, G., "The Big Panics Since 1837". The Magazine of Wall Street 14, September 1908.

Bakan, J. (writer) The Corporation. Dirs. Mark Achbar & Jennifer Abbott. Zeitgeist Films, 2004.

Birmingham, S., "Our Crowd": The Great Jewish Families of New York. New York: Harper & Row, 1967.

Bruner, R. & S. Carr, The Panic of 1907: Lessons Learned from the Market's Perfect Storm. Chichester: Wiley, 2009.

Bryan, W. & M. Bryan, The Memoirs of William Jennings Bryan. Chicago, IL: John Winston Co., 1925.

Butler, S., War is a Racket. Los Angeles: Round Table Press, 1935.

Chandler, L., Benjamin Strong, Central Banker. Washington, DC: Brookings Institution, 1958.

Chernow, R., The Warburgs: The Twentieth-Century Odyssey of a Remarkable Jewish Family. New York: Vintage, 2016.

Chisholm, H. (ed.), "Gage, Lyman Judson". Encyclopedia Britannica, eleventh edition. Cambridge: Cambridge University Press 1911.

Clews, H., Fifty Years in Wall Street. New York: Irving, 1908.

Dearinger, R., The Filth of Progress: Immigrants, Americans, and the Building of Canals and Railroads in the West. Los Angeles, CA: University of California Press, 2015.

Dodge, H., "The Aldrich-Vreeland Emergency Currency Act". Annals of the American Academy of Political and Social Science, January 1922.

Dykes, E. & M. Whitehouse, "The Establishment and Evolution of the Federal Reserve Board: 1913–1923". Federal Reserve Bulletin, April 1989.

Edmunds, R., "One of the Greatest Economic Problems the World Has Ever Faced". The Manufacturer's Record, 19 August 1926.

Edwards, R., *New Spirits: Americans in the "Gilded Age", 1865–1905*. New York: Oxford University Press, 2011.

Ellis, J., *The Life of Cardinal James Gibbons*. Milwaukee, WI: Bruce Publishing Co., 1963.

Farrer, D., *The Warburgs: The Story of a Family*. Ann Arbor, MI: Stein & Day, 1975.

Filler, L., *Crusaders for American Liberalism: The Story of the Muckrakers*. Yellow Springs, OH: Harcourt Brace, 1939.

Finlay, M., *Growing American Rubber: Strategic Plants and the Politics of National Security*. New Brunswick, NJ: Rutgers University Press, 2009.

Fraser, S., *Every Man a Speculator: A History of Wall Street in American Life*. New York: Harper Collins, 2005.

Friedman, M., *Money Mischief*. New York: Harcourt, Brace, 1992.

Gertenberg, C., "The Underwriting of Securities by Syndicates". *Trust Companies* 10 (1913), 328–32.

Ginger, R., *Age of Excess: The United States from 1877–1914*. New York: Macmillan, 1969.

Greider, W., *Secrets of the Temple: How the Federal Reserve Runs the Country*. New York: Simon & Schuster, 1988.

Griffin, E., *The Creature from Jekyll Island: A Second Look at the Federal Reserve*, fifth edition. American Media, 2010.

Groner, A., *The American Heritage History of American Business and Industry*. New York: American Heritage Publishing Co., 1972.

Hansen, A., *Gentlemen Volunteers: The Story of American Ambulance Drivers in the Great War August 1914–September 1918*. New York: Arcade Publishing, 1996.

Irwin, N., *The Alchemists: Three Central Bankers and a World on Fire*. New York: Penguin, 2013.

Ivry, B., *The Seven Sins of Wall Street: Big Banks, Their Washington Lackeys, and the Next Financial Crisis*. Philadelphia, PA: Public Affairs, 2014.

Josephson, M., *The Robber Barons*. San Diego, CA: Harcourt, Brace & Co., 1934.

Kane, T., *The Romance and Tragedy of Banking*. The Bankers Publishing Co., 1922.

Kellock, H., "Warburg the Revolutionist". *Century Magazine*, May 1915.

King, W., "Should a Federal Monetary Authority Be Established To Exercise Complete Control Over the Currency?". *Journal of the American Statistical Association* 30:189 (1935).

Kemmerer, E., *The ABC of the Federal Reserve System: Why the Federal Reserve System Was Called Into Being, the Main Features of its Organization, and How it Works*. Princeton, NJ: Princeton University Press, 1936.

Lamont, T., *The Record of a Useful Life*. New York: Harper, 1933.

Lane, C., *A Nation Wholly Free: The Elimination of the National Debt in the Age of Jackson*. Yardley, PA: Westholme Publishing, 2014.

Laughlin, J., *The Federal Reserve Act: Its Origins and Problems*. New York: Macmillan, 1933.

Leffingwell, R., "The Cavalcade of Greed". *Social Justice*, August 1936.

Liaquat, A., *Lords of Finance: The Bankers Who Broke the World*. New York: Random House, 2009.

Livingston, J., *Origins of the Federal Reserve System: Money, Class, and Corporate Capitalism, 1890–1913*. Ithaca, NY: Cornell University Press, 1986.

Lowenstein, R., *America's Bank: The Epic Struggle to Create the Federal Reserve*. New York: Penguin, 2015.

Macey, J., *The Death of Corporate Reputation: How Integrity Has Been Destroyed on Wall Street*. Upper Saddle River, NJ: FT Press, 2013.

Mayer, M., *The Fed: The Inside Story of How the World's Most Powerful Financial Institution Drives the Markets*. New York: The Free Press, 2001.

Mayer, R., "The Origins of the American Banking Empire in Latin America: Frank A. Vanderlip and National City Bank". *Journal of InterAmerican Studies and World Affairs* 15:1 (1973).

Mazuzan, G., "Our New Gold Goes Adventuring: The American International Corporation in China". *Pacific Historical Review* 43:2 (1974).

Meltzer, A., *A History of the Federal Reserve: Volume I, 1913–1951*. Chicago, IL: University of Chicago Press, 2002.

Milgram, S., *Obedience to Authority: An Experimental View*. New York: Harper & Row, 1974.

Moore, G. (ed.), *Business Cycle Indicators*, vol. II. Princeton, NJ: Princeton University Press, 1961.

Mullins, E., *The Secrets of the Federal Reserve: The London Connection*. Staunton: Bankers Research Institute, 1984.

Noyes, A., *Forty Years of American Finance: A Short Financial History of the Government and People of the United States since the Civil War, 1865–1907*. New York: Putnam, 1909.

Phillips, D., "The Treason of the Senate: Aldrich, the Head of it All". *The Cosmopolitan*, March 1906.

Postel, C., *The Populist Vision*. New York: Oxford University Press, 2007.

Roberts, P., "Benjamin Strong, the Federal Reserve, and the Limits to Interwar American Nationalism". *Federal Reserve Bank of Richmond Economic Quarterly* 86:2 (2000).

Rothbard, M., *The Case Against the Fed*. Auburn, AL: Mises Institute, 2012.

Sealander, J., *Private Wealth and Public Life*. Baltimore, MD: Johns Hopkins University Press, 1917.

Smith, B., *The Freedoms We Lost: Consent and Resistance in Revolutionary America*. New York: The New Press, 2010.

Spencer, R. & J. Huston, *The Federal Reserve and the Bull Markets: From Benjamin Strong to Alan Greenspan*. Lewiston, NY: Edwin Mellen Press, 2006.

Steffens, L., "Rhode Island: A State For Sale". *McClure's Magazine* 24:4 (1905).

Stephenson, N., *Nelson W. Aldrich: A Leader In American Politics*. New York: Charles Scribner's Sons, 1930.

Sternstein, J., "King Leopold II, Senator Nelson W. Aldrich, and the Strange Beginnings of American Economic Penetration of the Congo". *African Historical Studies* 2:2 (1969).

Sternstein, J., "Corruption in the Gilded Age: Senator Nelson W. Aldrich and the Sugar Trust". *Capitol Studies* 6:1 (1978).

Strouse, J., *Morgan: American Financier*. New York: Random House, 1999.

Suskind, R., *Confidence Men: Wall Street, Washington and the Education of a President*. New York: HarperCollins, 2012.

Vanderlip, F., "The Modern Bank", in *The Currency Problem and the Present Financial Situation: A Series of Addresses Delivered at Columbia University, 1907–1908*. New York: Columbia University Press, 1908.

Vanderlip, F., *From Farm Boy To Financier*. New York: Appleton-Century, 1935.

Warburg, P., "A Plan for a Modified Central Bank". *Proceedings of the Academy of Political Science in the City of New York* 4:4 (July 1914).

Warburg, P., "Principles That Must Underlie Monetary Reform in the United States". *Proceedings of the Academy of Political Science in the City of New York* 1:2 (January 1911).

Warburg, P., "The Owen-Glass Bill As Submitted To the Democratic Caucus: Some Criticisms and Suggestions". *North American Review* 198:695 (October 1913).

Warburg, P., *The Federal Reserve System: Its Origin and Growth: Vol. II, Addresses and Essays 1907–1924*. New York: Macmillan, 1930.

Wicker, E., *The Great Debate on Banking Reform: Nelson Aldrich and the Origins of the Fed*. Columbus, OH: Ohio State University Press, 2005.

Wiesen Cook, B., "The Impact of Anti-Communism in American Life". *Science & Society Quarterly* 53:4 (1989/1990).

Wuliger, R., "America's Early Role in the Congo Tragedy: How US Financiers Helped Belgium's King Leopold Rape the Homeland of 20 Million Africans". *The Nation*.

Index